The BOLD BRAHMINS

New England's War Against Slavery: 1831–1863

Books by Lawrence Lader

THE MARGARET SANGER STORY
THE BOLD BRAHMINS:
  NEW ENGLAND'S WAR AGAINST SLAVERY: 1831–1863

The BOLD BRAHMINS

New England's War Against Slavery: 1831-1863

By LAWRENCE LADER

ILLUSTRATED

E. P. DUTTON & CO., INC.,   NEW YORK,   1961

Contents

Illustrations

The BOLD BRAHMINS

New England's War Against Slavery: 1831–1863

CHAPTER I

Garrison's Bloody Year: 1835

THERE WAS a din of rushing feet through Boston's cobbled streets that afternoon of October 21, 1835. Men came running from Central Wharf and India Wharf where columns of proud masts etched the graying sky. They poured out of insurance offices and barrooms on State Street, from the Exchange Coffee House on Congress Square, from the prosperous, red-brick countinghouses of Merchants Row. Many still carried the handbill that two prominent merchants of Central Wharf had ordered from the editor of the *Commercial Gazette* that morning—"something to wake up the populace." The editor had minced no words. "A purse of one hundred dollars has been raised by a number of patriotic citizens to reward the individual who shall first lay violent hands on Thompson," he wrote, "so that he may be brought to the tarkettle before dark."

By one o'clock, most of Boston had read the handbill. The hunt was on. They would "snake out" George Thompson, the visiting, English antislavery leader, as the handbill exhorted. The proprietor of a leading oil-shop in the North End immediately closed his doors and ordered his assistants to procure "a bucket of green tar and be ready to tar and feather a ———— Abolitionist." By three o'clock State and Washington Streets held a swirling mob that soon numbered between six and ten thousand men, said the *Gazette*. More conservative officials counted five thousand or less, still a considerable figure in a city of seventy-eight thousand.

But all agreed on one point. It was a well-dressed mob—"a broad-cloth mob," the papers called it. Samuel Sewall, an eminent lawyer, wrote later that "the poor and laboring classes had little hand in it." One paper boasted that the mob contained "many of

13

our first citizens." Harriet Martineau, the English author, touring
the country, reported a university president saying "there had
been no mob, the persons assembled having been all gentlemen."

Hooting and jeering, they converged on the antislavery office
at No. 46 Washington Street, where the regular, monthly meeting
of the Boston Female Antislavery Society was scheduled for
three o'clock. For days a rumor had swept the city that Thompson
would address the meeting. And William Lloyd Garrison would
certainly be there. Thompson was the leading British proponent
of the Emancipation Act which had passed Parliament in 1833
and freed the slaves of the British West Indies. Lord Brougham
had proclaimed in the House of Lords: "I rise to take the crown
of this most glorious victory from every other head and place it
upon George Thompson's." Garrison, who had sponsored his
trip to America, was the editor of the *Liberator*, New England's
most radical advocate of immediate Negro emancipation. Here
were two rich prizes for a mob to catch together—"fanatical
wretches" and "scoundrels" the newspapers, both North and
South, had almost unanimously labeled them.

Had not the Boston *Morning Post* only a few weeks before reprinted a pointed warning from the Richmond, Virginia, *Whig?*
"The people of the North *must* go to hanging these fanatical
wretches, if they would not lose the benefit of the Southern
trade; and they *will* do it. They know too well which side their
bread is buttered on, ever to give up these advantages."

Boston was to prove that afternoon that Southern cynicism was
not misplaced. It had been only four years since Garrison had
opened his war against slavery, demanding in the first issue of
the *Liberator* on January 1, 1831, that "every chain be broken
and every bondsman set free." Now Boston would provide the
first, major battleground. Ironically enough, it would be the very
spot where Revolutionary patriots had fallen before British guns
in the 1770 massacre.

WHO COULD have predicted that slavery would become the nation's torment? "The great and foul stain upon the North Ameri-

can Union," John Quincy Adams called it in 1820. That year, Congressmen from both North and South had joined together, hoping to bury the ghost forever with the Missouri Compromise, preserving the balance between slave and free states.

Who could have predicted that the issue would rise to torment Massachusetts? Had it not gloried in being the first state to abolish slavery in 1780, the only state in the first census of 1790 not to have a slave within its borders?

But in the last fifteen years, the merchant aristocracy had come to learn "which side their bread is buttered on." As Boston's shippers, merchants, and manufacturers doubled and tripled their Southern trade, the leading politicians, Harrison Gray Otis and Theodore Lyman, Jr., showing the way, established a "conspiracy of silence" on slavery. No one could interfere with, or even criticize, an institution that was so crucial to the business of the North. By 1835 a man would have to be an enemy of the Union, a virtual traitor, if he even raised the subject in public discussion.

Garrison, it is true, disturbed this carefully regulated calm by demanding not just freedom for the slave but immediate emancipation. Garrison came from native soil, the town of Newburyport, forty miles north of Boston on the coast. He was born in poverty, so poor that he once had to beg leftover food from the mansions on State Street. Boston considered him little more than a crackpot editor, crying stridently, ". . . I will not retreat a single inch—AND I WILL BE HEARD." So Boston ignored him those first years when the paper's circulation was only a few hundred, mainly among Negroes. But as Garrison's support grew to include a handful of respectable citizens like Sewall and his cousin, the Reverend Samuel J. May, son of a prominent merchant, both Harvard graduates of 1817, it was time for a change in tactics. Boston decided to crush the abolitionists with a massive demonstration for slavery. If that didn't work, there were always stronger remedies.

Fifteen hundred of Boston's wealthiest aristocrats signed the call for a Faneuil Hall meeting on August 21st. It was an overflow meeting, "one of the largest ever held here," reported the *Morning Post*. The chairman was Mayor Lyman, its principal speakers

Otis and Peleg Sprague. Otis, the nephew of James Otis, the Revolutionary hero, was a former mayor and ex-senator from Massachusetts. His wife had long been one of the brightest adornments of Boston society. Sprague, who had just retired as a senator from Maine, had returned to his native state to practice law. Lyman ranked equally high in the firmament. A brigadier general in the State Militia, Lyman and his brother George, soon to be president of the Lowell Railroad Company, were among the city's leading capitalists.

Who could question Boston's unanimity when such men swore to "our countrymen of the South" that they stood solidly behind the perpetuation of slavery? The audience cheered wildly when the meeting went on record "to manifest the almost universal sentiment of regret and indignation at the conduct of the abolitionists. . . ." Only the wise and pungent John Quincy Adams had fears that ". . . the disease is deeper than can be healed by town-meeting resolutions."

And where public demonstrations left off, brickbats began. The handful of abolitionist speakers met growing violence all through New England in 1835. Something about slavery seemed to dissolve men's memory of free speech and the Bill of Rights. To quench antislavery discussion was becoming a patriotic duty. Thompson, honored in the halls of Britain's Parliament, was mobbed at Concord, New Hampshire, at Lowell, Lynn, and Abington, Massachusetts. A brickbat thrown from outside the window of one meeting narrowly missed his head. At another meeting a stone meant for Thompson struck a lady in the audience. Attempting to speak again the next night, he was attacked by three hundred people and only saved by the foresight of a dozen women who surrounded him quickly and hurried him out the back door.

Garrison was no less a target. His brother-in-law, Henry Benson, wrote on August 19th that the feeling in Boston and its vicinity was so tense that "Garrison nor May would not be safe there on an evening, and I doubt whether they would not meet with trouble in the daytime." Another associate wrote that Garrison, Thompson, and Arthur and Lewis Tappan, prominent New York abolitionists, were all marked for assassination. "I have not ventured into the city nor does one of us dare to go to church today," wrote Mrs. Lydia Maria Child after a New York antislavery meeting, "so great is the excitement here. . . . 'Tis like the times of the French Revolution when no one dared trust his neighbors."

Garrison was to wake up on the morning of September 18th to find that a model gallows had been placed threateningly in front of his home at 23 Brighton Street. "It was made in real work-manlike style, of *maple joist* five inches through—8 or 9 feet high for the accommodation of two persons," the *Liberator* described it. Although the gallows carried the inscription, "By order of Judge Lynch," Garrison laughed off the warning. After the city authorities destroyed it, he remarked, "I regret it was not preserved for our Antislavery Museum."

For a man who had been so hounded and vilified, Garrison presented a strange contradiction. "What," exclaimed a clergy-man who had traveled from Europe with him, "do you call such a man a fanatic? . . . For six weeks I have been with him, and a more discreet, humble and faithful Christian I never saw." As a young editor six years before, he had been labeled by a rival editor "Lloyd Garrulous" and "a great egoist," displaying "the pert loquacity of a blue-jay." And in a moment of explosive self-confidence he had written, ". . . My name shall one day be known to the world. . . . This, I know, will be deemed excessive vanity—but time shall prove it prophetic." Yet on meeting him for the first time, Dr. Abraham Cox was startled to find him "so mild and meek." Harriet Martineau found Garrison's face "wholly expressive of purity, animation and gentleness. I did not wonder at the citizen who, seeing a print of Garrison at a shop window without a name to it, went in and bought it, and framed it as the most saint-like of countenances. . . . Garrison has a good deal of a Quaker air; and his speech is deliberate like a Quaker's, but gentle as a woman's."

This saintlike aura, verging on "conscious rectitude," as Lewis Tappan noted, was intensified by Garrison's balding head, his silver-rimmed glasses without which he was almost blind, and the ear trumpet he often used in conversation because of increasing deafness. One critic a few years before claimed "his figure and

appearance are not unlike that of a dandy." Now at the age of
thirty, Garrison had retreated into somber clothes, almost Puri-
tanically severe. His face, Thomas Wentworth Higginson noted
later, had a "grave and iron strength." He was not reckless, but
he could face martyrdom almost joyfully, opening one letter, for
example, "My dear partner in the joys and honors of persecution."

That morning of October 21, 1835, Mayor Lyman was determined that Boston would have no more martyrs. As threats against
Thompson's life mounted, the mayor sent a deputy marshal to
Garrison's office. Garrison assured him that Thompson would not
address the Female Antislavery Society, that he was not even in
the city. Lyman breathed easier, omitting the precaution of increasing his slim police force or alerting the state militia. Garrison
himself went ahead with his plans to address the ladies' meeting.
Four years before he had promised not to retreat an inch, and he
was not changing his mind.

GARRISON arrived at 46 Washington Street shortly after 2 P.M.,
accompanied by Charles C. Burleigh, a Yale graduate and lawyer,
whose overgrowth of sandy beard, topped by a mane of flowing
ringlets, made him a favorite subject for abolition hecklers. More
than a hundred men were already gathered around the street door,
the crowd growing each minute.

By 2:10 P.M., almost twenty-five ladies, a few of them colored,
were seated in the meeting hall. That morning the ladies had sent
a message to the mayor, asking for protection in view of the
threatening handbills. "You give us a great deal of trouble," the
city marshal had told the messenger. By 2:20 the staircase and
passage leading from it to the hall were thronged with intruders.
A hundred women or more were prevented from getting up the
stairs to their own meeting. "They found no peace officers on the
spot," reported Mrs. Maria Weston Chapman who had arrived
early at the hall.

Garrison approached the intruders, warning them solemnly
that the meeting had been "called and intended exclusively for

ladies." They howled him down. Rather than antagonize the mob, Garrison went into the antislavery office, separated from the hall by a board partition, and sat down to work.

"The tumult continually increased with horrible execrations, howling, stamping, and finally shrieking with rage," recalled Mrs. Chapman. The mob in the street now numbered many thousands. They set up a steady shout, "Thompson! Thompson!" It was a few minutes before three when Mayor Lyman hurried up with a few of his constables. "The mob becoming more boisterous and inflamed, I was well satisfied that we were menaced with a serious riot," Lyman stated in a handwritten account published many years later.

The mayor now addressed the mob, told them that Thompson was not in the city, and asked them to disperse immediately. "As well might he have attempted to propitiate a troop of ravenous wolves," Garrison stated. "None went away."

Promptly at three, the president, Miss Mary Parker, called the ladies' meeting to order, read from the Scripture, and offered a prayer for "the forgiveness of enemies and revilers." "The clear, untremulous tone of voice of that Christian heroine in prayer occasionally awed the ruffians into silence," Garrison stated, "and was distinctly heard in the midst of their hisses, threats, and curses. . . ." The intruders now smashed the lower panel of the door to Garrison's office. Some cried, "That's Garrison! Out with the scoundrel!"

While the secretary of the meeting was attempting to read her report in the midst of tumult, the mayor entered. The following conversation, recorded by Mrs. Chapman, then took place.

Mayor: Ladies, do you wish to see a scene of bloodshed and confusion. If you do not, go home.

Mrs. Chapman: Mr. Lyman, your personal friends are the instigators of this mob; have you ever used your personal influence with them?

Mayor: I know no personal friends; I am merely an official. Indeed, ladies, you must retire. It is dangerous to remain.

Mrs. Chapman: If this is the last bulwark of freedom, we may as well die here as anywhere.

The mayor finally convinced the meeting that home was a better bulwark, and the ladies passed through the crowd, "greeted with taunts, hisses and cheers of mobocratic triumph," Garrison described it.

"When we emerged into the open daylight," recalled Mrs. Chapman, "there went up a roar of rage and contempt, which increased when they saw we did not intend to separate, but walked in regular procession. . . . As far as we could look either way the crowd extended. . . . We saw the faces of those we had, till now, thought friends; men whom we never before met without giving the hand in friendly salutation. . . ." With two white members escorting each Negro member, the group safely reached Mrs. Chapman's house where the meeting was continued.

The mob kept shouting: "We must have Garrison! Out with him! Lynch him!" Samuel Sewall, who had already helped two women from the building, was a descendant of Judge Samuel Sewall, notorious for his role in the Salem witchcraft trials and distinguished both for his public repentance and authorship of the first antislavery pamphlet in America in 1700. Sewall returned to see the rioters "rush towards the door of the building, which, however, the police officers prevented them from entering. The faces of these wretches while making these assaults seemed transformed with malice and passion. I never recollect seeing such a diabolical exhibition."

The immediate target of the mob's wrath now became the large sign hanging from the window announcing "Antislavery Rooms." Fearing that the rioters might bombard it, and then the police, with stones, the mayor "sent a person up the stairs to see if this sign could be taken into the room from the window. Instead of that being done, the man was interfered with by some of the lads and men already mentioned as being in the building, the signboard torn off the hooks and thrown down into the street."

The dismantling of the sign was to become one of the most controversial issues in the riot, for Garrison insisted it represented another step in Lyman's policy of appeasement. ". . . He ordered the sign to be hurled to the ground," Garrison wrote. ". . . The principle involved in its surrender and sacrifice is one upon which civil government, private property and individual liberty depend." Burleigh insisted that the mayor's representatives, "some of them, if not all, belonging to the police," took down the sign, "saying that such were the mayor's orders." The *New England Galaxy* reported that "two or three gentlemen, at the request of the mayor, took it down. . . ." Sewall, probably the best witness, wrote that it was thrown to the mob "either by the consent, or without objection, of the mayor."

Whatever the case, pieces of the sign were to become prized mementoes, the editor of the *Commercial Gazette* having one "cut up and distributed among his cronies," another being modeled into a coffin and sent to friends in New York.

"It was now apparent that the multitude would not disperse until I had left the building," Garrison stated. Both the mayor and Garrison's friends urged him to escape from the rear. With John R. Campbell at his side, he "dropped from a back window onto a shed, and narrowly escaped falling headlong to the ground. We entered a carpenter's shop, through which we attempted to get into Wilson's Lane, but found our retreat cut off by the mob." The carpenters obligingly secreted Garrison in an upstairs room and piled boards around him. Meanwhile, one of the sheriffs addressed the mob, told them that he had searched the building thoroughly and that Garrison had escaped.

The ruse, however, failed. One contingent of rioters broke into the carpenter's shop, and finding Garrison's hiding place, "furiously dragged me to the window, with the intention of hurling me from that height to the ground; but one of them relented and said—'Don't let us kill him outright.' So they drew me back and coiled a rope around my body—probably to drag me through the streets." One newspaper report the next day claimed that he fell on his knees and begged for mercy. Garrison stoutly insisted that while in the hands of men "who seemed to be insanely frantic —tearing my coat, shaking me fiercely," he calmly told them, "It is needless to make such extra efforts of violence—I shall go down to the mob unresistingly."

Garrison was brought down from the window by a ladder, then dragged through the street by the rope around his waist. "The plan," an anonymous participant wrote him later, "was to take you and Mr. Thompson to the Common, strip, tar-and-feather you, and then dye your face and hands black in a manner that would never change from a night negro color."

The mob had become almost frenzied, pressing "on every side as if eager to devour him alive," Burleigh described it. "One wretch," said Sewall, "struck a blow at Garrison with a club, which would probably have killed him, if Cooley had not warded it off with his arm." Cooley was one of two brothers, Daniel and Aaron, owners of a trucking firm on India Street, both of whom seized Garrison by either arm and formed a buffer as he was swept along the street—an unexpected mercy since they had previously been openly antiabolitionist.

Garrison, in fact, credits his life to their protection. "They led me along bareheaded, (for I had lost my hat), through a mighty crowd, ever and anon shouting, 'He shan't be hurt! You shan't hurt him! He's an American!' &c, &c. This seemed to excite sympathy among many in the crowd, and they reiterated the cry, 'He shan't be hurt!' I was thus conducted through Wilson's Lane into State Street, in the rear of the City Hall [Note: the Old State House], over the ground that was stained with the blood of the first martyrs in the cause of LIBERTY and INDEPENDENCE by the memorable massacre of 1770. . . . My offense was in pleading for LIBERTY—liberty for my enslaved countrymen, colored though they be. . . ."

Dr. Henry Ingersoll Bowditch, a prominent physician and son of Nathaniel Bowditch, internationally renowned mathematician, saw the mob at the corner of Court Street and, asking a bystander its purpose, was told, "They are trying to 'snake out' Garrison and Thompson to tar and feather them."

"Then it has come to this," Bowditch lamented, "that a man cannot speak on slavery within sight of Faneuil Hall. . . ." Seeing Samuel A. Eliot, a member of the city government, later mayor and Congressman, he offered to help him suppress the rioters. ". . . Instead of sustaining the idea of free speech . . . he rather intimated that the authorities, while not wishing for a mob, rather sympathized with its object which was to forcibly suppress the abolitionists. I was completely disgusted and I vowed in my heart as I left him with utter loathing, 'I am an abolitionist from this very moment. . . .' "

Charles Sprague, the banker and poet, whose office overlooked Wilson's Lane, said, "I saw an exasperated mob dragging a man along without his hat and with a rope about him. The man walked with head erect, calm countenance, flashing eyes, like a martyr gong to the stake, full of faith and manly hope."

Several people shouted to the mayor, who was hurrying from the antislavery office to City Hall, " 'They are going to hang him; for God's sake, save him!'—at least ten or fifteen said this. . . . I rushed to his rescue. . . . He was in the hands of two men. . . . I said to the men who held him, 'Take him into my office.' "

Colonels James W. Sever and Thomas C. Amory ran to help the mayor and his constables drag Garrison, still supported by the Cooleys, into the south door of City Hall. The door was slammed shut with what Lyman recalls as "the use of great physical strength." Part of the mob, however, forced its way into City Hall through the north door. Lyman stationed himself at the foot of the staircase leading to the Mayor and Aldermen's Room. "I spoke to the people and said in substance that the law must be maintained, the order of the city preserved, and that I would lay down my life on the spot to effect these objects."

As the mob continued to assault the south door, Lyman hurried to the window over it, got out on the ledge, and addressed them again. In the later controversy over the mayor's blundering, this must rank as his most determined stand.

Inside City Hall these few minutes of calm were used by the mayor's aides to replenish Garrison's clothing. Since his suit had been ripped and his hat lost, one man lent him a pair of pants, another a coat, a third a cap. Meanwhile, the mob was shouting furiously for Garrison, "greatly inflamed by having had him taken out of their grasp," the mayor said later. Lyman seemed to lose his nerve again in this crisis. After consulting with his aides, he decided on another retreat—to remove Garrison to the protection of the Leverett Street jail.

Garrison claimed later that this decision only put him in more personal danger. "What could have been more rash than the attempt to drive me in a carriage to the jail . . . ? That it was successful is truly a marvel; for the scene around the carriage was indescribably perilous."

Garrison was further embittered by the irony of jailing the victim of the riot rather than its instigators. Sheriff Parkman wrote a warrant for the arrest. "It is true, I made no objection," Garrison said, "because freedom of choice did not appertain to my situation." But until he heard the warrant in court the next day, Garrison claimed he "had not the slightest intimation or suspicion that I was incarcerated on a criminal charge."

The mayor now ordered one carriage brought to the south door to distract the mob's attention while Sheriff Parkman and Ebenezer Bailey hurried Garrison into another carriage at the north door. Bailey, a member of the Common Council, later reported the scene to a friend: "Fortunately I had with me a large strong umbrella, and as we tried to get him into the carriage, there was such a rush made upon him that I struck with my whole strength in every direction, and thus we cleared the way. . . . [Garrison] showed perfect courage and self-possession. He was only very absurd in one thing. He kept saying, 'Oh, if they would only hear me five minutes, I am sure I could bring them to reason.' . . . That was ridiculous, for they were all ready to tear him in pieces."

"A great multitude of neatly-dressed young men . . . said at the time by the multitude to be merchants' clerks," Ellis Ames reported later, "assailed the guard . . . and rushed with great fury to break through the lines and seize Garrison. . . . But their lines were kept so firm that the young men did not break through and after a fearful struggle, Garrison got into the coach. . . ."

"The hack seemed to me," said Sewall, "to be completely wedged in by a dense mass of people, some wishing to tear Garrison out and impede its motion, and some evidently pressing it forward. For some moments I felt very doubtful whether Garrison again would not be in the hands of the wild beasts who surrounded the carriage."

Some rioters managed to get a rope around the hack, intending to pull it over. "For a moment or less it seemed as though they

would succeed," an anonymous witness recalls, "for, by pulling on
the line outwardly, they lifted the coach from its perpendicular
so that it tilted on its off-wheels. I expected to see it go over; but
the owner lashed his horses, and their momentum was too great
for those holding the rope."

"Whenever the coach attempted to turn a corner," reported
Sewall, "people would spring on the horses and attempt to stop
them."

Colonel Sever recalled rioters "hanging on to the wheels and
calling out to *'Cut the traces! cut the reins!'* An individual drew
his knife and made an attempt to do this, when he was seized
by myself and thrust aside."

Garrison later described how the crowd "clung to the wheels—
dashed open the doors—seized hold of the horses—and tried to
upset the carriage. They were, however, vigorously repulsed by
the police—a constable sprang in by my side—the doors were
closed—and the driver, lustily using his whip upon the bodies of
his horses and the heads of the rioters, happily made an opening
through the crowd, and drove at a tremendous speed for Leverett
Street."

Careening through the narrow streets, the carriage scraped a
standing buggy on Court Street so closely that the rioters, clinging
to the door, were brushed off. At Bowdoin Square the driver got
rid of more pursuers by making a false turn for Cambridge Bridge.
But a howling crowd of about three hundred men had outguessed
the mayor's strategy and was waiting for the carriage at the jail
door. Lyman reached Leverett Street on foot. In a final moment
of crisis, he organized the police into a line from the jail door to
the carriage and fought back the mob. Garrison leaped to the
ground and was quickly locked in safety in his cell.

The ordeal had left him with a "good conscience and a cheerful mind," for his spirits always flourished in martyrdom. "It
seems to me a blessed privilege thus to suffer in the cause of Christ,"
he summarized his day. That evening John Greenleaf Whittier,
A. Bronson Alcott and his wife, who was a sister of Samuel J. May,
and Isaac Knapp, publisher of the *Liberator*, came to the grated
window of his cell to talk. Whittier recalls him saying playfully,

"You see my accommodations are so limited I cannot ask you to spend the night with me."

Always alert to the drama of his cause, Garrison took a few minutes the next morning to inscribe on the wall of his cell:

> Wm. Lloyd Garrison was put into this cell on Wednesday afternoon, Oct. 21, 1835, to save him from the violence of a "respectable and influential" mob, who sought to destroy him for preaching the abominable and dangerous doctrine that "all men are created equal," and that all oppression is odious in the sight of God. "Hail, Columbia!" Cheers for the Autocrat of Russia and the Sultan of Turkey!
>
> Reader, let this inscription remain till the last slave in this despotic land be loosed from his fetters.

Garrison's plea actually came within a few years of realization. For the Leverett Street jail, and its symbolic inscription, was demolished in 1852, eleven years before the Emancipation Proclamation.

The next morning a friend called to present Garrison with a new hat. But the "best suit" was not so easily replaced. About two weeks later he was to write his wife, "Yesterday (Sabbath) forenoon, I concluded not to go to church, because, to confess the truth, I had not replaced my torn pantaloons, and as the weather was too warm to justify the wearing of a cloak."

In the afternoon a judicial hearing was held at the jail since the mayor feared another riot at the courthouse. The final irony was the reading of the warrant which neatly reversed the roles of the innocent and guilty. Garrison, it stated, "did disturb and break the peace of the Commonwealth, and a riot did cause and make, to the terror of the good people of the Commonwealth. . . ."

Garrison was free now, but the mayor insisted he leave Boston for a while "to tranquillize the public mind." It was certainly not fear that made him agree, for his "nerves never knew what it was to shiver and vibrate with irritation or with fear," Mrs. Harriet Beecher Stowe once said. But his wife was expecting a child, and

he saw no reason to put her under any further strain. All that day
knots of rioters were combing the trains and stages leaving Boston
for the prey that had eluded them. Sheriff Parkman had to drive
Garrison to Canton where he joined his wife. Together they took
the train for Providence.

GARRISON was relentless in his attacks on Mayor Lyman's conduct. Why had he not done more to protect the meeting of a
handful of women? If he was honestly interested in the city's
safety, why had he not increased the police force or alerted the
state militia? Why had he not made decisive attempts to disperse
the mob instead of a few speeches of "useless persuasion"?

Even after the riot, Lyman made no attempt to prosecute its
instigators, who were well known. "No efforts have been made to
arrest the leading rioters," Garrison complained. "The mayor has
made no public appeal to the citizens to preserve order; nor has
he given any assurance that the right of free discussion shall be
enjoyed without molestation. . . ."

What Garrison failed to realize was that Boston had no interest
in whether the riot was right or wrong, in whether free speech
should be protected, in whether the culprits should be punished.
The only issue was to rid the city of Garrison and his ilk, and
if Lyman's bumbling had helped that objective, so much the
better.

Boston was simply proving the thesis that a prominent New
York businessman had laid down to the Reverend Samuel J. May
a few months before. "Mr. May," he had said, "we are not such
fools as not to know that slavery is a great evil, a great wrong. But
it was consented to by the founders of our Republic. . . . A great
portion of the property of the Southerners is invested under its
sanction; and the business of the North, as well as the South, has
become adjusted to it. There are millions upon millions of dollars
due from Southerners to the merchants and mechanics of this city
alone, the payment of which would be jeopardized by any rupture
between the North and the South. We cannot afford, sir, to let
you and your associates succeed in your endeavour to overthrow

slavery. It is not a matter of principle with us. It is a matter of business necessity. . . . We mean, sir, to put you abolitionists down,
—by fair means if we can, by foul means if we must."

"The state of things here is lamentable," Sewall wrote Garrison
on October 27th. "The *most respectable* people either openly
justify or coldly disapprove the riot. . . ."

The press, in fact, went a step further, not only justifying the
riot, but blaming Garrison for its outbreak. The *Daily Advertiser*
considered "the whole transaction as the *triumph of the law* over
lawless violence." For the abolitionists "ought not to defy public
opinion, however wrong," preached the *Christian Register,* a
Unitarian paper. "In what terms of indignation," cried the Boston
Evening Transcript, "can we speak of the man, who, by rancorous
denunciations, and his brawling, ferocious abuse, together with
the disorganizing tendencies of his doctrines, has excited the people
to such an ebullition of their deeply exasperated feelings."

Since the very act of holding an antislavery meeting was "the
signal for the assemblage of a mob," the *Mercantile Journal* demanded that the government prohibit future meetings "by the
strong arm of the law."

The "broad-cloth mob" had succeeded in driving Thompson
out of the country. Late in November he was secretly rowed by
two friends from a Boston wharf to a small, English brig, which
by fortunate coincidence had been consigned to Henry G. Chapman, husband of Maria Chapman and one of the rare abolitionists
among the merchant class. The brig carried him to St. John, New
Brunswick. From that port he sailed for England on November
28th.

More significant, the "broad-cloth mob" had united government and business behind the principle of open violence against
the abolitionists. The floodgates were open, not just in Boston but
throughout New England. Two days later, May was mobbed in
Vermont. On October 26th, rioters broke up an abolitionist prayer
meeting in Salem, Massachusetts. The Reverend Cyrus Grosvenor
was attacked in Worcester; the Reverend George Storrs was arrested during a New Hampshire meeting and hauled before a
judge as a vagrant and disturber of the peace.

On October 21st at Utica, New York, six hundred abolitionists were meeting in the Second Presbyterian Church when church bells began tolling across the city to call out the rioters. One thousand men with fire hooks, ropes, and ladders invaded the meeting, sent the delegates scurrying and then demolished the building.

"They *know* that so long as they confine their plunder and violence to the property and persons of the antislavery men, they can act with perfect impunity," Isaac Knapp concluded in a letter to Garrison. The abolitionists had passed through an ordeal of blood in 1835, but it was only the beginning.

CHAPTER II

Seeds of Violence—The Constitution

WHAT HAD SO twisted the American dream by 1835 that Boston citizens could be prevented from speaking their minds within sight of Faneuil Hall, the "Cradle of Liberty"? What strange forces, forty-five years after Massachusetts had become the first state without a slave, could impel the highest levels of business and society to support mob brutality against an antislavery meeting?

The seeds of this violence go back to the Constitutional Convention itself, to the debates at Philadelphia during the broiling summer of 1787. The Continental Congress had already agreed that no more slaves should be imported. Yet two concessions would soon be made.

In his first draft of the Declaration of Independence, Jefferson condemned King George III of Britain for obstructing Colonial attempts to halt "this execrable commerce"—the slave trade. But, Jefferson complained, "the clauses were struck out in compliance to South Carolina and Georgia who had never attempted to restrain the importation of slaves and who, on the contrary, still asked to continue it."

Meeting in New York on July 13, 1787, Congress passed the Northwest Ordinance, prohibiting slavery forever from the territory from which Ohio and other states would soon be carved. But again it yielded to the South by including a fugitive slave clause.

From such slim precedents, the South demanded and won three crucial clauses in the Constitution for the protection of slavery, although the word "slavery" is never mentioned. The fifth paragraph of Article I, Section 2, states that "representatives and direct

31

taxes shall be apportioned among the several States . . . according to their respective Numbers" which shall include "three fifths of all other Persons," these being slaves. Not only is slavery thus recognized, but the slave-holding states rewarded. For three-fifths of the slave population, although given no rights of citizenship, are added to the Southern white population represented in the House.

In the Convention debates of July, 1787, over this clause, a part of the "great compromise," the lofty language of the Declaration of Independence is painfully absent. The key word has suddenly become "property." Pierce Butler of South Carolina insists this is "a government which was instituted principally for the protection of property." John Rutledge of South Carolina declares property "was certainly the principal object of society."

Only a handful of delegates contend that the government is also concerned with human rights. James Wilson of Pennsylvania "could not agree that property was the sole or primary object of Government and Society. The cultivation and improvement of the human mind was the most noble object."

"Upon what principle is it that the slaves shall be computed in the representation?" demands Gouverneur Morris of Pennsylvania. "Are they men? Then make them citizens and let them vote. . . . The admission of slaves into the representation comes to this: that the inhabitant of Georgia and South Carolina shall have more votes in a government instituted for protection of the rights of mankind, than the citizen of Pennsylvania or New Jersey who views with a laudable horror so nefarious a practise."

Under the three-fifths clause, the Northern states with eight hundred thousand people will have one third fewer representatives in the House than four Southern states with about seven hundred thousand people, Rufus King of Massachusetts points out. "I can never agree to let them [slaves] be imported without limitation and thus be represented in the National legislature."

This crisis was only part of the major crisis of representation, for the demand of the smaller states for an equal voice in the Senate was as strong as the South's demand for added representation in the House for slave property. The one dominant objective of the Convention was to preserve the Union. How could it be done except by compromise? The tragedy was that the three-fifths clause involved a compromise not just of power but of a basic principle of human rights.

Morris himself supplied the path for compromise on July 12th by urging that direct taxation should be apportioned according to representation. With these elements linked, the South would have to pay more direct taxes on slave property if it were to gain by including them in representation.

With many Northern delegates representing rich seaboard areas whose shipowners had a heavy stake in the slave trade, expediency could be placed ahead of human rights. In the key vote on July 12th, six states backed the three-fifths compromise. Only New Jersey and Delaware were unanimously opposed. The Massachusetts delegation was split, part opposing the compromise. Although the final vote on the "great compromise," which established equal votes for the small states in the Senate, was not taken until July 17th, the first slavery concession had been made.

In the turbulent debates over the admission of Missouri as a slave state in 1819, Rufus King, then a senator, was to conclude: "The concession [the three-fifths clause] was, at the time, believed to be a great one, and has proved to have been the greatest which was made to secure the adoption of the Constitution."

WHILE historians have generally labeled the chief conflict at the Convention as that between large and small states, an equally serious cleavage had already developed between North and South.

"It seemed now to be pretty well understood," James Madison of Virginia stated on July 14th, "that the real difference of interests lay, not between the large and small but between the N. & Southn. States."

Morris warned "that the Southn. Gentlemen will not be satisfied unless they see the way open to their gaining a majority in the public Councils."

In the face of such portents, why did the Convention accept

such a dangerous compromise? There were other alternatives. Morris, for example, suggested that "I would sooner submit myself to a tax for paying for all the negroes in the United States than saddle posterity with such a Constitution."

The most obvious alternative was to let the Southern states separate immediately. Inflexible support for slavery came only from South Carolina and Georgia which held less than 130,000 of about 698,000 slaves in the country. Virginia and Maryland, which had already abolished the slave trade, held together almost 400,000 slaves. North Carolina, which had partially abolished it, held about 100,000. Reviewing their stand in the debates and in key Convention votes, therefore, it is a reasonable assumption that only South Carolina, Georgia, and perhaps North Carolina, would have been lost if the Convention had refused protection to slavery.

Morris estimated "two States might be lost to the Union. . . ." Oliver Ellsworth of Connecticut figured "two States with others that may stand aloof. . . ."

How strong was the bargaining power of the inflexible slave states? How long could they have remained out of the Union on their own terms? General Pinckney answered these questions himself in his report to the South Carolina legislature after the Convention: "We are so weak by ourselves that we could not form a union strong enough for the purpose of effectually protecting each other."

In the August debates over the continuation of the slave trade, South Carolina constantly appealed to the North's investment in shipping. "Religion and humanity had nothing to do with the question. . . ." Rutledge insists. "If the Northn. States consult their interests, they will not oppose the increase of slaves which will increase the commodities of which they will become the carriers." General Pickney dangles the bait again and again. "The more slaves, the more produce to employ the carrying trade. . . ."

Many Northern delegates agreed. "The morality and wisdom of slavery," states Ellsworth, who would be named Chief Justice of the Supreme Court in 1796, "are considerations belonging to the States themselves—what enriches a part enriches the whole, and the States are the best judges of their particular interest."

George Mason of Virginia warned that continuation of the slave trade meant immediate expansion of slavery. "The Western peoples are already calling out for slaves for their new lands. . . . [Slaves] bring the judgment of heaven on a country."

"I think it wrong to admit in the Constitution the idea that there can be property in men," proclaimed Madison.

In a letter to Jefferson in May, 1788, Mason bitterly condemned the Southern states, branding the slave trade "a more favourite Object with them, than the Liberty and Happiness of the People." Before the Virginia ratification convention in 1788, he called abolition of the slave trade "a principal object of this State, and most of the States in the Union. . . . As much as I value a Union of all the States, I would not admit the Southern States into the Union unless they agree to a discontinuance of this disgraceful trade, because it would bring weakness and not strength to the Union."

The deadlock was finally resolved on August 24th by allowing the South to import slaves until 1800 and granting the North an advantageous navigation clause. General Pinckney enlarged the South's gains the next day by winning extension of the slave trade until 1808. Thus the second major compromise over slavery was incorporated in Article I, Section 9 of the Constitution. A coalition of seven Northern and Southern states backed the compromise. Only the Middle states, New Jersey, Pennsylvania, Delaware, and Maryland, opposed it!

On August 28th with almost no debate, the South gained further protection for slavery, the fugitive slave clause of Article IV, Section 2. General Pinckney had good reason to exult before the South Carolina legislature a few months later: "We have obtained a right to recover our slaves in whatever part of America they may take refuge, which is a right we had not before. In short, considering all circumstances, we have made the best terms for the security of this species of property it was in our power to make."

And the three North Carolina delegates in a letter to Governor Caswell on September 18th summarized the Southern gains: "When it is also considered that five Negroes are only to be charged the same Poll Tax as three whites the advantage must be considerably increased under the proposed Form of government."

THE TRAGEDY was that the future of slavery had been left in suspense. At worst a basic principle of human rights had been bargained away. At best the delegates had held the Union together with a flimsy skein of compromises. The language of the three clauses was inherently hypocritical in its refusal to mention the word "slavery." The clauses inferred intentions without defining policy. Both sides could read into the Constitution whatever their interests demanded. In their effort to keep the states together, the Convention had given North and South a grab bag of illusions.

The North could cling to the illusion that it had delayed a real crisis until slavery would dwindle and disappear through natural death. "As population increases," Ellsworth summarized this empty optimism at Philadelphia, "poor laborers will be so plentiful as to render slaves useless."

Already eyeing the Western lands hungrily, and hopeful of a vast slave population to exploit them, the South could develop the illusion that the Constitution permanently guaranteed slavery. But it said not a word about slavery in the territories or the future states. Such purposeful omissions in 1787 only stirred Southern ambitions to an explosive point by 1820. The gamble of the founding fathers was a direct invitation to the Missouri crisis and each succeeding crisis.

". . . The bargain between freedom and slavery contained in the Constitution of the United States," John Quincy Adams wrote in his diary in 1820, "is morally and politically vicious, inconsistent with the principles upon which our Revolution can be justified. . . ."

CHAPTER III

Conspiracy of Silence: 1820–1831

IF ELLSWORTH of Connecticut helped convince the Convention that slavery would die of its own uselessness, Eli Whitney of Connecticut would destroy the illusion forever within six years. With Whitney's gin, cotton would revolutionize the South. A good field slave, valued at a few hundred dollars in 1787, would sell for over five hundred dollars in 1800 and fifteen to eighteen hundred dollars by 1858. The siren song of gradual emancipation quickly dwindled to a whisper.

IT WAS no accident that cotton became King, for Southern planters had been searching intensively for a staple crop to replace the languishing tobacco and indigo industries. Britain supplied the first market. Its thriving textile mills, mechanized by Arkwright's spinning frame and other inventions, consumed 5 million pounds of raw cotton in 1775 and 56 million by 1800. Large-scale production of Southern cotton, however, had to wait until the development of an easy device to separate the seed from its closely-adhering lint.

Whitney, a Yale graduate of 1792, solved the problem only a year later. His gin could clean fifty pounds of lint each day, a slave only one pound by hand. With cotton selling for thirty-five cents a pound in the decade before 1800, fortunes would soon be made overnight. On his plantation near Columbia, South Carolina, Wade Hampton with eighty-six slaves in 1799 turned out a crop worth ninety thousand dollars.

Cotton released the South from the confines of the coastlands and tobacco belt, and gave it an inexhaustible hunger for new land. A wave of immigration pushed inland to the "upper country" of Georgia and South Carolina.

The plantation system reached the Appalachians by 1820, ceaselessly pushing South and West. Mississippi bottom land, worth two dollars an acre in 1800, was selling for one hundred dollars by 1819. In the two decades after 1810, population increased 142 per cent in Alabama, 81 per cent in Mississippi, and 41 per cent in Louisiana. Small farmers, younger sons, land-hungry adventurers deserted the older states by the thousands. The ease of crop-raising and higher yield per acre soon placed the deep South far ahead of the Atlantic coast.

Cotton output soared from one hundred and fifty thousand bales in 1812 to over 5 million in 1859. Speculation not just in land but slaves became a mania. Slaves were imported in frantic haste before the 1808 deadline, almost forty thousand arriving at one port in a twelve-month period. Even after 1808 the slave trade flourished illegally, many American ships, often manned by New England captains, sailing under foreign flags. A single slave cargo after expenses could bring the owners one hundred and fifty thousand dollars, an immense fortune then. Between 1808 and 1860, between two hundred and fifty thousand and two hundred and seventy thousand illegal slaves were smuggled into the country.

Forced slave-breeding, particularly in Virginia and Maryland, also supplied the planters. By 1832 Virginia, selling at least six thousand slaves a year, resembled "one grand menagerie where men are reared for the market like oxen for the shambles," said Thomas Jefferson Randolph.

The plantation system's hunger for new soil where cotton could be grown more profusely, inextricably linked Southern economy with the nation's expansion and fanned continual crises. With little respect for treaties, settlers pushed the Creeks, Choctaws and Chickasaws out of Georgia, Alabama and Mississippi. The fierce Seminole wars of 1834–1842 opened up huge cotton tracts in Florida, ceded by Spain in 1819. The grand objective, however, was Texas.

Although the Mexican government determined to eliminate slavery, American settlers forced an act through the Texas legislature in 1828, permitting peonage contracts. When Mexican rule was overthrown in 1836, the new Republic established slavery without restriction.

The westward drive of these tough pioneers excited the patriotic fervor of a nation, which already envisioned its boundaries stretching from coast to coast. America's territorial ambitions, soon labeled Manifest Destiny, marched under many banners. They were not all cotton planters or even slaveholders. Many were small farmers from the free states, many simply adventurers carving a new life from the frontier. Slavery, therefore, advanced by the side of Manifest Destiny. The Southern planter conveniently cloaked his system in the radiance of national glory.

IN 1789 Samuel Slater, a former apprentice in the English cotton mills, landed in New York. Britain had guarded the secrets of textile production so zealously that even the shrewdest New England mechanics had failed to duplicate its intricate machinery. But Slater was a mechanical genius with a long memory. Backed by Moses Brown, a Quaker merchant of Rhode Island, he built America's first efficient spinning mill.

By 1815, Francis Cabot Lowell of Boston, a master of finance and industrial production, added a second essential ingredient, the fractionalized and continuous-flow system. With each step in manufacture minutely divided and handled by different machines, raw cotton entered at one end of the production line and emerged as finished goods at the other.

In the next decade, New England mills increased their purchases of Southern cotton by 600 per cent. Textiles made Massachusetts the nation's leading manufacturing state. Boston's prosperity was thus linked firmly with the South's, its commercial aristocracy drawn into an inevitable alliance with the slave system.

The shortage of ships in the Southern states to carry its vast exports further strengthened this link. Northern ships, particu-

larly from Boston and New York, carried cotton both to England
and New England and returned to the South with textile goods,
machinery, and other New England manufactures. The South
probably imported ten dollars' worth of goods from the North
for every dollar's worth from Europe.

The textile industry was dominated by a closely-linked group
of Boston families. Francis Lowell sold stock in the Waltham mill,
which paid almost 19 per cent dividends from 1817 to 1826, to only
a handful of business associates and relatives by blood and marriage.
When the great new Lowell mills were financed in 1821, and
later the Hamilton Company, Lowell Manufacturing Company,
and Appleton Company, the same Lowell, Cabot, Appleton, Lyman, Sears, Otis, Thorndike, and Jackson families with a sprin-
kling of uncles and cousins monopolized the list. In 1828, Boston's
most powerful East India merchants, Thomas Handasyd Perkins
and Ebenezer Francis, previously opposed to textiles as a threat
to their business, entered the inner circle. The fusion of manufacturing and merchant capital was complete.

The power of the "Boston Associates," a name first used when
leading merchants joined in a real estate combine, penetrated the
entire New England economy. They controlled every Boston
bank but one. They dominated the insurance companies. They
used a concentration of trusts and annuities to funnel the flow of
capital into new ventures, particularly a half dozen New England
railroads.

With such centralized economic control in a few hands, it is
hardly surprising that the merchant aristocracy could achieve a
complete reversal of Boston's attitude toward slavery. Boston
was now buying enough Southern cotton to impress John C. Calhoun, then a Congressman from South Carolina. When Francis
Lowell went to Washington in 1816 for the tariff hearings, he
convinced Calhoun of the advantages of mutual cooperation. The
planters had no liking for the tariff, but Calhoun supported Lowell
in tariff benefits highly favorable to the Waltham mills.

The struggle over Missouri's admission as a slave state cemented
the alliance. Both Massachusetts Senators voted for the Missouri
Compromise of 1820. In the House, eleven Massachusetts repre-

sentatives supported it, only three opposed. Six refrained from voting. A few dissidents like John Quincy Adams continued to rail against the evils of slavery, but Boston had made its convenient peace with the South.

SOUTHERN power hinged on a precarious balance of expanding territory and political domination. Territorially, the outlook was optimistic. Arkansas was organized as a federal territory in 1819. Texas lay ahead. But control in Washington was another matter.

With the South's added three-fifths slave representation, the populations of both sections were almost identical in 1790. But by 1820 the South's 2,685,095 white population, and 1,496,189 slaves, lagged far behind the North's 5,133,372. Rapid industrialization in the North was constantly expanding the gap.

Even with 60 per cent more representation in the House and its resulting advantage in the Electoral College, the South could control the House and the Presidency only with the help of key Northern states. Its center of power had to be the Senate.

With the admission of Illinois as a state in 1818 and Alabama in 1819, the balance of free and slave states had been maintained at eleven each. Then Missouri applied for statehood. Congressman James Tallmadge of New York promptly proposed an amendment which prohibited further introduction of slaves into Missouri and emancipated all slave children at the age of twenty-five.

The Constitution had carefully avoided the issue whether Congress could impose restrictions upon a state entering the Union. Now the South refused to admit Maine, which had been a district of Massachusetts, unless Missouri came in without limitation.

A year of bitter and increasingly violent debate ended in the drastic compromise of March 2nd and 3rd. On the bill to eliminate slavery restrictions in Missouri, passed in the House by 90 to 87, many Northern Representatives, soon labeled "dough-faces," voted with the South. The North had surrendered for "a bauble of insignificant promises," claimed John Quincy Adams.

The bauble was the eighth section of the Missouri Act—a provision that divided the Louisiana territory at the latitude 36°30′ and prohibited slavery "for ever" north of this line. The North had not only yielded on Missouri. More important, it had indirectly rewritten the Constitution as it applied to Congress' power over the territories by conceding that everything south of this line was reserved for slavery. The division of the nation into two equal parts had now been established by law.

In addition, the South's grip on the Senate was secured. It could look forward to new slave states in Arkansas, Florida, its half of the Louisiana territory and eventually Texas.

Henry Clay, who had steered the Missouri Act through Congress, was hailed as the "great peacemaker."

"But this is a reprieve only, not a final sentence," the aged Jefferson noted. On April 13, 1820, he wrote a friend sadly: "I have been among the most sanguine in believing that our Union would be of long duration. I now doubt it much."

ALTHOUGH the Missouri Compromise had simply legalized slavery below a geographic line, the South now asserted that no further attacks on the institution could be tolerated. Even public discussion of slavery should be eliminated from the political arena, public meetings, and newspaper columns.

If this was a brazen infringement of free speech, Boston's commercial aristocracy disregarded such niceties. A "conspiracy of silence" was clamped on the city and most of New England. For a decade nothing was allowed to disturb the calm until Walker's *Appeal*. David Walker was a free Negro born in North Carolina, who had traveled widely, observed the degradations of slavery, and now ran a second-hand clothing store in Boston. For a few years he had held Negro discussion groups in his shop, unobserved by the authorities. But in 1829 the publication of a small pamphlet of seventy-six pages sent a paroxysm of fear through the South.

In fiery language Walker's *Appeal* exhorted the Negro to strike back against his oppressors. It preached the principle, "kill or be killed," and demanded immediate revolts among the slaves. Three editions, each more militant than the last, were published before Walker's death in 1830.

The specter of slave revolts had always haunted the South. Prosser and Boxley had led revolts in Virginia at the turn of the century, Vesey in South Carolina as recently as 1822. The mayor of Savannah, Georgia, demanded that Mayor Harrison Gray Otis of Boston imprison Walker and confiscate the pamphlets. Otis complied by warning sea captains against carrying the pamphlet South on their ships. But he could find no law under which to prosecute the author.

The bloody Nat Turner revolt of 1831 brought Southern reactions to a climax. For three days in August, Turner's followers terrorized a whole Virginia county, killing about sixty people. After the revolt was quelled, seventeen slaves and three free Negroes were hanged and many transported.

The slave codes were strengthened and severely enforced—two Louisiana missionaries to the Cherokees, for example, were imprisoned for admitting colored children to their Indian school. The South was determined that no antislavery literature would reach its post offices. Georgetown in the District of Columbia decreed imprisonment and fines for any free Negro receiving abolitionist mail. Maryland passed a similar law. After a mob in Charleston, South Carolina, sacked the post office in 1835, the local postmaster agreed to stop delivery of antislavery material. Although his decision had no legality, it was supported by Postmaster General Amos Kendall, a Massachusetts politician and member of President Jackson's "Kitchen Cabinet."

Garrison had never met Walker and disapproved of his policy, but the Georgia legislature immediately voted five thousand dollars for Garrison's arrest and trial on its soil. South Carolina established a fine of one thousand five hundred dollars for the conviction of anyone who circulated the *Liberator*.

Boston cooperated by harassing Garrison's meetings. "The patriotism of all classes must be invoked to abstain from discussion, which by exasperating the master, can have no other effect than to render more oppressive the condition of the slave," Governor

Edward Everett, a favorite disciple of the textile and shipping magnates, told the Massachusetts Legislature in 1834. When Garrison's followers refused to abstain from discussion, Everett invoked the law. "Whatever . . . is calculated to incite an insurrection among the slaves . . . ," he announced, "may be prosecuted as an offense against the people of the Commonwealth."

Theodore Lyman had already tried to force two bills through the Massachusetts Legislature in 1821 and 1822, which would have excluded migratory Negroes from the state. This attempt failed. But in 1835 Everett attacked the Commonwealth's law of 1787 guaranteeing trial by jury to all persons under duress— a law occasionally used in the defense of runaway slaves. At the very time that abolitionist speakers were being mobbed throughout New England, the Massachusetts Legislature made its grand gesture to slavery by repealing the law.

GARRISON came out of Newburyport, where he was born in 1805, the Puritan past in his mother's lineage, the stamp of rigorous, Puritan dedication on his boyhood of poverty. His father left home when he was three and never returned. His mother, who "loved me so intensely that no language can describe the yearning of her soul," brought up three children, taking any job, traveling even to Baltimore to work in a shoe factory. At thirteen Garrison became an apprentice on the Newburyport *Herald*. At twenty, editing his own paper, he had already announced editorially the subject "that should be dwelt upon till our whole country is free from the curse—it is SLAVERY." In 1828, editor of a Bennington, Vermont, paper, he demanded that New England be roused from its "lethargy as by a trumpet call."

The early antislavery newspapers and societies before Garrison had been characterized by quiet respectability. They were often led by eminent statesmen like Chief Justice John Jay and his son, Judge William Jay, and Benjamin Franklin. By 1827, an estimated one hundred and forty to one hundred and eighty societies were in operation, at least half, significantly enough, in Southern States.

But in the violent Southern reaction after 1831, even Southern Quakers, the backbone of these groups, were silenced. By 1837 not one society remained in slave territory.

With only a vague program of future emancipation, they were a pale contrast to Garrison's decisive stand. They lacked militancy. Above all, they were thwarted by the popular acceptance of the American Colonization Society, founded in 1817 with the ostensible purpose of resettling Negroes in their own colonies, particularly Liberia.

Under the banner of philanthropy, Colonization in effect sought to remove the most intelligent slaves and free Negroes, the most obvious troublemakers, from the country. It not only drained the money of Northern philanthropists from productive antislavery work but lulled the public with the impression that the slavery problem was being intelligently solved. Garrison himself supported Colonization until he grasped its dangers and attacked it vehemently in a pamphlet, "Thoughts on African Colonization."

The most aggressive early crusader against slavery was Benjamin Lundy. A Quaker and editor of the *Genius of Universal Emancipation,* Lundy preached in almost every state, making most of his trips on foot, his papers on his back, walking as much as seven hundred miles on a single trip. Impressed by Garrison's editorials on slavery, Lundy walked from Baltimore to Vermont to enlist him as a partner in the *Genius.* Within a few months after he joined Lundy in Baltimore, Garrison struck hard, not just at New England but at his own birthplace.

If Boston's commercial aristocracy was a tacit ally of the South, many shipowners profited openly from the domestic slave trade, which carried an estimated fifty thousand Negroes yearly from one state to another. On November 13, 1829, Garrison attacked "this horrible traffic," singling out the ship *Francis,* owned by Francis Todd of Newburyport. Such men, cried Garrison, are *"highway robbers and murderers;* and their final doom will be, unless they speedily repent, to *occupy the lowest depths of perdition."*

Todd brought suit for libel against Garrison. In a Baltimore court in April, 1830, he was found guilty and fined fifty dollars and costs, a total of over one hundred dollars, more than he had probably ever possessed at one time. On April 17, Garrison entered the Baltimore jail and ended his partnership in the *Genius*. Even behind bars he kept up the attack, writing Todd, "I am in prison for denouncing slavery in a free country! You, who have assisted in oppressing your fellow creatures, are permitted to go at large and enjoy the fruits of your crime!" After forty-nine days, Garrison was released on bail supplied by Arthur Tappan, a wealthy New York merchant, native of Northampton, Massachusetts, who had long supported religious and antislavery causes.

In Boston, Garrison formed a partnership with Isaac Knapp, and began to plan the *Liberator*. At No. 11 Merchants Hall, in one room with "dingy walls; the small windows bespattered with printer's ink; the pressing stand in one corner . . . , the bed of the editor and publisher on the floor," as Oliver Johnson, an associate described it, they lived "chiefly upon bread and milk, a few cakes, and a little fruit."

The first issue of the *Liberator* appeared on January 1, 1831, Garrison's editorial flinging out its strident challenge to the land:

> Let Southern oppressors tremble—let their secret abettors tremble—let their Northern apologists tremble—let all the enemies of the persecuted blacks tremble.*** I *will be* as harsh as truth, and as uncompromising as justice. On this subject, I do not wish to think, or speak, or write, with moderation. Tell a man whose house is on fire to give a moderate alarm. . . . I am in earnest.—I will not equivocate—I will not excuse—I will not retreat a single inch—AND I WILL BE HEARD.

Rarely has the sound of one man's voice so disturbed a nation. It shattered the "conspiracy of silence" that had lasted from 1820 to 1831. People had forgotten the meaning of moral wrath. They were startled by this avenging angel, an inflexible figure from a Puritan mold. His language was furious, almost Biblical. He whipped and goaded the conscience of a people. He made them listen. He was all will, a symbol of the moral torment of his times.

His self-confidence was monolithic, "the selfless egotism of supreme self-assertion," John Jay Chapman described it.

Garrison raised the struggle against slavery above politics and compromise. He admitted no shadings of right and wrong. Slavery was total evil and had to be obliterated immediately and forever. "He did the work of a man of iron in an iron age," said Thomas Wentworth Higginson. The founding of the *Liberator* was a knife stroke cutting all ties with the past. Now the nation had to face itself.

CHAPTER IV

Mobs and Mad Women: 1833–1838

By 1831, the hustling merchants and farmers of Canterbury, Connecticut, located strategically on the Worcester and Norwich Turnpike, had built a town of classic beauty. A ring of majestic, white-framed houses with two-story pilasters and triple-arched, fanlight windows radiated from the village green to the lush farms beyond. The demands of their womenfolk for glitter and refinement even brought the town a prospering jewelry store. Now they lacked only one essential for complete respectability, a private seminary where their daughters could be given education and polish challenging the standards of Boston or Providence.

The search for an ideal headmistress finally settled on a brilliant and comely local teacher of twenty-seven named Prudence Crandall. She had the further merit of impeccable Puritan heritage, her mother claiming descent by marriage from Governor Bradford of Plymouth Colony. Supported by the wealthiest citizens, Prudence purchased a spacious house on the village green. The Canterbury Female Boarding School opened without incident and flourished for over a year. Then a seventeen-year-old girl named Sarah Harris applied for admission, and Prudence Crandall came to a decision that horrified Canterbury and most of New England.

For Sarah Harris was a Negro, and obviously a danger in Canterbury's eyes to its sacrosanct Boarding School. As a devout Quaker, however, Prudence had been "taught from childhood the sin of slavery," as she wrote the Reverend Samuel J. May who held a ministry six miles away. She was also a regular reader of the *Liberator* and an admirer of Garrison. Further, Sarah was eminently qualified. The daughter of a prosperous farmer, she had excelled in the district school and needed this advance education to prepare herself for a teaching career.

It is not surprising that Miss Crandall's Quaker conscience made her admit this first Negro pupil. And not unexpectedly, a parade of angry parents, led by the wife of the Episcopal minister, swarmed through Prudence's door the next day. But if Prudence thought their protests would dwindle away, she was wrong. Canterbury considered the social status of its school besmirched. Merchants feared the town's real estate values would tumble. One after another the leading citizens removed their daughters from the school until Prudence found herself with an empty building.

Facing financial ruin, Prudence now made a momentous decision—to convert the boarding school completely to Negro education. In January, 1833, she wrote Garrison for advice. A few weeks later she visited him in Boston and then went to Providence and New York to get the backing of other antislavery leaders. Advertisements were taken in the *Liberator*, soliciting students. By April, twenty colored girls arrived in Canterbury to begin their studies.

The presence of these students meant catastrophe as far as Canterbury was concerned. Three town meetings were held in one week to develop a plan for driving Miss Crandall out of town. The leader of the opposition was a prominent lawyer, Arthur T. Judson, soon to become a Congressman and eventually judge of the United States District Court. His indignation was personal, for he owned a fine home next to the school. He was also chief spokesman of the local Colonization Society, and Connecticut was a Colonization stronghold, equally bitter against abolitionists and free Negroes whom it intended to eradicate as a "curse and a contagion." Further, Judson was an ambitious politician. The Crandall case could be nicely exploited for his own purposes.

Garrison, too, recognized its significance, and immediately wrote the Reverend May that "Miss C. must be sustained at all hazards." While Prudence had not foreseen that she would soon become the focal point of abolitionist propaganda, she was a lone woman against a whole town. When May and George W. Benson, Garrison's future brother-in-law, hurried over from Brooklyn, six miles away, she accepted their help.

The crucial town meeting took place on March 9th. Since it was hardly acceptable for a woman to defend herself in public, May attended as Prudence's representative. Still hoping to avoid a fight, she approved a plan to move the school to the outskirts of town. But Judson whipped the meeting into such fury against her that May was unable to present the compromise plan. He was surrounded and almost beaten by a fist-shaking mob. When he tried to return to the hall to address the last stragglers, the trustees ordered the doors locked in his face.

A reign of terror was now launched against the school. When Prudence or her pupils walked down the street, they were followed by urchins and raggamuffins, screaming and blowing horns in their ears. The gentry had their own weapons—local merchants refusing Prudence's purchases, doctors refusing to treat the students. Rocks were constantly thrown through the school windows. Manure, dumped in the school well, permanently poisoned its water supply.

Prudence survived those months only through the determination of her father, brother, and a Negro merchant from a nearby town. Each day through a gantlet of curses and stones, they carried supplies and water to the school.

Once it was apparent Prudence could not be driven out by violence, Canterbury turned to the courts. An ancient Vagrant Act gave the town selectmen authority to fine any out-of-state resident who had been warned to leave town but refused. If the fine remained unpaid, the offender could be whipped "on the naked body not exceeding ten stripes."

Since most students came from other states, the town brought charges against one sixteen-year-old girl from Providence. She upset Canterbury's strategy, however, by insisting on the whipping. Even the Reverend May had not looked for such martyrdom and blocked execution of the penalty by posting bond for all students.

Judson, however, was determined not to be licked at legal in-fighting. On May 24, he rushed a bill through the Connecticut

Legislature. Known as the "Black Law," it provided that no
school for out-of-state pupils could be established in any town
without the approval of local officials. Canterbury greeted its
passage with ringing church bells and booming cannon.

Since Prudence still refused to close the school, she was arrested under the law in late June. She had come a long way from
her simple insistence on education for Negroes. Jail would bring
abolitionism its first woman martyr, and the Reverend May was
ready to exploit the chance. He arranged with the jailer that
Prudence should occupy the same cell that had just been vacated
by a murderer named Watkins, executed a few days previously.
The bed and mattress on which Watkins had slept, however, were
tactfully removed and replaced with new ones. For twenty-four
hours the cell doors closed behind Prudence Crandall. The next
day May supplied bail, and she was released. Garrison and abolition had their martyr. The *Liberator's* headlines cried, "Savage
Barbarity!"

Martyrdom, however, needs a public, and the majority of the
nation's press simply ignored the story. Newspapers in the neighborhood counties were particularly fearful of Judson and Canterbury's rulers. At this crucial moment, Arthur Tappan in New York
heard of Prudence's lonely fight. He was a rabid reformer who
specialized in education and helped found Kenyon and Oberlin
colleges. Hurrying to Canterbury himself, he located an old
printing press, purchased it, and hand-picked young Charles C.
Burleigh to publish a new paper dedicated to the Crandall cause.

Tappan's almost bottomless resources were doubly helpful because for almost a year Prudence would be enmeshed in a propaganda and legal war. Three times her case came to trial. By July,
1834, Judson and Canterbury had still not won court authority
to close the school.

Anger at this delay boiled through the town, and violence was
its inevitable result. For two years a lonely woman had successfully resisted a whole community. Her bravery even amazed Garrison who wrote that she was "as undaunted as if she had the whole
world on her side." But late that summer a group of ruffians set

fire to the school. The flames were extinguished with a minimum of damage, and Prudence kept the school going until the final attack on the night of September 9th. Then a large mob, carefully organized, broke into the school. Armed with clubs and iron bars, they shattered ninety panes of glass and virtually wrecked the front rooms of the building.

It was too much to expect a group of girls to live under daily physical violence. Further, repairs of the building would require sizable capital, and Prudence was penniless. There was a final irony in this inevitable retreat. During the last hectic months, Prudence had fallen in love with Calvin Philleo, a minister from Ithaca, New York. The Reverend Philleo seemed to lack her nerveless stamina and devotion to Negro education. They had been married five days before the attack, and he strongly objected to spending any more of his honeymoon as the target of mobs. Prudence sadly consented to give up the school, and the Reverend May reluctantly concurred, writing, "The words almost blistered my lips. I felt ashamed of Canterbury, ashamed of Connecticut, ashamed of my country, ashamed of my color."

Prudence Crandall and her husband disappeared into the Midwest. She had fought on a single issue, the right of education for Negroes. Standing alone against violence even before Garrison faced the mob in Boston in 1835, she had lifted women from obscurity to the forefront of antislavery. But as far as the record shows, she neither spoke nor wrote on abolition during the next fifty years.

Then in 1886 Canterbury and Connecticut sought to make amends. A group of prominent citizens, led by Judson's nephew, got the State Legislature to pass a resolution of apology. Another town resident, Mark Twain, conceived the plan of buying Prudence Crandall's old school and presenting it to her as a home for her declining years. She turned down the offer but finally accepted a State pension. When a reporter located her in Elks Falls, Kansas, she told him wistfully, "Here in Elks Falls there is nothing for my soul to feed upon. . . . No one visits me, and I begin to think they are afraid of me."

AFTER exploring the American political scene in the summer of
1834, Harriet Martineau, the prominent English writer, concluded: "The country people are abolitionists by nature and education, and they see the inequity of mob law." The Canterbury
mobs would seem to render her judgment premature. Rural New
England at this point welcomed neither abolition nor Negro
education. Only a year later, when Noyes Academy at Canaan,
New Hampshire, admitted a few colored students, the village
wasted no time on legal procedures. Three hundred men, assisted
by a hundred yoke of oxen, simply attached ropes to the school
building and hauled it outside the town limits. It would be almost
1840 before the economic decline of New England farms, the
vast, agricultural expansion of the West and Southwest, and the
increasing dominance of the textile and factory economy, directed
the frustrations of the rural areas against slavery.

Prudence Crandall was indeed a phenomenon, the authentic
mold from which future women rebels were formed. For American women were still second-class citizens. In marriage they had
no legal rights over their own property. They could not even
execute a contract. Economically, there were few job openings
except as schoolteachers although thousands of the less-educated
were deserting the farms to work for about two dollars a week in
Francis Cabot Lowell's mills.

It was too early for feminine rebellion on a broad front. The
rare exception like Frances Wright, who had bewitched Lafayette
with her beauty on his American tour in 1824, could shout noisily
for liberalized divorce laws, free thought, and Robert Owen's
brand of socialism. But after all, she had been born and brought
up in Scotland and the public quickly damned her as a free-lover
and an anticlerical crackpot. The less flamboyant rebels like Lucy
Stone and Lucretia Mott were frustrated at every turn by the
bullying world of men. Only in the antislavery movement, and
not always here, could they find an outlet. Thus they were forced
to channel their energies against slavery. It gave them scope and
status. It provided flame for their souls.

They learned to make good use of every feminine weapon from
the knitting needle to the tea table. Furious at the proslavery

sermons of her minister, Mrs. Almira Swett of Ipswich, Massachusetts, carried her knitting to church and clicked her needles noisily in protest all through the service. After a few Sundays of such obstructionism, Mrs. Swett was arrested for "contempt of worship" and sent to the House of Correction. But the chivalrous jailer, reported a contemporary observer, "declined to receive her."

Even children were utilized in the knitting brigade, Boston girls crocheting samplers with such appropriate messages as, "May the points of our needles prick the slaveholders' consciences!"

The tea table became a major battleground. On their social calls women recruited new prospects and secured signatures for the omnipresent petitions, their only access to Congress. By 1837, thirty-two Female Antislavery Societies had been organized in Massachusetts alone. On one petition, opposing the expansion of slavery in Texas, New England women collected forty-five thousand signatures.

The power of the tea table has been adroitly eulogized by one feminine poet:

> We know, to our sorrow, that over their tea,
> These ladies, for months, have been brewing
> A plot to dismember the Union and free
> Your slaves to their positive ruin.

Soon the ladies plunged into more active combat, many serving as key agents on the Underground Railroad, hiding escaped slaves at great risk at key "stations" in Providence, Boston, and more rural routes on the path to Canada. Mrs. George S. Hillard, an aristocratic Bostonian, built a secret compartment in her Pinckney Street home. Her husband, first sympathetic but soon an enthusiastic Webster Whig, was either ignorant of her lawbreaking or ignored it. Mrs. Elizabeth Buffum Chace, a devout Quaker whose home near Providence was a frequent "station," often disguised escaped slaves in severe, stiff-collared Quaker dress to expedite their escape. She also carried on a ceaseless campaign against the segregationist policies of the Rhode Island railroads by forcing her way into "Jim Crow" cars and sitting with the Negroes.

Abby Kelley, the brashest and probably prettiest woman abolitionist, maintained a pivotal Worcester "station" on her farm, a
secret cellar vault connecting by tunnel to an abandoned well.
Like most abolitionists, she came from old Puritan stock. One of
the first women graduates of Oberlin, she was an unquenchable
feminist, splitting the American Antislavery Society, as we shall
see, by her demands for feminine equality.

With her husband, Stephen Foster, an equally fiery abolitionist
and feminist, they made up a stormy team. At Dartmouth he was
jailed for his pacifism and refusal of military service. Afterward,
he gave up the Congregationalist ministry to become a full-time
antislavery agent. He was still a rebel in 1872, refusing to pay
taxes on his farm unless his wife was given the vote.

These women could handle their share of physical combat, Mrs.
Thankful Southwick of Boston, aided by a band of Negro women,
engineering the escape of two slaves from the brig *Chickasaw*
in 1836. After the slaves were discovered in Boston harbor and
the captain insisted on returning them to Baltimore, Mrs. Southwick got them into court on a writ of *habeas corpus*. Fearful that
if the judge released them the owner might have them immediately
rearrested under another legal process, she packed the courtroom
with her followers. As soon as the claimant darted forth his arm,
women surrounded the slaves. One portly Negress threw her arms
around the court officer. "A lane had been made. . . . At a given
signal, the slaves were spirited away from the crowded courtroom
and out of the city," reported Miss Martineau.

Lucy Stone has been credited with saving the life of the Reverend May. When a mob attacked the Haverhill, Massachusetts, hall
where he was delivering an abolition speech, Lucy took his arm
and led him through the mob, daring them to touch her first. And
just in time! For at the corner, May relates, they met "a posse of
men, more savage than the rest, dragging a cannon, which they
intended to explode against the building. . . ."

Lucy, born on a Massachusetts farm, a granddaughter of a
leader of Shays' Rebellion, was an Oberlin graduate, later expelled
from her church for abolitionism. Above all, she was a feminist,

carrying her fight for equality to the altar. When she married Henry B. Blackwell, she omitted the word "obey" from the ceremony and promised only to "love and honor." The couple even prepared an elaborate document, protesting the male's legal dominance in marriage. To make sure the world knew where they stood, the document was published in all local papers. But the moment the ceremony concluded, relates the Reverend Thomas Wentworth Higginson, who married them, "Lucy, the heroic Lucy, *cried* like any village bride. . . ."

Lucretia Mott, Nantucket-born but transplanted to Boston at eighteen, was a delegate to the World Antislavery Convention in London in 1840. "A glorified presence," Frederick Douglass, an escaped slave and antislavery leader, called her. Lucretia Mott and Elizabeth Cady Stanton were shocked to find British abolitionists as determined to keep women in a subservient role as most of their American colleagues. With other women delegates from England they were forced to sit apart from the men, screened discreetly by a heavy curtain. Lady Byron, the poet's widow, protested vehemently. And Garrison, who had been devoting so much space in the *Liberator* to the feminist cause that John Greenleaf Whittier warned he was weakening abolitionism, made his protest by refusing to join the convention and sat alone in the gallery.

Lucretia and Elizabeth, demanding equal participation, laid siege to the male delegates at their hotel. Three British clergymen hopped excitedly around the women, thrusting the Bible in their faces and declaiming passages to prove the Lord's desire to maintain feminine segregation. But the ladies wore them down. To get some peace, the men were forced to move to another hotel— all except the Reverend Nathaniel Colver of Boston, who fortified himself each morning by eating six raw eggs. Walking home alone the last night of the convention, Lucretia and Elizabeth vowed than an open feminist rebellion could no longer be postponed. The first Women's Rights Convention, held at Seneca Falls, New York in 1848, was conceived then and there by two bedeviled women three thousand miles from home.

The most powerful feminine weapon was the pen. And no

one wielded it more forcefully than Mrs. Lydia Maria Child! Granddaughter of a Revolutionary soldier, daughter of a wealthy baker, she had achieved unprecedented fame and was easily the largest-selling woman author in the country by 1833. In South as well as North, her books were household classics. *The Frugal Housewife* went into thirty-three editions. *The Mother's Book* and *The Little Girl's Own Book* instructed a whole generation in such rudiments of life as the saving of twine, the merits of hard gingerbread, and the thrifty use of the backs of old letters for further scribbling.

What a thunderbolt was then unleased in 1833 when this revered spokesman of Puritan homilies suddenly switched to politics and published a savage and erudite attack on slavery, *An Appeal in Favor of That Class of Americans Called Africans!* Until *Uncle Tom's Cabin* in 1852, no book reached so wide an audience.

Southern ladies publicly burned her previous works and deluged her with scathing letters. One Atlanta belle, inviting Mrs. Child to visit, promised her "lodgings in the calaboose with as much nigger company as you desire." The reaction at home was equally harsh. Formerly the idol of Boston, she was now ignored by most booksellers. Boston had bestowed upon her that supreme badge of achievement—a free card at the Athenaeum, library and meeting place of the intellectual aristocracy. Now her card was withdrawn. One prominent member, disdaining to soil his hands, is said to have lifted *The Appeal* from the shelves with a pair of fire tongs and flung it from the window.

In the face of such bitterness, Mrs. Child retorted mildly that if the book had advanced abolition "even one single hour," she would not exchange it "for all Rothschild's wealth or Sir Walter's fame."

The Appeal was not only the first remarkable challenge by a woman in the slavery debates. But through Mrs. Child's prominence, it "reached thousands who had given no heed to us before," as the Reverend May pointed out. Its impact was felt even in the Brahmin world. The Reverend John Palfrey, who had inherited slaves from his father's Louisiana plantations, testified that *The Appeal* made him give them their freedom. Charles Sumner stated that it influenced his whole career in Congress. Higginson wrote that this book alone had converted him to abolitionism.

The workhorse of the movement was Mrs. Maria Weston Chapman, one of Boston's dazzling Weston sisters. She roamed the state ceaselessly, organizing Female Antislavery Societies; edited the *Liberator* when Garrison was away; and served on the executive committee of the American Antislavery Society. For twenty-five years she kept replenishing the empty coffers of abolitionism with her women's fairs and bazaars. "The Joan of Our Ark," the poet James Russell Lowell, momentarily resorting to pun, called her.

Everyone who met her waxed wildly eloquent over Mrs. Chapman's beauty. One observer described her "slender, graceful form, the golden hair which might have covered her feet; the brilliant complexion, noble profile, and deep purple eyes." Another always remembered her voice, "clear and sparkling as a running brook."

At the National Antislavery Convention of American Women in Philadelphia in 1838, Mrs. Chapman, although ill with a high fever, insisted on making her scheduled speech. Mobs circled the hall, which they eventually burned to the ground. Bricks smashed through the windows. The brilliant, crimson shawl around Mrs. Chapman's shoulders was like a beacon to the panicky audience. "I kept my eye on that shawl . . ." one delegate wrote. "I made up my mind until that shawl disappeared, every man must stick to his guns."

Mrs. Chapman was the most glittering symbol of this new breed of women in rebellion. "Something about her," her grandson, William Jay Chapman, recalled years later, "reminded me of a gladiator. . . . I cannot help thinking of all the antislavery people as being earth-born, titanic creatures, whom Nature spawned to stay a plague and then withdrew them and broke the mold. Heroic they remain."

CHAPTER V

The Grimké Sisters—Southern Belles on a Rampage

THEY WERE an almost unbelievable phenomenon, these two fragile sisters from Charleston, South Carolina. Sarah and Angelina Grimké were the ultimate rebels. Born to the highest purple of Charleston's slave-holding aristocracy, they deserted the South and invaded New England like screaming banshees. They were tormented souls, proof that an evangelistic conscience does not necessarily spring from Boston soil. From 1835 to 1838 they were the anguish and fury of the abolition movement, driven by inner devils that made them the most passionate of all Puritans.

Sarah was born in 1792, Angelina thirteen years later. Their father, Judge John Faucheraud Grimké, a descendant of Charleston's earliest French and German settlers, inherited great wealth, plantations, and slaves. But his own brilliance as a lawyer made him Senior Associate, comparable to Chief Justice, of the State's Supreme Court.

Their mother, Mary Smith, a dominant figure in the social hierarchy of Charleston as well as the Episcopal Church, came from an equally distinguished English family. Two of her forebears had been Colonial governors. Her great-grandfather was Second Landgrave of South Carolina, a resplendent title bestowed on a few major landholders under South Carolina's early feudal system.

Heirs to all Charleston could bestow, both girls rebelled from childhood. At five, after watching the whipping of a family slave, Angelina ran to a local sea captain and begged him to carry the slave to freedom. At night she would steal off to the slave cottages and rub oil on the wounds of those who had been whipped. She taught her dressing maid to read, noting in her diary: "The light was put out, the key-hole screened, and flat on our stomachs before the fire, we defied the laws of South Carolina."

Already she envisioned her future crusade, writing: "If I could only be the means of exposing the cruelty and injustice. . . ." Even at thirteen she was repelled by the hypocrisy of religion's approval of slavery and refused to be confirmed in the Episcopal Church.

Sarah, the elder, had first rebelled against Charleston's "circles of dissipation and folly," and scandalized her family by wanting to study law. This revolt found some outlet when she accompanied her father to Philadelphia for medical treatment and was deeply impressed by the Quaker families she met. After Judge Grimké died, she became a Quaker, the sole woman in Charleston's society of two old men. Dressed in rigidly simple Quaker costume, she was the city's prime symbol of dissent.

Their hunger for salvation must have made both girls terrifying bores in their own home. They removed from their clothing all laces, flounces, veils, and trimmings, even the bows of their shoes. Since they considered the novels of Walter Scott in the family library a sentimental indulgence, they destroyed the complete set. Angelina made her mother call the servants together at a set time each day for religious instruction. Mrs. Grimké was further cajoled to share a half hour of brooding silence with her daughters before tea, and when she dared to repaper the drawing room, they attacked her "luxury and ease."

It is little wonder that Mrs. Grimké was appalled by what she called her "alien daughters." For Sarah and Angelina had virtually taken the whole guilt of the South on their shoulders. Their ascetic devotions provided a temporary release, but Sarah soon fled to her Quaker friends in Philadelphia. Angelina followed her in 1829.

Remarkably, neither sister had yet become the stern-visaged heretic that later photographs reveal. They were tall graceful girls with blue eyes and chestnut hair set in buoyant ringlets. The next five years, however, were a period of tortured and desperate searching. They practiced Quakerism diligently, hoping to become leaders in the Society of Friends. They worked with the poor.

They spent long days, even weeks, in harsh isolation. Their diaries in this period are filled with the frenzy of neurotic despair as they groped their way toward salvation.

It was Angelina, the younger, who found it first by breaking not only with her past but with the Friends, and giving herself completely to the abolition movement. Her final commitment took the form of a letter which she sent Garrison on August 30, 1835. "It is my deep, solemn, deliberate conviction that this is a cause worth dying for," she wrote. ". . . Yes! let it come—let us suffer, rather than insurrection should arise."

The letter brought a week of excruciating pain. For two days she held it. "On my bended knees," she wrote in her diary, "I implore Divine direction. . . ." Finally she mailed it, then sank into despair again until the fifth day when, after constant prayer, she reported that God seemed "to open the windows of Heaven."

Garrison himself had no such doubts. Delighted at this unique recruit, he published the letter in the *Liberator*. Overnight Angelina created national turmoil. In Charleston she was damned by the press which linked her with Garrison as the No. 1 target. Even her friends in Philadelphia considered the letter "the ravings of a fanatic." Her Quaker associates, who at best favored Colonization and strongly opposed Garrison, demanded she recant. Sister Sarah joined them.

But instead of recanting, Angelina sat down and wrote *An Appeal to the Christian Women of the South*, the most devastating attack against slavery since Mrs. Child's book three years before. She demanded that Southern women take the lead by setting their slaves free and flooding Congress with a campaign of speeches and petitions against the institution. It was a passionate, furious book, burning with the insight and personal observations of a former aristocrat who had seen slavery make of her home "a whited sepulchre, full of dead men's bones and all uncleanness."

Charleston turned violently on one of its proudest daughters. A few copies of Angelina's book reached the city. Mobs seized them and burned them in the streets. When Angelina announced she was returning home for a short visit, the mayor informed Mrs. Grimké that her daughter would not be allowed to set foot on

South Carolina soil, and if she managed to evade the harbor police, she would be immediately jailed.

In antislavery circles, however, Angelina was hailed as an avenging angel. She followed her first literary triumph with a second book in 1838, *An Appeal to the Women of the Nominally Free States*. Then Elizur Wright, secretary of the American Antislavery Society, invited her to New York to address women abolitionists. Sarah had now emerged from five years of inner turmoil, following Angelina out of the Friends and into the abolition movement. Henceforth the sisters would be a team.

Their names were not even included in the notices of their first parlor meeting. But the word got around. When three hundred women tried to crowd into the parlor, the meeting had to be moved to a nearby Baptist Church. It was a significant event, probably the first time except for Fanny Wright that American women had addressed a public gathering in a public hall.

Elizur Wright sent them to Hudson, Poughkeepsie, and upstate New York, speaking on a weekly schedule to overflow audiences. That spring the Massachusetts Antislavery Society invited them on a tour that opened in Dorchester. As usual the meeting, scheduled for a parlor, had to be moved to the Town Hall to accommodate the crowds. Accidental as it may have been, there were explosive consequences. A few men, listening through the windows, finally squeezed into the back of the hall. All that week, more and more men joined the ladies in what horrified New Englanders would soon call "promiscuous audiences." After the first mixed audience, Angelina noted in her diary, "Nearly twenty men present, pretty easy to speak." At Lynn on July 21st, men came by invitation for the first time. A thousand people packed the hall. To accommodate the overflow, a second meeting was held the following night.

Even the Reverend May, who at first admitted "a miserable prejudice" against women speakers, was swept away. He invited the sisters to his South Scituate pulpit, where they were so successful he scheduled them at churches in Hingham, Duxbury and surrounding towns.

Soon the sisters were speaking six nights a week, the demand

Left. William Lloyd Garrison, founder of the *Liberator,* and symbol of the abolitionist movement *(Widener Library, Harvard). Below.* Wendell Phillips, a magnificent orator who became known as the "golden trumpet" of abolition *(Widener Library, Harvard)*

THOMPSON,
THE ABOLITIONIST.

That infamous foreign scoundrel **THOMPSON**, will hold forth *this afternoon*, at the Liberator Office, No. 48, Washington Street. The present is a fair opportunity for the friends of the Union to *snake Thompson out!* It will be a contest between the Abolitionists and the friends of the Union. A purse of **$100** has been raised by a number of patriotic citizens to reward the individual who shall first lay violent hands on Thompson, so that he may be brought to the tar kettle before dark. Friends of the Union, be vigilant!

Oct 21. 1835

Boston, Wednesday, 12 o'clock.

Distributed through Boston October 21, 1835, this handbill roused a "broadcloth mob" of merchants and clerks whose interests lay with the South against George Thompson, visiting British abolitionist. When the mob failed to find Thompson, it almost lynched Garrison *(Bostonian Society, Old State House)* finally forcing them to separate, Angelina appearing in one town, Sarah in another. When a thousand people packed one church and the joists began to slip, the audience was warned to leave. But no one moved! In another church, space was at such a premium that men propped ladders against the window sills and stood on the rungs.

Although both sisters were superb speakers, Angelina particularly probed and wrung the deepest passions of her audience. "An eloquence such as never had been heard from a woman," Wendell Phillips described it. Even more essential was her skill at "laying bare her own heart to search the hearts of others," Phillips concluded.

Angelina, the first feminine abolitionist in the North who had lived intimately with slavery, knew how to translate her own revulsion into a virtual orgy of pain and guilt. She considered herself an instrument of God. Her mission was to immerse each audience in her own neurotic suffering. They wept with her as she hit the sawdust trail in town after town, flooding New England in an ocean of tears.

One night in Groton, Massachusetts, a gang of boys pelted the sisters with apples. In Bolton, every church was closed against them, and when their meeting was scheduled in a private home, their placards were ripped down. At Worcester the minister of a Congregational Church threatened to resign if Angelina spoke in his parish house. Suddenly the sisters were surrounded by enemies, attacking them not as abolitionists, at least not openly, but as women who had dared to speak in public and, even worse, to mixed audiences.

The spearhead of the opposition was the Reverend Nehemiah Adams, who had been dubbed "Southside" Adams since his passionate apology for the institution, *A Southside View of Slavery*. Behind him was the omnipotent General Association of Congregational Ministers of Massachusetts, which passed a resolution censuring the Grimkés and forbidding any minister to open his church to women speakers. "If the vine . . . thinks to assume the independence and overshadowing nature of the elm," proclaimed the Association's pastoral letter, "it will not only cease to bear fruit, but will fall in shame and dishonor in the dust. . . . The power of a woman is her dependence."

Angelina retorted angrily, "Are we aliens because we are women?" To a friend she wrote, "My idea is that whatever is morally right for a man to do is morally right for a woman to do."

Overnight, the abolitionist crusade became a tangle of screaming, hair-pulling hellions. Garrison plunged gaily into the fray. At the annual meeting of the New England Antislavery Society, he forced through a resolution allowing women to sit on the convention floor. The delegates from the Andover Theological Seminary protested vehemently. Eight orthodox clergymen resigned, seven others made written protests. "The whole land seems aroused to the discussion of the province of woman," Angelina exulted. The "ultimate result," she predicted, "will most certainly be 'the breaking of every yoke' . . . an emancipation far more glorious than any the world has ever yet seen. . . ."

Maria Chapman satirized the ruckus over the Grimkés in biting verse:

> They've taken a notion to speak for themselves,
> And are wedding the tongue and the pen;
> They've mounted the rostrum; the termagant elves,
> And—oh horrid!—are talking to men.

It was exhaustion, not the orthodox clergy, that finally stopped the sisters. After a year of ceaseless campaigning, Sarah's voice had become dangerously strained. Angelina was ordered by her physician to rest every moment away from the platform. She said she was "sometimes so sick before I rise that it seems almost impossible for me to speak ten minutes." After a brief period of seclusion in the country, they returned to Boston for a whirlwind climax, six successive evenings at the Odeon Theater. The press lampooned them as "Devilina" and "Grimalkin." But each night, two to three thousand people jammed the hall. Most important of all, it was the first time a major Boston auditorium had been opened to abolitionist speakers.

Angelina went on to one final triumph. Two years before, the Lunt Committee of the Massachusetts Legislature, bowing to

Southern demands for an investigation, had denied Dr. Charles Follen and other abolitionists the chance for equal testimony. But in February, 1838, Representative James C. Alvord opened the State House to Angelina. Not only could she reach the highest policy-makers of Massachusetts; it was the first time the State House had admitted a woman speaker. Above all, the invitation marked a dramatic shift in official attitude toward abolition.

Angelina made the most of it. On three successive days, hundreds of standees packed the hall, hundreds more were turned away. Her vivid testimony against the horrors of slavery, reported Wendell Phillips, was "the wail of a broken-hearted child." Phillips noted that the audience clung to her words in "painful silence." Angelina wrote in her diary, "the chairman was in tears almost the whole time I was speaking."

On the second day an antagonistic legislator tried to stop the meeting on the excuse that overflow crowds imperiled the safety of the gallery. Another legislator from Salem retorted wryly that a committee should be appointed "to examine the foundations of the State House to see whether it will bear another lecture from Miss Grimké."

All these months Angelina had worked closely with Theodore Dwight Weld, a Connecticut abolitionist who had led the rebellion at Lane Seminary in Ohio and established himself as the most dynamic abolitionist in the West. At the height of her career, like Prudence Crandall, Angelina was courted and won. She married Weld in Philadelphia on May 14, 1838, turning even the ceremony into a brilliant propaganda display. Six former slaves of the Grimké family were among the guests, "our testimony against the horrible prejudice," Sarah noted. Since liberal Pennsylvania laws made a marriage legal if witnessed by twelve people, Angelina and Weld dispensed with a minister to bind the nuptials. Garrison read the marriage agreement. Angelina and Weld themselves officiated, Weld reading into the record a biting attack against "the unrighteous power vested in a husband by the laws of the United States over the person and property of his wife." The only clerical attendants, two Negro and white ministers, were allotted a few minutes to pray for the union.

The honeymoon was equally bizarre. While Prudence Crandall defended her school against the Canterbury mobs, the Welds journeyed to Philadelphia to attend the opening of the Antislavery Convention of American Women.

It met at Liberty Hall, a sumptuous, new, gaslit building financed by abolitionists and other reformers. The opening night drew three thousand Negro and white delegates, seated together. This infringement of social custom particularly inflamed the mob gathered outside. An appeal for protection was sent to the mayor, but he blandly insisted there was no danger.

Maria Chapman, as we have seen, calmed the audience while rocks hurtled through the windows. Then Angelina rose to her last hour of public glory. "The calmness and impassioned earnestness of Angelina Grimké speaking nearly an hour amid that howling mob," one delegate testified fervently, "was not surpassed in courage or consecration by Paul among the wild beasts at Ephesus."

The mob returned the following night, fifteen thousand strong. Again the convention appealed to the mayor for police protection. He came himself and addressed the mob, insisting they were good citizens. Shortly after the mayor left, the convention adjourned. The mob broke into the building, sacked it, and burned it to the ground.

Angelina and Sarah descended to earth like exhausted meteors. The Welds moved to a New Jersey farmhouse, accompanied, of course, by Sarah. All three continued to write vigorously against slavery. But the fury of their rebellion seemed to have dissipated itself among a maze of new causes. Every new and daring fad, mysticism, Mrs. Bloomer's clothes, the diets of Sylvester Graham, they automatically embraced and championed. The Welds even practiced on their infant son, Charles Stuart, feeding him only a tablespoonful of milk an hour according to Grahamite principle until a friend insisted he was starving to death.

A final irony haunted the sisters after the Civil War when they discovered a namesake, Archibald E. Grimké, on the student roster of Lincoln University, a Negro institution in Pennsylvania. Their investigation turned up a brother, Francis. More startling yet, they found that the boys were the sons of their brother, Henry, by a Negro mistress!

Never ones to flinch from facts, the sisters publicly acknowledged the boys as their nephews and helped them complete their studies. And now it was the colored Grimkés who would keep that proud, Charleston name before the nation! Archibald, a prominent writer, went on the become United States Consul in Santo Domingo and vice president of the National Association for the Advancement of Colored People. Francis established an honored career as Presbyterian minister in Washington, D.C.

Thus the whole lives of these sisters were plagued by ironies. Outcasts from birth in their own homeland, they brought their fierce moral standards to a Boston that had nurtured the Puritan ethic but could never accept the rampages of two unfettered women. Their tortured souls thrived on the martyred air of abolition. Yet even Boston abolitionists thought them a little mad. By spreading their torment across the headlines, they gave New England its first intimate contact with the horrors of slavery. There would be other proud Southerners, James G. Birney particularly, who fled their homes to preach the antislavery gospel in the North. But no one struck with the fire of the Grimkés. And New England recoiled for years from their wrath.

CHAPTER VI

Boston Rebels and the Martyrdom of Lovejoy: 1837

IT WAS A passionate time when passionate men gave up wealth and position for their faith. "I was called upon by a voice from heaven as Saul of old was," Dr. Bowditch declared when he joined the abolitionist band. Francis Jackson, a conservative businessman, underwent conversion with no less fervor. Appalled by the attack on the Female Antislavery Society the day of the Garrison riot, he offered the ladies his luxurious home to "perpetuate the right of free discussion," aware he was subjecting his family and possessions to the fury of the mob.

"And if in defense of this sacred privilege, which man did not give me, and shall not (if I can help it) take from me," he wrote, "this roof and these walls shall be levelled to the earth, let them fall! . . . They cannot crumble in a better cause."

If their passion often reached a hairline from eccentricity, Higginson insisted that "without a little crack somewhere, a man could hardly do his duty to his times." The cultists and the mystics stood shoulder to shoulder with hard-headed lawyers like Ellis Gray Loring. "Father Lamson," a patriarchal figure in flowing white beard, who conceived himself the symbol of hurrying Time, carried a scythe and stood at meetings, silent and awesome, resting his chin on its handle. By contrast, Abby Folsom generally dominated meetings with such endless tirades that one contemporary "longed for the authority of the Puritan elders to banish her from the state." After she had refused repeated admonitions of silence at one meeting, three men finally hustled her from the hall. But Abby, clinging to the last word, cried, "I'm better off than Jesus— He had one ass to carry Him, I have three!"

Nothing could dampen their personal eccentricities. Henry C.

Wright, a Congregational minister in Newburyport, incurred the
wrath of his parish by removing his clothes in broad daylight and
swimming the Merrimack River. John Humphrey Noyes, whose
impeccable background included the Yale Divinity School and a
wealthy father, a Vermont Congressman, first startled his family
by renouncing, like Garrison, his allegiance to the national government as a tool of Southern slaveholders. As if this wasn't enough,
he proceeded to organize the Oneida colony in upper New York
state, one of the most daring social experiments of the century.
Noyes not only abolished the institution of marriage, but established "scientific breeding" under which men and women needed
the prior approval of their elders before joining together as child-
bearers. Noyes, however, was proof that commercial success and
eccentricity were delightfully compatible. For his Oneida Community Plate, manufactured at the colony, grew into a million-
dollar business which still flourishes today.

The Tappan brothers, Lewis and Arthur, were protagonists of
the same principle. Although they had made a fortune as merchants
in New York, they were born in Northampton, Massachusetts
of solid Puritan stock. Gladly they contributed much of their
fortune to the abolitionist cause, and flung themselves into such
personal crusades as discharging employees who smoked, played
cards, or attended the theater. No chair ever appeared in the office
of either brother. They were convinced business could be carried
on more efficiently when customers were denied a seat.

If sin was an endless challenge to reformers like Dr. Samuel
Gridley Howe, equally noted for his battle against slavery as his
work for the blind, it had considerable drawbacks for his family.
Julia Ward Howe's pet name for her husband was "The Comet-
Apostle." During his long absences from home, while his sword
and pen were engaged against the Devil, she would sing to their
children:

> Rero rero riddlety rad,
> This morning my baby caught sight of her Dad.
> Quoth she, "Oh, Daddy, where have you been?"
> "With Mann and Sumner a-putting down sin!"

THE EARLY abolitionists paid dearly for their faith through professional and social ostracism. David Child, husband of Lydia Maria, lost most of his legal practice. Henry Chapman, one of the rare Boston merchants to support Garrison before 1835, was boycotted by business associates both in New England and the South.

The Reverend Theodore Parker stated, "I am as much an outcast from society as if I were a convicted pirate." The Reverend John Palfrey, after bringing his freed slaves North at his own expense, walked up Beacon Street, saying, "Once I was invited to those fine houses, but now I never enter them."

"It ostracized me as it did others . . . ," wrote Dr. Bowditch. "Captain Oxnard, one of my father's old and respected friends, . . . would even stare and scowl without speaking when we met. . . ."

Bowditch's associates warned him that abolitionism was ruining him professionally. After he was selected admitting physician of the Massachusetts General Hospital, the trustees suddenly changed their minds. It was five years before he was placed on the staff.

His enemies took an advertisement in the Boston *Courier*, stating: "If a physician . . . is secretary of . . . political meetings, if he makes speeches on the street, we do not ask him to come and see us when we are sick." On this newspaper clipping, Bowditch scrawled, "I will live or die in Boston, practicing my profession here or nowhere. I will always have an opinion on any subject and express that opinion when and where I choose."

In one Boston street clash over an escaped slave, Bowditch relates that, "the marshal stepped up to me from behind and said, as I stood upon the sidewalk, 'Dr. Bowditch, you would do to be more careful of your speech. Every word you have uttered this morning has been officially noted.' I instantly retorted, 'Marshal Tukey, you may do your worst, and then we shall learn that men cannot utter their honest opinions under the brow of Bunker Hill.' "

Bowditch always treated Negro associates as equals. After being introduced to Frederick Douglass, he invited him home to dinner. On the way the doctor met an aristocratic friend who showed "by her look of regret that she thought me 'all wrong.' " Douglass never forgot the incident. Speaking at a meeting in Boston years

later, he said, "Dr. Bowditch I greet joyfully here, for he first
treated me as if I were a man."

Harvard, equally a pillar of conservative Unitarianism and State
Street Commerce, did its best to stifle antislavery agitation. Charles
Follen, a distinguished German liberal who had been forced out of
the Universities of Jena and Basle by his opposition to the Bona-
partist rule, finally found refuge on the Harvard faculty in 1825
and was given a professorship a few years later. But when he
joined the abolitionists in 1833, his professorship was terminated.

The ostracism of Boston's aristocracy pursued him to his grave.
After his tragic death in the sinking of the steamer *Lexington* on
Long Island Sound in 1840, memorial services were announced at
the Federal Street Church by his close friend, the Reverend William Ellery Channing. But the church board objected to prayers
for an abolitionist, and the services were banned. This "great refusal," as it was known, virtually broke Channing's heart and
helped bring his own death shortly afterward.

As late as 1848, the rising Whig politician, Charles Sumner,
himself a Harvard graduate, was virtually hissed out of Cambridge.
When Sumner criticized slavery in a speech to the student body,
Henry Wadsworth Longfellow records that "the shouts and hisses
and the vulgar interruptions grated on my ears," and the poet
finally fled the hall.

Channing's tragedy even surpassed Follen's, for his life was torn
between allegiance to the aristocracy that made him and abolition
which he admired but feared. "Selected by a set of money-making
men as their representative for piety," as an early observer wrote,
Channing had broken with a Calvinism that debased man and
sought to placate a terrifying God. At the Federal Street Church,
he became New England's most distinguished minister, the leader
of the new Unitarianism which preached man's perfectibility under a compassionate and loving God.

But when perfectibility touched the issue of slavery and the
pocketbook of his parishioners, Channing wavered. His friends,
Follen, Sewall, Loring, and Mrs. Child, knew his hatred of the
Southern system and begged him to oppose it. In 1834 he admitted
to the Reverend May, "I have been silent too long." A year later

he published his *Essay on Slavery*, which was to be a turning point in his life. Although damning the institution, it also criticized abolitionists for "exaggerating their object."

Garrison, angry at his timidity, claimed that Channing "preferred to attack sin in the abstract than to deal with it personally." On the other hand, Southern fire-eaters abused him violently. On the floor of Congress, General Waddy Thompson of South Carolina called him an enemy more despicable than Garrison. Channing's wealthy parishioners passed him coldly on the street. Soon his name became anathema in aristocratic Boston. He lived out his last few years, a lonely giant, broken by the ostracism of former admirers.

"WE HAVE the lion-hearted, invincible Weld at the West," Garrison wrote. For Theodore Dwight Weld, who would marry Angelina Grimké, was leonine in physique as well as spirit. His face was dark and scowling. A twisted nose gave him the almost permanent appearance of anger. His voice was heavy and sonorous; few audiences could resist the power of its conviction. Even a liquor merchant, one listener commented, could be persuaded after an hour of Weld to go home and empty all his vats.

Born in Hampton, Connecticut, his ancestry stocked with distinguished Congregational ministers from the Edwards, Dwight, and Hutchinson families, Weld carried abolition westward. At Ohio's Western Reserve College, his one-man crusade virtually indoctrinated the whole faculty. In 1834 he moved on to Lane Seminary near Cincinnati, a theological center of such standing it was now headed by the venerable Dr. Lyman Beecher, fresh from his battles against liberal Unitarianism in Boston.

Garrison's teachings had already made deep inroads among the students when Weld led the demand for immediate emancipation and helped organize an abolition society. The overseers ordered the society abolished. Almost as a body, the students, mature men in their late twenties, refused and requested honorable dismissal.

The Lane "revolt" thus unleashed a trained group of abolitionist speakers throughout the Midwest, the famous "Seventy" who set

forth to inflame the countryside against slavery. Some went to
Oberlin College and made it a principal antislavery center. Marius
Robinson, crisscrossing Ohio, was once dragged from his bed at
night, tarred and feathered, and left by a mob almost dead by the
roadside. Weld himself, continually battered by rocks and eggs
in his tour of Ohio and Pennsylvania, was soon labeled the "most
mobbed man" in America. Speaking in a church one day, a stone
hurled through the window knocked him almost senseless. But as
soon as his supporters blocked the windows against further
missiles with their jackets, he went on calmly with his speech.

New England remained abolition's organizational center. But
the West now became a major battleground. Even Garrison recognized this. Although the New England Antislavery Society was
organized in a basement room of a Negro church on Beacon Hill
in 1832, the American Antislavery Society met for the first time
in Philadelphia a year later with many delegates coming from Midwest states.

Yet significantly enough, the Midwest abolition movement came
straight from the Puritan mold. In 1835, a young man named
Elijah Lovejoy, born in Maine while it was still a district of Massachusetts, the son of a Congregationalist minister, began to edit a
religious paper in St. Louis. Lovejoy, transplanting his hatred of
slavery from Maine to Missouri, was soon attacking the institution
in his editorials. "The cry of the oppressed has entered . . . into
my soul so that while I live I cannot hold my peace," he announced.
With Lovejoy, abolition would have its first bloody martyr.

St. Louis was no place for a righteous Presbyterian minister who
insisted on using the columns of the *Observer* to slash away at
slavery. A tough, brawling river port, it specialized in Southern
trade and was dominated by Southern businessmen who warned
Lovejoy bluntly of the recklessness of his editorials. He refused to
diminish his attacks. When they accused him of sending abolition
literature to Jefferson City, he denied it.

Lovejoy, a broad-shouldered, heavily muscled man of thirty-
three with dark, burning eyes and even darker hair combed back

severely from his forehead, now stepped boldly into the McIntosh case. McIntosh was a mulatto boatman who inadvertently killed a white man while resisting arrest. Without trial, a mob dragged him from jail, chained him to a tree, and burned him alive. Lovejoy attacked the lynching. And even worse, when one of the city's prominent judges defended such mob law, Lovejoy turned his editorial wrath on the judge.

The citizens of St. Louis decided that Lovejoy had gone too far. They sacked the *Observer* office and tossed his press in the Mississippi River.

In June, 1836, a group of Presbyterian clergymen invited Lovejoy to bring his paper to Alton, Illinois, twenty-five miles up the river from St. Louis. Illinois was a free state, of course. But Alton was also a booming river port near the mouths of the Missouri and Illinois rivers. Its four thousand population rivaled Chicago's, and it had pretensions of becoming the foremost city in the state. Politically, the city was dangerously split between the Southern businessmen, slave-traders and waterfront toughs, a faction known as the "Mint Juleps," and the New England emigrants, sternly religious Puritans mockingly called the "Teetotallers."

Lovejoy's press arrived at Alton by riverboat on Sunday, July 24th. The captain unloaded his cargo, and since Lovejoy maintained the Sabbath scrupulously, the press sat unprotected all day on the landing. The "Mint Julep" faction, wanting no part of this troublemaker who would invariably damage their Southern trade, dumped the press in the river.

Lovejoy's supporters purchased a new press, and as abolitionism gained strength, the paper's circulation grew from five hundred to two thousand five hundred between January and August, 1837. The "Mint Juleps" now turned to personal violence. On the night of August 21st, Lovejoy was returning home with medicine for his wife when a masked band, later admittedly led by Dr. T. M. Hope, accosted him at a lonely spot on the high bluffs above the Mississippi. They gave Lovejoy two choices; either leave town immediately, or they would tar and feather him and cast him adrift in a canoe on the river.

Lovejoy faced the mob coolly, saying "I am in the hands of

God and ready to go with you." He handed the medicine to Dr. Hope, asking only that it be delivered to his wife "without intimating what is about to befall me." Unnerved, his attackers retreated, returned to town, sacked the *Observer* office, and destroyed the press.

Again Lovejoy's supporters raised money for another press. Again on its arrival the mob broke into the warehouse and destroyed it.

In late September the Lovejoys visited St. Charles, Missouri, where his wife's mother lived. A mob broke into the house, trying to drag Lovejoy outside. His wife boldly struck one man, armed with a dirk, threw her arms around her husband and dared the mob to kill her first. Then the mob retired to the yard, but three times during the night, they attacked the house. Finally friends came and secretly conducted the Lovejoys to another part of town.

The Lovejoy faction was now convinced they could only defend their constitutional right to publish by force of arms. Henry Tanner, one associate, insisted later that Mayor John Krum was "not only cognizant of all our doings but had stated to us that we had a right to defend the press. . . ."

Their first test came in October when the Illinois Antislavery Convention held its initial meeting at Alton. Fifty-nine of the delegates were Congregational or Presbyterian ministers and elders. Among them, significantly enough, were the Reverend Edward Beecher, president of Illinois College, whose abolitionist leanings ran strongly counter to Dr. Lyman Beecher, his father; and Dr. David Nelson, president of Marion College in Missouri, once a slave holder and atheist who had freed his slaves and become a Presbyterian minister. To close the convention, Beecher preached at Lower Alton's Presbyterian Church. A mob gathered outside and began to hurl bricks through the windows. Instantly, Lovejoy's supporters seized their arms, and in perfect military formation, escorted Beecher and the congregation safely to their homes.

The mob increased its pressure daily. Two men broke into Lovejoy's house when he was away and were fought off by his younger brother, Owen. A brick, hurled through the window,

narrowly missed Lovejoy's sister. Again a mob stoned the house
with Lovejoy away and drove his wife and child into hiding in the
garret. The largest mob came for Lovejoy personally and were
only dispersed when the editor leveled his rifle at them and threatened to open fire.

The Reverend Beecher convinced business and civic leaders of
Alton to call an emergency meeting. Lovejoy's only support came
from one merchant, Winthrop S. Gilman. Every other participant,
including Mayor Krum and the State Attorney General, pleaded
for Alton's commercial prosperity at the expense of a free press.
If Alton wanted peace, it must oust Lovejoy. As one State Legislator concluded: "We must mutually sacrifice our prejudices."

Tanner answered bitingly: "And has it come to this? Is it in our
land that freedom of the press is called a *prejudice?*"

Lovejoy went before the meeting and made a final plea whose
eloquence rings boldly through the years:

> I have asked for nothing but to be protected in my rights
> as a citizen. . . . This right [to publish] was given me by my
> Maker; and is solemnly guaranteed to me by the Constitution
> of these United States and of this State . . . But if I have
> been guilty of no violation of law, why am I hunted as a
> partridge upon the mountains? . . . Why am I waylaid every
> day . . . my life in jeopardy every hour? . . . Where can I
> be safe if not here? . . . Sir, the very act of retreating will
> embolden the mob to follow me wherever I go. . . . If the
> civil authorities refuse to protect me, I must look to God, and
> if I die, I have determined to make my grave in Alton.

Nothing moved the committee. Alton's leaders were determined
Lovejoy must go, and the meeting ended by passing a resolution
prohibiting the publication of his paper. But significantly, no decision was made as to who would enforce the order. This was an
open invitation to mob action, and the city immediately became an
armed camp. Mayor Krum continued to waver dangerously. When
Lovejoy's supporters informed him that a new press was arriving

from Cincinnati the night of November 6th, he affirmed their right
to defend their property but refused to take command of the
armed citizens who had sworn to uphold the law.

The press arrived at three in the morning, escorted by thirty
men to the warehouse of Godfrey and Gilman, stoutly built of
native stone. Soon the defending force was increased to sixty under
command of Captain Enoch Long, a veteran of the War of 1812.
Many had no abolition sentiments but were simply determined to
protect a free press. The day passed quietly, and by nine o'clock
the night of November 7th, most of the defenders grew weary
and returned home. Only Lovejoy, Long, Gilman, and Tanner
and about fifteen others remained on guard.

The news quickly reached the waterfront bars where the mob
had been drinking heavily all evening. Dr. Horace Beall, a South-
erner and "Mint Julep" leader, egged them on. Lit by flares, an
angry column marched on the warehouse. First they pelted the
windows with rocks and broke open one door with sledge ham-
mers, and the defenders quickly barricaded the door. Then they
opened fire, their aim enhanced by a bright moon which hung low
over the river.

Captain Long had ordered the defenders to hold their fire until
his order. This was the first error. At that point, the mob was
small enough to be dispersed, but it was constantly re-enforced
with recruits from the bars along Tontine Row. Further, they now
had the support of Alton's leading citizens. "Merchants of Second
Street, doctors and lawyers, and even such ministers of the Gospel
(heaven save the mark!) as John Hogan and Charles Howard either
egged on the mob, or were, at best, coldly indifferent," Dr. Samuel
Willard, an observer, wrote later.

The attackers approached under a flag of truce and demanded
the press be surrendered. Lovejoy refused and demanded that
Mayor Krum be summoned as intermediary. Krum tried to address the mob but only succeeded in having his hat knocked off
by stray buckshot and hastily fled the scene.

"Kill every damn abolitionist in town!" shouted Dr. Beall. The
mob prepared for its final attack. While riflemen fired at three
sides of the building to keep the defenders' attention, an attack

party set ladders against the east wall, which had no windows or observation points.

Meanwhile, Mrs. Graves, wife of the Presbyterian minister, had been tolling the church bell frantically. Unexplainably, no help came.

The attack party climbed their ladders and set fire to the roof. But defenders on the third floor stifled the blaze. Now the attackers improved their strategy, placing four riflemen behind barrels near the ladder to cover the torchbearers.

This time the attack party set a roaring fire to the roof. Captain Long asked for volunteers to douse it, and Lovejoy, Royal Weller, and Amos Ruff accepted. As they reached the roof, their bodies, silhouetted by the moonlight and flames, made easy targets. The group, hidden behind the barrels, opened fire.

Weller and Ruff were wounded. Lovejoy was hit in the chest by a blast of buckshot, probably five balls. He stumbled inside the building, crying, "I am shot, I am shot. I am dead!"

The mob surged into the warehouse and destroyed the press. Lovejoy's body was left all night on the stone floor, Weller and Thaddeus B. Hurlbut standing guard over it. The rest of the defenders went home.

Along Hunterstown Road, Lovejoy's horse trotted dutifully to its stable. Mrs. Lovejoy and Owen, watching from the window of their house, saw the riderless horse and got their first warning of disaster. At dawn Lovejoy's friends carried his body up Second Street, followed by a jeering crowd. "If I only had a fife, I would play the Dead March for him," Dr. Beall taunted. The body was placed in a plain pine box in the Lovejoy parlor. Over it young Owen swore an oath he would never give up the fight; soon he would make his mark as a brilliant abolitionist and antislavery Congressman from Illinois.

Ironically, it was Lovejoy's birthday, his thirty-fifth.

The funeral took place the next day in a heavy rain. For fear that a mob would gather, it was held in secret. There was no oration, not even flowers scattered on the coffin. The grave was dimly marked. Soon after, when a road was cut through the cemetery, the site was lost completely and not rediscovered until 1864 when it was moved to the top of the bluff. Then a marble memorial was erected, but Lovejoy's friends, obviously doubting he had found final peace, inscribed on it: "Here lies Lovejoy. Spare him now in his grave."

ALTHOUGH the Illinois press barely mentioned Lovejoy's death, the news rocked New England. "A shock as of any earthquake throughout this continent," John Quincy Adams called it. And in New York, the *Evening Post* warned: "To say that he who holds unpopular opinions must hold them at the peril of his life . . . is to strike at all rights, all liberties, all protection of law."

Even opponents of abolition quickly recognized the lesson: Not freedom of the press, nor any constitutional liberty, was secure against the demands of slavery.

Richard Fletcher, a supporter of Mayor Otis during the Garrison riot in Boston two years before, quickly offered a third of the money needed to establish another Alton *Observer*. Dr. Channing issued a call for a protest meeting at Faneuil Hall. He was backed by a hundred prominent citizens who would previously never have lent their names to such a cause. Cautious as always, Channing insisted that the meeting concerned not slavery but freedom of speech and press. "What I desired," he stated, "was that the citizens of Boston of all parties should join as one man in putting down the reign of terror by the force of opinion."

Still, the mayor and aldermen denied the use of Faneuil Hall. "And has it come to this?" Channing demanded in an open letter. "Has Boston fallen so low? May not its citizens be trusted to come together to express the great principles of liberty for which their fathers died?" Channing's Committee of One Hundred exerted such pressure through delegates in each ward that the meeting was finally approved for December 8th.

At ten that morning, five thousand people, many with strong Southern sympathies, jammed Faneuil Hall. After Channing, speaking from a lectern in the center of the standing crowd, had introduced the opening speakers, a squat, red-faced man pushed his way to the front of the gallery. He was an unscheduled speaker, but the audience quickly recognized James T. Austin, Attorney General of the Commonwealth.

Austin unleashed a stinging attack on Boston's own Negroes—"lions, tigers, hyenas, an elephant, a jackass or two and monkeys in plenty," he called them. He praised the South for subjugating their own "wild beasts of the menagerie." The Alton mob—"an orderly mob," he called it—was as glorious as the Revolutionary patriots who had dumped English tea into Boston Harbor. In a bombastic climax, obviously intended to disperse the meeting, he insisted that Lovejoy had received his just reward. "He died as the fool dieth!" he proclaimed.

There was near pandemonium while Channing gaveled helplessly for order. Then a young man, his face strikingly handsome, almost classic with a "careless, buoyant patrician air as if nothing in the way of mob violence was worth considering," Higginson said, tore off his overcoat and fought his way to the lectern. At twenty-six, having attended his first abolition meeting only six months before, Wendell Phillips was making his first public speech. In a few minutes he would win back the audience with an eloquence rarely heard in Boston. His voice would soon be known as the "golden trumpet" of abolition. Higginson would marvel at the way his "sentences would come in a long, sonorous swell, still easy and graceful, but powerful as the soft stretching of a tiger's paw." Other observers would praise "this marvellous voice, sweet as a song, clear as a flute."

The Phillips name represented supreme wealth and social position in New England. Wendell could trace his ancestry to 1630, to the Puritan minister, the Reverend George Phillips. All his forebears had been distinguished judges and governors; two of them had founded the Phillips academies at Andover and Exeter. His father, John Phillips, had been Boston's first mayor. Wendell himself, born and raised in a sumptuous Beacon Street mansion, had attended Harvard where he became president of the aristocratic Porcellian Club, and graduated from Harvard Law School in 1833. Now one speech in Faneuil Hall was to sever his ties forever with this privileged past.

Wendell had married only recently, a beautiful girl, Ann Terry

Green. Although Boston commentators were apt to wax eloquent over their prized women, the description of her "magnificent long hair, Hebe's complexion and the form of Juno" was fully justified. Ann was the daughter of a wealthy shipping merchant, but her parents had died early and she had been brought up by her uncle, Henry G. Chapman, a close friend of Garrison's. Thus Ann had become a devoted abolitionist, and quickly lured Wendell into the ranks. "Yes," he admitted later, "my wife made an out-and-out abolitionist of me. . . ."

Phillips was not a scheduled speaker. He was interrupted and heckled ferociously. But he stood his ground, pointing to the portraits of the Revolutionary heroes which adorned the walls of Faneuil Hall. "Sir," he cried, "when I heard the gentleman lay down the principles which place the murderers of Alton side by side with Otis and Hancock, with Quincy and Adams, I thought those pictured lips would have broken into voice to rebuke the recreant American—the slanderer of the dead."

Masterfully, he broke down Austin's arguments. How compare the Boston Tea Party with the Alton mob? The Revolutionary patriots were demanding their rights under Colonial law; the Alton mob had murdered an editor, protected by the guarantees of the Constitution. "The question that stirred the Revolution touched our civil interests," he proclaimed. "*This* concerns us not only as citizens but as immortal beings."

Slowly the audience yielded. The heckling ceased. Soon they were clapping and cheering as point after point was driven home with passionate clarity. Few Bostonians left Faneuil Hall that day without realizing that a few rifle shots in Alton had threatened their own liberties. "When liberty is in danger," Phillips thundered, "Faneuil Hall has the right, it is her duty to strike the keynote for these United States."

Not only was it a remarkable performance that "electrified the mighty assembly," rhapsodized Boston's *Independent Messenger* the next day, "It was sublime, irresistible, annihilating." More significantly, it brought a new giant to the abolition band. All the wealth, talent, and authority that Phillips possessed would be thrown from that day into the movement. Reviled by his friends, an outcast in a city where he was born to leadership, Phillips never wavered. Along with Garrison, he would symbolize an epoch.

"Garrison was the executive of the antislavery movement," one associate concluded. "The other was to supply the eloquence that would melt the fetters from a race and transform a nation."

John Quincy Adams—
"Mad Man from Massachusetts": 1831–1848

DEFEATED FOR reelection to the Presidency in 1828, John Quincy Adams cloistered himself in his Quincy home and wrote anguishedly, "I have no plausible motive for wishing to live when everything that I foresee and believe of futurity makes death desirable, and when I have the clearest indication that it is near at hand."

Old before his time, short, paunchy, and almost bald despite a fringe of whiskers, Adams bitterly resigned himself to the political graveyard, believing, "My whole life has been a succession of disappointments. I can scarcely recollect a single instance of success to anything that I ever undertook."

Infirmities overwhelmed him. His hand shook almost uncontrollably when he wrote. He complained about his "smarting, bloodshot eyes" so weak and inflamed that rheumy tears often trickled from the corners. His voice, always shrill, tended to crack irritatingly. He slept little and badly, his diary was filled with continual laments of "disturbed, unquiet sleep—full of tossings." His temper was increasingly short. "Fierce as ten furies, terrible as hell," Andrew Johnson described it. And Adams admitted in his diary, "I have need of a perpetual control over passion."

It was like being born anew, therefore, when a group of devoted friends, National Republicans, convinced him to run for Congress in 1830. He was sixty-three, a retired President, son of the second President, the nation's last link of stature with the Revolution, for Adams as a boy had watched the cannon smoke roll over Bunker Hill. It was unprecedented, and remains so today, for an ex-President to return to the brawling forum of the House. Adams not only won his election and entered Congress: for the next eighteen years until the end of his life, he would be continually reelected. Instead of the bucolic solitude sought by Washington and other ex-Presidents, Adams would carve out a radical new career. He had carefully dodged the slavery issue in the White House. Now he would plunge into it almost recklessly, drawing a whirlwind of controversy around his head. No former President, then or now, would suffer such abuse, newspapers even branding him the "Mad Man from Massachusetts." Solitary and indomitable, he would emerge as a new symbol. The old Puritan warhorse, aloof as a President, would become the foremost champion of popular liberties, surrounded by warmth and devotion that had never come to him in the White House.

ADAMS was steeped from birth in the Puritan's tortuous devotion to principle, devoured by moral preoccupation with good and evil, molded by his father for public service whose ultimate target was the Presidency. At twenty-six he was appointed Minister to the Netherlands, ten years later elected to the United States Senate. Madison made him Minister to Russia. Monroe made him his Secretary of State, a position he filled brilliantly from 1817 to 1824 when he won the Presidency from Andrew Jackson, a bitterly fought contest that had to be decided in the House of Representatives. John Adams lived to see the family destiny completed, his son in the White House. He died on July 4, 1826, the same day as Jefferson, the fiftieth anniversary of the Declaration of Independence.

It was the end of an epoch. Only one Congressional elector had voted against Madison in 1816. But John Quincy Adams was a minority President, struggling to hold the National Republicans together. In 1828, a combination of Southern planters and conservative Republicans of the Middle states behind Jackson and Calhoun crushed the two Northern candidates, Adams and Richard Rush. Slavery was already the hidden issue.

No man had condemned slavery in more blistering words than Adams—"the great and foul stain upon the North American Union!" No man had better gauged the tragic consequences of the

Missouri Compromise. "Oh, if but one man could arise . . . to lay bare in all its nakedness that outrage upon the goodness of God, human slavery," he wrote in 1820, "now is the time, and this is the occasion, upon which such a man would perform his duties of an angel upon earth!"

It would be sixteen years before Adams would attempt these duties. And even then, inadvertently! In his maiden speech to Congress, he presented fifteen petitions from citizens of Pennsylvania, praying for abolition of slavery and the slave trade in the nation's capital. Although the petitions caused a bedlam of Southern protests, few Congressmen, and not even Adams, foresaw the consequences.

The petition to Congress, a right guaranteed by the Constitution, would soon become the major weapon of the abolitionist movement. As petitions poured upon his desk, Adams presented them in increasing numbers to the House. Hating slavery, he was still far from an abolitionist. But he doggedly defended the right of petition and each petition from towns and villages all over New England stirred new debate. It was a provocative device, a constant knife jabbing at Congress. Abolition at last had a national forum. Adams and his petitions would soon turn the House into an inferno.

Ironically enough, the petition campaign was developed by peace-loving Quakers and launched in Essex County, Massachusetts, by the Quaker poet, Whittier. The abolitionists were tireless collectors. In one year alone, 1837, their petitions would carry over two hundred thousand names; Theodore Weld coordinated the campaign from the New York headquarters of the American Antislavery Society. One petition, demanding the abolition of slavery in the District of Columbia, carried 130,200 names; another to prohibit slave trade between the states, 23,160; a third to prohibit slavery in United States territories, 21,200; and so on down the line. In Massachusetts, petitions to free the slave, Latimer, drew 51,862 signatures. Dr. Bowditch described "the immense roll of paper" as "about the size of an ordinary barrel."

Adams calmly presented each petition to a fuming House. On January 15, 1838, he introduced fifty separate petitions; on February 14, three hundred and fifty. Each interrupted the business of the House. Each roused Southern Representatives to increased fury. They had intended to bury slavery as an issue of debate with the Missouri Compromise. They had even tried to ban abolition literature from the United States mails—the bill had passed the House with Jackson's backing, failing in the Senate. But here were the abolitionists, exploiting the petition device, forcing the slavery issue into national debate, turning the House into a constant bedlam!

The dominant slavery bloc, not only Southern Representatives but their Northern allies, decided to crush these agitators. On May 18, 1836, a committee headed by Henry Laurens Pinckney of South Carolina presented three resolutions, all quickly passed. The key resolution ruled that any petition or memorial to Congress relating to slavery should be automatically laid on the table without being printed or referred. It was a sweeping Gag Rule! And it would be renewed at every session until 1840 when the House would tighten the Gag by making it a standing rule!

Adams rose to protest, shouting, "I hold the resolution to be a direct violation of the Constitution of the United States, of the rules of this House, and of the rights of my constituents." But he was howled down. The slavery bloc had clamped its Gag on the nation. Not one petition, not one word of debate on slavery would henceforth be tolerated by the people's Representatives!

ADAMS NOW took on virtually the whole House in one of the wildest struggles in Congressional history. Refusing to be gagged, he resorted to every trick and parliamentary device to bring the slavery issue to the floor. One Washington correspondent described him, "creeping through this rule and skipping over that" while the Speaker angrily gaveled him down. Week after week, he infuriated the House with "tit-bit speeches, which were so short and so quickly said that, though they were out of order, nobody could call him to order; and when they did, he would say, 'My speech is done.'"

He would leap to his feet, his face flushed, "throwing himself into the attitude of the veteran gladiator . . . immovable as a pillar until he has completed his task," another correspondent described him. He had never been an accomplished speaker, admitting in his diary, "I am so little qualified by nature for an extemporaneous orator that I was at this time not a little agitated by the sound of my own voice." Now his shrill words exploded with new power. His epithets lashed the House unmercifully. One Representative, a leading proponent of the Gag, was attacked for "emitting a half hour of his rotten breath." Another was branded, "the very thickest skull of all New Hampshire." A third, cried Adams, kept "butting his head against the air like a he-goat."

One day Adams presented a petition from 228 women, praying for the abolition of the slave trade in the District of Columbia. When Speaker Polk demanded its contents be stated, Adams provoked the usual pandemonium, described by the *National Intelligencer:*

> Adams: I am doing so, Sir.
>
> Polk: Not in the opinion of the Chair.
>
> Adams: I was at this point of the petition, "Keenly aggrieved by its [slavery's] existence in a part of our country over which Congress possesses exclusive jurisdiction in all cases whatever"—
>
> *Cries of "Order! Order!" shook the House.*
>
> Adams: "Do most earnestly petition your honorable body"—
>
> *John Chambers of Kentucky rose to a point of order.*
>
> Adams: (rushing to complete his sentence before the House drowned him out) "Immediately to abolish slavery in the District of Columbia."

When the Speaker's gavel or the furious chorus of "Order! Order!" stopped him, Adams employed other devices—amending the House *Journal,* or presenting a petition that ingeniously skirted the slavery provisions of the Gag Rule.

Frequently he even refused to tell the Speaker the contents of a petition, crying, "I refuse to answer because I consider all the proceedings of the House as unconstitutional." Adams in his diary reports that, "While speaking these words with loud, distinct and slow articulation, the bawl of 'Order! Order!' resounded again from two thirds of the House. The Speaker with agonizing lungs screamed, 'I call upon the House to support me in the execution of my duty.' I then coolly resumed my seat."

In February, 1837, Adams presented a petition from nine Negro women of Fredericksburg, Virginia, not knowing himself whether they were slaves or free. The Speaker immediately tabled it. Adams then announced he was presenting another petition, signed with scrawls and marks. An uproar rose through the House. No petition from slaves had ever been presented. Southern Representatives screamed that Adams was destroying the Union; one demanded he be indicted by the District grand jury for inciting rebellion. The storm continued for three days, Adams cagily fanning it.

Biding his time until the House let him speak, he blandly announced that the petition had nothing to do with freedom. Just the opposite! The slaves had petitioned the House to protect them from the abolitionists lest their welfare be harmed. "It remains," wrote one historian a half century later, "the best and most effective practical joke in the history of Congress."

Since Adams tenaciously insisted his petition battle was based on the freedom of petition, his enemies put him to the test. They sent him a petition, praying Congress that all free Negroes be deported or sold as slaves. Adams methodically presented it. When the citizens of Rocky Mountain, Virgina, sent him a petition praying Congress to expel the Honorable John Quincy Adams, he never hesitated to present it.

Such Puritanical devotion to principle brought an increasing flood of ferocious letters to his desk. ". . . Your damned guts will be cut in the dark," warned a Georgia correspondent. "On the first day of May next I promise to cut your throat from ear to ear," threatened an Alabama writer. Nearing his seventy-fourth birthday, still unflinching in his lonely struggle although he complained privately of his "drowsy brain" and "my faculties dropping from me one by one as the teeth are dropping from my head," Adams already ranked as the nation's most vilified ex-President.

When General Sam Houston's victory over Mexico's Santa Anna on April 21, 1836, stirred the nation's dream of annexing Texas to the point of mania, Southern leaders grasped hungrily at this vast, new territory from which to carve an array of slave states.

The Texas mania, however, seriously alarmed the North. And the alarm spread to segments of the population far beyond the abolitionist groups. Dr. Channing published a scathing tract against annexation which reached an immense audience. Anti-Texas petitions began to flood the House conjointly with abolition petitions. Anti-Texas resolutions by the State Legislatures came from Massachusetts, Michigan, Ohio and Vermont.

Although Adams as President had twice tried but failed to purchase Texas from Mexico, he was now convinced that the Texas revolution was a plot by Jackson, the plantation-owners, and their Northern allies. "The Texas land and liberty jobbers," he would soon charge, "had spread the contagion of their land-jobbing traffic all over the free states throughout the Union. Land-jobbing, stock-jobbing, slave-jobbing, rights-of-man-jobbing were all hand in hand, sweeping over the land like a hurricane."

In the closing months of 1837, Adams forced these anti-Texas petitions to the floor, deftly slipping in a number of abolition petitions. Although Speaker Polk struggled to shut him off, he got the House floor during morning hours for committee business and held it tenaciously each day for three weeks. His one-man campaign and the flood of petitions stalled the Administration; annexation had to be postponed.

Still, the Southern bloc kept its Gag clamped on the House although it was slowly losing ground. In January, 1837, The Gag Rule was passed by 115 to 47; in January, 1840, by only 114 to 108.

THE LACK OF unified support even from abolitionists intensified Adams's solitary struggle. "He [Lundy] and the abolitionists generally are constantly urging me to indiscreet movements, which would ruin me, and weaken and not strengthen their cause," he wrote on September 2, 1837. ". . . I walk on the edge of a precipice almost every step I take." Two years later he was still complaining of their "senseless and overbearing clamor."

The abolitionists, unfortunately, were skilled propagandists but reckless politicians. While Adams was still battering at the petition Gag, they demanded other immediate challenges—a test vote, for example, on abolition in the District of Columbia. But Adams was too sharp a strategist to be pushed into political suicide. A test vote was "notoriously impracticable," he wrote on November 8, 1838. "There is in the present House of Representatives [a majority] of nearly two to one opposed to the consideration or discussion of the subject." A month later he insisted he could not collect five votes on such a test.

When the abolitionists kept bullying him, he complained they "have already given me repeated warnings that they will desert and oppose me if I do not come over to them in the creed of immediate abolition."

If Adams fended them off politically, he warmly recognized the justice of their cause. "George Washington was abolitionist; so was Thomas Jefferson," he wrote the Rhode Island Antislavery Society in 1838. "But were they alive, and should dare to show their faces and to utter the self-evident truth of the Declaration within the State of South Carolina, they would be hanged."

Despite repeated tension between Adams and the abolitionists, he would soon be lionized with their rapturous enthusiasm for his new battle, not on the House floor but before the Supreme Court. In April, 1839, fifty-three Africans, recently delivered to Cuban slave-runners, broke their chains, killed the captain and cook and seized the ship transporting them, the *Amistad*. After reaching the Long Island coast, the Africans on the *Amistad* were captured by Lieutenant Thomas R. Gedney, commanding a United States brig. The slave trade was prohibited by a Spanish-British treaty. And since the Africans had already been illegally landed in Cuba, their status provided a thorny issue.

The Cuban slave-runners claimed them as lawful property. Gedney claimed them and the ship as salvage. The case was fought to the Supreme Court.

Lewis Tappan and other New York abolitionists raised defense funds for the Africans and begged Ellis Gray Loring to secure Adams as their counsel. It had been years since he had tried a case. Although plagued by poor health and doubtful that his mind could meet the rigorous challenge of a trial, he finally accepted.

Adams's brilliant defense proved that the Africans were free men of an illegal cargo under Spanish law and ridiculed the government's thesis that the United States Fugitive Slave Law had any force in a trans-Atlantic slave trade outlawed by Spain. "The world, the flesh and all the devils in hell," Adams proclaimed, "are arraigned against any man who now in this North American Union shall dare to join the standard of Almighty God to put down the African slave trade."

On March 9, 1841, the Supreme Court submitted its decision— the Africans were freed! The abolitionists were jubilant. "Praise be to the God of *Justice*," Joshua Leavitt, a leading abolitionist, wrote Adams from New York.

THE ELECTION in 1840 of the first Whig President, William Henry Harrison, and Whig control of the House would soon bring the petition struggle to a climax. Opponents of the Gag Rule were picking up strength. The Gag passed by only six votes in 1840; of 128 votes from the free states, only 26 were still supporting it.

Further, an antislavery coalition of insurgent Whig Congressmen had formally organized for the first time. The chief spokesmen of this "Select Committee on Slavery," which established itself at Mrs. Sprigg's boardinghouse near the Capitol, were Joshua Giddings and Sherlock J. Andrews of Ohio, William Slade of Vermont, and Seth M. Gates of New York. Theodore Weld was sent to Washington to work with them, marking a new solidarity between abolitionists and moderates.

But it was Adams who dominated the group and kept its energies concentrated on the petition struggle. And it was Adams whom Whig leaders feared most, for his chairmanship of the House Committee on Foreign Affairs gave him a pivotal role in the Texas dispute.

Organized in the spring of 1834, the Whigs were a hodgepodge of former National Republicans, anti-Jacksonites, States' Rights men, and above all, the aristocracy of Southern plantation owners who had been badly hurt by Jackson's removal of deposits from the United States Bank. Thus the South, already a dominant influence in the Democratic party, now largely controlled Whig policy. The alignment between Northern and Southern Whigs was dramatically evident in the Gag votes, all Northern and Southern Whigs without exception supporting the 1837 Gag.

Southern dominance over the Army had prolonged the savage Seminole War in Florida, aimed at crushing escaped slaves as well as Indians. Southern influence in Washington had made a mockery of federal control over slave-running. Bitterly Adams listed in his diary the key government offices filled by slaveholders in 1842— the President, President of the Senate, Speaker of the House, Chief Justice of the Supreme Court, Commander-in-Chief of the Army, and three of the six heads of executive departments.

The Whig leaders had decided that Adams must be destroyed once and for all. The moment he rose on the House floor, they badgered him incessantly as Weld reported to his wife, "screaming at the top of their voices: 'That is false.' 'I *demand*, Mr. Speaker, that you *put him down*.' 'I demand that you shut the mouth of that old Harlequin.' 'What are we to sit here and endure such insults?' "

Adams fought back doggedly. "A perfect uproar like Babel would burst forth every two or three minutes as Mr. A. with his bold surgery would smite his cleaver into the very bones," Weld added. ". . . Mr. Adams would say, 'I see where the shoe pinches, Mr. Speaker, it will pinch more yet.' 'I'll deal out to the gentlemen a diet they'll find hard to digest.' "

Adams finally gave the Whigs their long-sought opening—a petition from Haverhill, Massachusetts, praying for the peaceable dissolution of the Union. No petition so drastic had ever been introduced. Southern members rose in fury, demanding it be burned in the presence of the House. Henry A. Wise of Virginia called for censure, and Thomas F. Marshall of Kentucky, nephew of the Chief Justice, immediately drafted the resolution of indictment. The crisis had come; Adams was fighting for his life.

Left. Angelina Grimké, South Carolina aristocrat and abolitionist *(Woman's Archives, Radcliffe College). Right.* Abby Kelley Foster, most fiery of feminine abolitionists *(Woman's Archives, Radcliffe College)*

Left. John Quincy Adams *(Widener Library, Harvard). Above.* Reverend Theodore Parker, militant anti-slavery Unitarian *(Bostonian Society, Old State House)*

The Legal Committee of Vigilance Dr

Explanatory

On the 15th Feb. 1851 Shadrach, a fugitive slave from Virginia was arrested at the instance of his Captor, a slave-hunter from Norfolk Va, and taken before Commissioner Curtis; who after the adjournment of the first examination, was rescued from the Suffolk Court house, by the colored people & sent to Canada. In this brave act Lewis Hayden, Robert Morris, James Scott & Elizur Wright were arrested & tried before Judge Sprague of the US Court. Some all acquitted; the expenses of these trials, are herewith recorded. Some defrayed by donations contributions entered on the opposite pages of this book.

Hon Arthur P Hale, Richard H Dana & Geo Hurley were the Lawyers employed to defend the rescuers.

1851			
May 21	Nath Colver for services in collecting money	11	50
" 24	Wm C Nell do do do	15	
"	Nath Colver do	14	
	Amount carried over	40	50

Francis Jackson Treasurer Cr

Donations for the Rescue Cases (collected by Austin Bearse)

1851			
May 16	Deborah S Plagg Boston	10	
"	Friend (Hal. S.O.) "	10	
"	George W Bond "	10	
"	Benj. P Winston "	10	
"	James W Stone "	5	
"	N Davis Cotton "	5	
"	John Scheeler "	5	
"	Carrie Lies Brannhall "	5	
"	John T Sargent "	5	
"	Daniel J J Child "	5	
"	John S May "	5	
"	Thomas T Bruce "	5	
"	Jonathan Brown "	5	
"	A Friend "	2	
"	Dana D Walsh "	1	
"	Luther Parks Jr	1	
"	J G Dodge	1	
"	Bourne Spooner Plymouth	5	
17	Richard P Waters Salem by Edward		95
"	Samuel Butler & Friend 2 & Friend 3		25
18	Catharine Hunt with Sargent Boston		6
"	Edward Winslow & Friend 1		3
"	Franklin King		3
"	E D Loring		4
20	Amasa Walker Brookfield		3
	Amount carried over		149

At seventy-five, plagued by a hacking cough, pimples, and boils, Adams plunged eagerly into preparations for his defense. His energy was "astonishing," Weld, who assisted him, wrote his wife. "Last Friday, after he had been sitting in the House from twelve o'clock until six, and for nearly half that time engaged in speaking with great energy against his ferocious assailants, I called at his house in the evening, and he came to me as fresh and elastic as a boy. I told him I was afraid he would tire himself out. 'No, not at all,' said he, 'I am all ready for another heat.' . . . He went on for an hour, or very nearly that, in a voice large enough to be heard by a large audience. Wonderful man!"

Adams had become a one-man symbol of the struggle against slavery. "A hundred men of the House represent slaves; four-fifths of whom would crucify me if their votes could erect the cross," he wrote in his diary. "Forty members, representatives of the free in the league of slavery and mock Democracy, would break me on the wheel if their votes or wishes could turn it round. . . ."

Day after day, Adams held the floor in his defense, seemingly inexhaustible, his shrill voice slashing away at his enemies. Although literally a man without a party, new allies suddenly flocked to him. The long, tortuous petition struggle, and now the censure trial, at last captured the imagination of the North. News of the trial filled the headlines, most New England papers backing him. Petitions against his censure began pouring into the House. His support reached far beyond the abolitionist groups now. At a mass meeting in Faneuil Hall on January 28, 1842, many leading men of Boston cheered his name and voted a resolution in his honor. At the most desperate moment in his life, Adams had actually reached the zenith of his power.

After two weeks of tumult on the House floor, the Whigs were tiring. Even their leaders despaired of putting down this furious figure who had now been aptly named, "Old Man Eloquent." On February 7, he announced he would need a week more for his defense. The opposition completely crumbled. A motion to table the resolution of censure was quickly passed 106 to 93. Even then Adams wasn't finished! He held the floor the rest of the day, happily presenting two hundred petitions. Then he went home, "scarcely able to crawl to my chamber," he wrote, "but with the sound of *Io triumphe!* ringing in my ears."

The South recognized the significance of its defeat. Marshall, one of the prime movers of censure, went home to Kentucky never to return to Congress. "The triumph of Mr. Adams is complete," Weld perceptively wrote his wife. "This is the first victory over the slave-holders in a body ever yet achieved since the foundation of the government and from this time their downfall takes its date."

ADAMS WAS welcomed like a hero in Boston and Quincy. When he set out with his wife the next summer for a vacation through Western New York, the trip unexpectedly became a festival of homage. In Buffalo there was a torchlight parade and an address by Millard Fillmore, soon to ascend to the Presidency. In Syracuse and Utica, he was the guest of the city. When his train stopped for food and water in Batavia, the whole town turned out. In Rochester he was greeted with booming cannon and ringing church bells.

Invited to Cincinnati to lay the cornerstone of the Astronomical Society, he was besieged by welcoming crowds across Ohio. At a reception in Akron, he was greeted with a kiss by the prettiest girl and noted happily, "I returned the salute on the lips and kissed every woman that passed. . . ." At Covington, Kentucky, he recorded, "a very pretty woman . . . whispered, 'the first kiss in Kentucky'—which I did not refuse."

One slight setback marred the year. Frustrated by Adams, the Whigs now took a small measure of revenge on his associate, Joshua Giddings. After a group of Virginia slaves on the ship *Creole* mutinied and escaped to Nassau, Giddings introduced a resolution declaring they were not subject to Virginia law and thus had attained their natural freedom. For what the Whigs called a fiendish resolution, the House censured Giddings. He resigned his seat, went back to Ohio and was promptly reelected by a stunning majority.

Nothing, however, could halt Adams in the final stages of his triumph. The Democrats swept the nation in the fall of 1843, taking control of the House. The Gag Rule could muster only a slim majority of 91 to 94. "The truth is that the slaveholders got so smitten with consternation at the bolts of father Adams hurled through the ranks at their last session," Weld proclaimed, "that they have never been able to rally."

At the opening of the new session in December, 1844, Adams was convinced he had the votes for a final showdown. After eight years under the lash of the Gag Rule, he confidently submitted a motion to rescind it. The motion was passed that very day, 105 to 80.

It was the most spectacular battle any Congressman had waged, and for most of the eight years he had stood alone. He had opened the halls of Congress to the slavery debate, taken it from the moral arena of Garrison and forced it into the very fulcrum of national politics. Younger men like Giddings would press the attack, and on a state and local level, the Liberty party had already made slavery the crucial political issue. "Blessed, ever blessed be the name of God," Adams wrote in his diary that night.

He had made himself the dominant figure of the antislavery movement although shrewd realism kept him from complete alignment with the abolitionists. As early as 1839 he had submitted three radical resolutions to the House. The first set July 4, 1842, as the date after which any child born to slave parents would be declared free. The second prohibited any future slave states but Florida. The third declared slavery and the slave trade illegal in the District of Columbia after July 4, 1845. It was an eminently practical plan of gradual abolition, but the House ignored it. With it probably disappeared one of the last comprehensive chances for a peaceful settlement of the crisis.

ON THE morning of November 20, 1846, after rising as usual before 5 A.M. and breakfasting with his family, Adams took a brisk walk to the new Harvard Medical College. On the way he was stricken, probably a light cerebral hemorrhage. Yet his recovery was remarkably quick. In a few months he was riding around Boston in his carriage. When he returned to his seat in Congress, sectional differences were momentarily forgotten. The whole House, North and South alike, stood as one man. "Old Man Eloquent," the nation's last great link with its Revolutionary heritage, was back.

On Monday, February 21, 1848, Adams, now eighty-one, reached the House early. Polk had just received the treaty of peace with Mexico. A roll call was going on, the House filled with clatter. Suddenly a member nearby saw Adams' face redden, his right hand clutch at the corner of his desk. Then he slumped over.

Someone cried out and caught Adams in his arms to prevent his falling. They carried him to the cleared area in front of the Speaker's table while the House adjourned. There he was placed on a sofa and moved to the Speaker's Room. Clay stood by, weeping. For a few minutes Adams revived. Leaning close, John Palfrey, the former Unitarian clergyman and Harvard professor, now a stanch antislavery Congressman, heard him say, "This is the end of earth, but I am composed."

His wife, Louisa, arrived but Adams, half paralyzed, had lapsed into a coma and gave no sign of recognition. He lingered through Washington's Birthday, and at 7:20 on the evening of February 23, he died.

The service three days later was probably the greatest public tribute since Franklin had been buried in Philadelphia. Thousands of people had filed by his coffin while it lay in state in the House; Southern leaders joined the North in homage. "Where could death have found him but at the post of duty," proclaimed Senator Thomas Hart Benton. That morning, a cannon salute started at sunrise and continued through the procession. Then the body was taken to Faneuil Hall in Boston, and over the entrance, where thousands more paid homage, they placed the inscription: "Born a citizen of Massachusetts. Died a citizen of the United States."

He was buried in Quincy in the old family tomb in the churchyard. At the last moment a Southern Congressman in the funeral party stepped forward, and stooping before the vault, called out, "Good bye, Old Man!"

CHAPTER VIII

Torrey and the Proper Price of Liberty: 1841–1846

HOURS BEFORE three thousand mourners crowded into Boston's Tremont Temple on the morning of May 19, 1846, Dr. Bowditch paid an early visit with his six-year-old son, Nathaniel. Named for his grandfather, the celebrated mathematician, the boy was too short to get a good view of the pale, wasted face beneath the glass cover of the cherry-wood coffin. The doctor had brought his son to "teach him to swear eternal enmity to slavery," he wrote in his diary. "Like Hamilcar of old, I determined to make the young Hannibal remember, as one of his earliest associations, his father taught him to hate slavery. . . . I raised the little fellow on my knee and allowed him to look, and when I took him down, he asked to be allowed to look once more."

"I think he will remember," Dr. Bowditch added, not knowing how prophetically he wrote. Less than twenty years later, Nathaniel, a cavalry lieutenant, would be killed in Virginia, in a charge against Confederate cavalry.

What was unique about the "revered face" of the Reverend Charles T. Torrey was not only his martyrdom but the course he had chosen. The Boston abolitionists had already buried Lovejoy. But while Lovejoy could be said to have resisted on principle, Torrey assaulted slavery directly and violently. He had invaded the South on frequent trips, a pattern soon followed by others like the former slave, Harriet Tubman. He had conducted a one-man campaign among the border states, mingling with slaves and plotting their escape. It was dangerous enough for a New England abolitionist on the "Underground Railroad" to hide a fleeing slave in his cellar. But here was a far more radical weapon that brought the struggle to the plantation itself.

Torrey well knew the havoc he wrought. "If I am a guilty man, I am a very guilty one," he wrote later from prison, "for I have aided nearly Four Hundred slaves to escape to freedom. . . ."

He came from a Puritan family, a long line of Calvinist ministers, the awareness of evil deep in his blood. Born in Scituate on Boston's South Shore where James Torrey had settled in 1629 to escape religious persecution, he was educated at Phillips Academy, Exeter, at Yale, and at Andover Theological Seminary. Ordained a Congregational minister, he held brief pastorates in Massachusetts and Rhode Island. But the church could not hold him long.

His first assault on slavery took place in Boston in 1841. A local seaman, who discovered an escaped slave on his ship, was returning the slave to his North Carolina master. Torrey organized a Vigilance Committee, the forerunner of more significant committees, and brought court action to stop the seaman. The action failed, but Torrey had found his work.

Supporting his family as an antislavery editor, he went to Annapolis, Maryland, to cover a convention of slaveholders. He sat in the gallery taking notes when officials collared him and flung him from the hall. In the street he was attacked by a mob, threatened with hanging, and finally jailed on the grounds that he had incited the riot. "In that cell, God helping me, if it stands," he consecrated himself to the task ahead, "I will celebrate the emancipation of the slaves of Maryland before ten years more roll away."

Torrey might have better judged how little time was left. Released from the Annapolis jail, he risked his life constantly in the next two years, darting back and forth through Virginia, Delaware, and Maryland, holding hurried nightly conferences in slave cabins, plotting scores of escapes. Once the police almost caught him on a Virginia plantation, but he raced his horse and carriage to the Pennsylvania border. A few months later in Baltimore his luck ran out. He was arrested and imprisoned in the Baltimore City Jail on June 24, 1844, the same jail that once held Garrison.

The charges were brought by a Winchester, Virginia, planter. But there was only one witness who had seen Torrey at a Winchester hotel the day of the slave escape. Torrey might have evaded sentence except for a Maryland planter who brought new charges against the minister for plotting the escape of his slave, Hannah Gooseberry, and her two children.

While Garrison stirred a fury of protest meetings throughout Massachusetts, Torrey took more direct action. With improvised tools, he sawed halfway through the bars of his cell. But the escape was betrayed by another prisoner, and Torrey was clapped into irons, "weighing, I judge, twenty-five pounds, so twisted I could neither stand up, lie down, nor sleep." Sick with fever, he wrote his wife, "The last nine nights I have slept in all less than fifteen hours. I have not been able to eat what would support an infant."

The trial in late November, 1844, was a major social event, drawing Baltimore's leading citizens to the crowded courtroom. The outcome was preordained; Torrey was sentenced to six years at hard labor. Soon he contracted tuberculosis, describing in his letters his "continued pain in the brain," the agonizing struggle "to repress the impulse to utter insane ravings." His body was wasting away, his sight disappearing. ". . . I am not able to sit up or get up alone from my bed," he wrote his wife early in 1846.

The Massachusetts abolitionists fought desperately for his release. Money was raised at a dinner given by the Reverends John Pierpont and Joseph C. Lovejoy, one of two younger brothers of the martyred Elijah. Negotiations were begun with the governor of Maryland to pay for Torrey's freedom, but they broke down. Torrey seemed little affected. "The chain that is riveted to my ankle will not hinder our Lord from communing with me," he wrote. When his friends begged his release on the pledge he would never return to Maryland, Torrey stopped them. "I cannot afford to concede any truth or principle to get out of prison," he wrote them. "I am not rich enough."

On May 4, 1846, a friend visiting the jail reported that, "he is a happy man." Five days later, at the age of thirty-three, the Reverend Torrey was dead.

Even then, Boston would bring the tragedy full circle. The funeral was scheduled for the Park Street Church where Torrey's brother-in-law worshiped. But at the last minute the Board of

Directors, representing the city's commerical aristocracy, prohibited the service.

They buried Torrey in Cambridge's Mount Auburn Cemetery.
"The young, the beautiful, the brave," Whittier's funeral psalm
described him. He had chosen a calculated martyrdom, and Reverend Lovejoy measured the cost for the mourners at Torrey's
grave. "The *proper price* of one man's *liberty*," he said quietly,
"is one man's life."

FROM New England soil, which bred Lovejoy and Torrey for
martyrdom, came hundreds of abolitionists equally dedicated to
the same risks. Jonathan Walker, a sea captain and boatbuilder
of East Harwich, Massachusetts, had undertaken a construction
contract for a section of Florida railroad. In the spring of 1844,
three of his Negro laborers begged him to help them escape by
boat to the British Bahamas where slavery had been abolished.
Captain Walker agreed. They slipped out of Pensacola the night
of June 22, four other desperate Negroes joining them at the last
minute.

After a week of violent squalls and intense heat, Walker took
sick, delirious for long periods, "my strength and flesh . . .
nearly gone," he wrote later. But he kept sailing ahead, making
seven hundred miles by July 8 when his boat was spotted by two
sloops, captured and taken to Key West.

In double irons, Walker was sent back to Pensacola, thrown
into a cell, chained and "secured in my cage like some rabid dangerous animal." He had lost so much weight from illness and virtual starvation in jail that his bones "were covered with little more
than the skin wrapped around them."

On November 11, he was taken to court, ordered to the pillory
and pelted for an hour with rotten eggs. Then the judge ruled
that he was to be branded on the right hand with the initials,
"SS," standing for "Slave Stealer." The marshal took the hot
branding-iron from the fire and, as Walker described it later,
"applied it to the ball of my hand and placed it on firmly for
fifteen or twenty seconds. It made a spattering noise like a hand-

ful of salt in the fire as the skin seared and gave way to the hot iron."

Walker was returned to jail and kept in irons nine of the next eleven months. But when news of the branding reached Boston, the indefatigible Dr. Bowditch began raising funds. Soon Walker's branded hand became a glorified symbol in the abolitionist press, Whittier eulogizing it in his poem:

> Take it henceforth for your standard, like the
>   Bruce's heart of yore;
> In the dark strife closing round ye; let that
>   hand be seen before.

Unlike Torrey, Walker survived the ordeal. By June his friends raised enough money to negotiate with the Florida courts and secure his release. He returned to Boston, lionized by the abolitionists, telling his story repeatedly to audiences who came in droves to gape at the seared flesh.

At this point, it must strike us as more than coincidence that the abolition movement itself was overwhelmingly concentrated in New England. At least half the active abolitionists came from this area, at least a third from Massachusetts alone. We may well inquire what unique combination of factors brought such a volcanic eruption to one corner of the nation, centered on Boston.

"The new race is stiff, heady and rebellious; they are fanatics in freedom," Emerson described the phenomenon. Yet we must immediately recognize how deeply this new race was rooted in the old. Almost every abolitionist came from original Puritan stock, and the Calvinist's concern with sin remained deep in their bones. If their ancestors warred on the sins of flesh and frivolity, the abolitionists were tortured by one overwhelming sin—the sin of a nation, the devouring stain of slavery.

"A sin against God," Garrison ceaselessly called slavery. Again and again he demanded "the purification of the nation from the guilt of slavery." Like an endless drum, *sin, guilt,* and *purification* reverberate through the abolitionist litany. It was the ultimate battle for the true abolitionist. He was not just opposing a system. He had taken God's side against the Devil. Above all, as Angelina

Grimké wrote and martyrs demonstrated, it was "a cause worth dying for."

If there was pain in the struggle, there was also regeneration. "I seemed transformed, 'regenerated' as your friends would style it," wrote Dr. Bowditch after exhausting months of struggle to block the return of an escaped slave to his Southern master. "It was a curious psychological phenomenon never to be forgotten by me. Work saved me perhaps from insanity."

We might even suspect that many abolitionists were as much concerned with saving themselves as the slave. The Garrisonian rigidity, the refusal to enter the political arena against slavery, the dis-Union policy and denunciation of the Constitution were all part of a strictly moral platform based on this almost hysterical hunger for self-purification.

But sin and purification were just one aspect of a broader religious evangelism from which the antislavery movement sprang. Abolition was essentially a religious outburst. "Like a meeting of early Christians," Higginson described it.

The religious revival in New England and western New York after the turn of the century, often called "The Great Awakening," helped sweep the old dogmas from the churches. Fear of eternal damnation was replaced by a new belief in the doctrine of good acts. Salvation was no longer limited to the chosen few but within reach of every man through continuing, daily goodness. Charles Grandison Finney made the Oneida Institute a center of this Perfectionist gospel. Boston ministers like William Ellery Channing and John Pierpont breathed new life into the Unitarian Church. By 1830, most of New England had freed itself from the old religion. Harvard went Unitarian, Yale swung part of the way.

The natural result of this Perfectionist search was a tumultuous period of soaring reform. For if good acts brought salvation, religion and reform were inextricably linked. Thus Finney's teaching at Oneida soon produced an outpouring of abolition agents. And in Boston, reform became a positive mania.

It was a time when almost every thinking Bostonian was convinced that the world could be remade at his doorstep. It was an age of unbounded confidence when Boston set out to re-create its own image of heaven on Beacon Hill. Societies for the promotion of reform sprouted endlessly. Horace Mann revolutionized public education, Samuel Gridley Howe, the training of the blind and deaf. Dorothea Dix transformed poorhouse and prison conditions. Theodore Parker inveighed against capital punishment.

If some crusades had a quixotic air, so much the better. Amelia Bloomer demanded a drastic change in women's clothing. The eminently respectable Josiah Quincy doggedly defended the outcast Joseph Smith and his Mormons. Edward Beecher rescued delinquent girls. Garrison even dabbled in mesmerism and spiritualism. Theodore and Angelina Weld, as we have seen, expounded Graham's health foods.

Boston, in fact, manufactured reform societies so efficiently that when an epidemic of smallpox broke out, one contemporary writer observed, a society was instantly organized to oppose it.

The eventual result of this outburst of reform was the Utopian communities, the ultimate expression of New England's dream of heaven on earth. Their prototype was George Ripley's Brook Farm outside Boston. Inspired by a dazzling array of philosophies from Fourier socialism to transcendentalism, these colonies were often allied to the antislavery movement, Noyes at Oneida and John A. Collins at Skaneateles, New York, for example, starting as abolitionists. Garrison's brother-in-law, George Benson, founded the Northampton, Massachusetts, colony where Garrison frequently lived.

Closely linked to evangelism and reform was transcendentalism. Its core was the Transcendental Club, organized in 1836, with a distinguished membership including Emerson, Hawthorne, and Thoreau. But it was far more than a literary sect. It was a philosophy, a way of life that helped mold the outlook of a generation.

The transcendentalists were the ultimate optimists, the party of hope. They had unlimited faith in man's perfectibility, his "infinite worthiness," as Emerson called it, coming from an upward surge of mind and heart. It was this inborn capacity to grasp truth and right that produced "the godlike nature of the human spirit." The transcendentalist visualized society as a drama of endless progress with man ascending from one triumph to another. "What is man for but to be a Reformer, a Remaker of what man has made?" asked Emerson.

Revolt was an integral part of optimism. For the transcendentalists were harsh critics of the Industrial Revolution so drastically uprooting the old New England values. They hated the new materialism, the vulgar money-grubbing of State Street. Their revolt took many forms. At Walden Pond, Thoreau turned his back on all exploitation of man and nature and searched for freedom under nature's laws. At Brook Farm the Utopians sought freedom through a mystique of the soil. Noyes's Colony, rejecting most basic laws of society, built a world on radically new standards of Christian love, marriage, and procreation.

Eventually all currents of this soaring period mingled and reinforced one another so that it was impossible to tell where one started and the other left off. As Mrs. Child explained it, the Unitarian "looks upward for the coming dawn and calls it Transcendentalism." The Calvinist too "looks upward, sees the light, and calls it Perfectionism."

All roads to perfectionism, no matter what their labels, brought new converts to the abolition movement. Abolition was the all-consuming struggle. It gave purpose and direction to the age, unifying the energies of every shade of reform and revolt. The keenest minds quickly saw that slavery outweighed all other issues. John Palfrey and Horace Mann plunged into politics and carried the antislavery fight to Congress; Samuel Gridley Howe would exhaust his strength in the antislavery wars. Abolition soon became the one concrete form of action through which thousands of New Englanders could hope to achieve the perfectionist dream.

A REMARKABLE cohesiveness of class and economic status held the abolitionists together. They were highly educated, almost always college graduates. They were primarily ministers, teachers, doctors, lawyers, and editors, professional men respected by their neighbors and earning good livings. In the rural areas, they owned substantial farms. But with rare exceptions like Wendell Phillips and Edmund Quincy, they ranked at the top of neither the financial nor the social hierarchy. And except for a handful like Henry Chapman and Francis Jackson, they had no links with the business world.

Thus they comprised an essentially professional élite whose position in community leadership had been established by their forebears even before the Revolution. By 1835, however, they had been rudely displaced by the new class of merchant princes. They had become, as Professor David Donald * has pointed out, "an élite without a function." In two decades, the industrial colossus had swept away many New England values. It was the lords of the loom and State Street who ruled Boston, Lynn, and Worcester now; the relentless struggle for money, no matter how made, had become the preeminent goal. Once Massachusetts had prided itself on being the only State without a slave within its borders. Now the textile magnates and merchants had solidified a happy partnership with the South, little concerned with the horrors of slavery as long as it enlarged their bank accounts.

It was against these tawdry values that many of the old professional élite revolted. "It is high time our bad wealth came to an end," demanded Emerson. "Our great capitalists are speculating . . . in the liberties of the people," protested William Jay. It was a revolt echoed constantly in literature, speeches, and from the pulpit where Theodore Parker thundered against greed and corrupt morality. The hatred of this class for the new tycoons was paralleled and reinforced by their hatred of slavery. "Seeking freedom for the Negro in the South," Professor Donald concludes, "these reformers were also attempting a restoration of the traditional values of their class at home."

What has been overlooked, however, is that this was a conservative revolt, directed not against aristocratic wealth but the hustling and ambitious men just coming to power. As late as 1846, the "old rich" of the Commonwealth, a category which can be conveniently defined as holding over one hundred thousand dollars in capital, had surprisingly few connections with textiles, Southern trade, or any business profiting from slavery.

* *Lincoln Reconsidered*, Alfred A. Knopf, New York, 1956.

With a few noteworthy exceptions among the textile giants like the Lawrence and Appleton brothers, the "old" money stemmed mainly from importing, shipping, finance, real estate, and particularly the China trade. John P. Cushing, worth two million dollars, and Thomas Perkins, worth a million and a half, were China traders. Robert G. Shaw became a millionaire as senior partner in Boston's largest commercial house. Nathaniel P. Russell was an insurance broker. Peter Chardon Brooks, probably the wealthiest man in New England, had vast real estate holdings.

Moreover, the old aristocracy, while rarely antislavery themselves, often developed strong links to the movement. Perkins's nephew, John Murray Forbes, was one of the stanchest supporters of the Free Soil and Republican parties. Russell's daughter would marry Reverend Palfrey. Shaw's whole family would become militantly abolitionist. John Quincy Adams's son, Charles Francis, enlarged the family holdings by marrying Brooks's daughter and continued the family tradition by running for Vice President on the Free Soil ticket. And Josiah Quincy, mayor of Boston, president of Harvard and listed at three hundred thousand dollars, denounced slavery unstintingly in his later years.

While Brooks never openly attacked the South, his moral position was clear. When his son-in-law, Edward Everett, who fought the abolitionists as governor in 1836, told Brooks he intended to buy a South Carolina plantation, the old man was deeply shocked. ". . . Nothing could be more mortifying to me, my son," he wrote Everett, "than to be told that you are the owner of a plantation and slaves."

The inflexible hatred of the abolitionists for the "new rich" and their tainted profits was equaled only by their bitterness over the vanishing promises of the Revolution. For them the abolitionist struggle was a logical continuation of the "unfinished" Revolution. What had their fathers fought for at Bunker Hill if a slaveholder could seize a Negro on Boston soil and drag him back to chains? "Are you the sons of the men of 1776?" Josiah Quincy demanded after one such seizure. "Or do you 'lack the gall to make oppression bitter'?"

"I keep in my study two trophies of the American Revolution,"

Theodore Parker wrote an English friend. "One is a musket which my grandfather fought with at the battle of Lexington, the other is a great gun which he captured in that battle." Parker, who had recently smuggled two escaped slaves, temporary residents of his parish, to England, added cryptically: "But now I am obliged to look to the 'British' for the protection of the liberty of two of my parishoners. . . ."

What Parker called "these symbols . . . these memories in me" was a constant goad to the abolitionists. Their ties to the Revolution drove them relentlessly to complete the unfinished work of their ancestors. If the presence of Captain John Parker, who commanded the Minute Men at Lexington, hovered constantly over Theodore's shoulder, William L. Chaplin referred equally often to his grandfather, Colonel William Prescott of Bunker Hill fame, while jailed for plotting the escape of two slaves from the nation's capital. Dr. Bowditch "longed to shoulder my grandsire's old King's arm" when Garrison was mobbed. Mrs. Child waved "the spirit of the Puritans and of '76" like a banner in her speeches and writing.

This Revolutionary fury, this necessity to achieve the dream which slavery dissipated, gave the abolition movement deep roots in New England. To complete the work of their ancestors was their own unique mission—"a mission to lead the way in redemption of the relapsed nation . . . ," Palfrey proclaimed. "We men of Massachusetts of this age have a function, the accomplishment of which, for better or worse, will stand long after . . . the thief of time shall have pilfered all this generation's heaps of gold."

CHAPTER IX

Slave Hunt in Boston—
The Come-Outers Shake the Walls: 1842–1844

"BOSTONIANS! friends of the rights of man! descendants of the Pilgrim Fathers!" cried the placards and handbills which flooded the city in late October, 1842. "Shall Boston, shall MASSACHUSETTS, be made the hunting ground of HUMAN KIDNAPPERS? Shall our soil be polluted by the footprints of HUMAN SLAVERY?"

The slave being hunted was George Latimer, a mulatto who had escaped many months before with his wife and child from Norfolk, Virginia, and had just been seized on the streets and clapped into Leverett Street jail. There was no warrant, not even proof of Latimer's identity. The arrest was simply made on order of his alleged owner, James B. Gray, countersigned by Elbridge Gerry Austin, a Boston lawyer representing him. Gray requested the Suffolk County jailer, Nathaniel Cooledge, to hold Latimer until his arrival, and Cooledge meekly complied.

To complicate matters, the fiery Stephen S. Foster was arrested for interfering with the constables taking Latimer to jail and locked up himself. Foster, whom Wendell Phillips called "a pure, eloquent, John-the-Baptist character," insisted he was "simply remonstrating" with the constables as they walked along.

It was a crucial test, Virginia versus Massachusetts, the first time that a Southern slaveholder had used the law to penetrate Boston soil and drag a Negro back to the plantation. The abolitionists, appreciating its significance, appointed Samuel Sewall chief defense counsel. Sewall immediately petitioned Chief Justice Lemuel Shaw to release the prisoner under a writ of personal replevin, citing the 1837 Massachusetts law which guaranteed trial by jury. Shaw refused, stating that the Constitution's fugitive slave clause and its recent interpretation by the U.S. Supreme

Court in the Prigg case superseded the law of the Commonwealth.

The Latimer case brought a wave of terror to Boston's colored population, mainly congregated on the north side of Beacon Hill. Under the leadership of Lewis Hayden, a lawyer, and the Reverend Leonard Grimes of the "Fugitive Slave Church," they formed a devoted core of Boston abolitionism. But many were fugitive slaves themselves who had lived there peacefully for years. If Latimer's seizure set a precedent, any Southern master could pursue his former property even to the stronghold of Beacon Hill. Hundreds of Negroes, dreading the risk, quickly packed their bags and fled to western Massachusetts, Vermont, and Canada.

Even the free Negro, of course, had always suffered from his own brand of local persecution. The railroads continually forced colored passengers with first-class tickets into "Jim Crow" cars. Only the year before a colored woman had been violently ejected from the stage near Cambridge Common. After he had been thrown off a white car on the Boston and New Bedford Railroad, David Ruggles, a leading Negro abolitionist, brought suit against the line, but the judge dismissed the case. Frederick Douglass was dragged off a car of the Eastern Rail Road, clinging to the seats so determinedly that he wrenched two or three from the floor. James N. Buffum, a white abolitionist, boarded the train at Lynn with Douglass a few days later. They were both thrown off. The abolitionists of Lynn protested the indignity so vehemently that no trains stopped at their station for the next month.

The law gave free Negroes little equality. A ban on interracial marriages in Massachusetts was not repealed until 1844. Segregated schools throughout the Commonwealth were not abolished until 1855 when the Massachusetts Legislature repudiated a State Supreme Court decision barring a Negro girl from a white school.

The prejudice of Boston's aristocracy even caused a minor crisis on Belknap Street which ran across Beacon Hill to the Negro section. To preserve their exclusiveness, the town-house residents convinced the city to change their part of Belknap to Joy Street. The Negro community promptly countered by getting the rest of the street renamed Joy.

Once Chief Justice Shaw demonstrated that state courts would not protect an escaped slave, the abolitionists worked feverishly to rouse public opinion behind Latimer. A mass meeting was called for October 27 at Faneuil Hall. But Southern sympathizers jammed the meeting and quickly turned it into a fiasco. Three abolitionist speakers were shouted down. When Charles Lenox Remond, a Negro abolitionist, mounted the platform, he was greeted with cries of "Damn nigger!" and "Tip him into the pit!"

Wendell Phillips finally attempted to sway the rioting audience. He lashed out at "ambitious lawyers panting to see their names blazoned in Southern papers as counsel for slave-catchers." His voice thundered over the shouts and catcalls as he accused his listeners of being "the guilty ones . . . the white slaves of the North." In the fury of the moment, Phillips then took the decisive step which would isolate him and the Garrison wing for the next two decades. Branding the Constitution an instrument of slavery, he announced his dis-Union policy to the enraged audience.

"Yes, silly men that we are! We presume to believe the Bible outweighs the statute book," he cried. "When I look upon these crowded thousands, and see them trample on their consciences and the rights of their fellow men, at the bidding of a piece of parchment, I say my CURSE be on the Constitution of these United States!"

The meeting broke up in chaos, one newspaper the next morning in possibly the mildest comment calling Phillips's speech "shameless abuse . . . from the lips of this fanatic madman." Phillips now was virtually a man without a country. Until emancipation in 1863, he refused to vote, practice law, or perform any legal responsibility under the Constitution. He had faced the ultimate decision: union or freedom for the slaves. The only choice for him was freedom.

When such spectacular methods brought Latimer no nearer release, Dr. Bowditch from a special office on Washington Street organized a new campaign. Through *The Latimer Journal and North Star*, published by him for the next six months, he hammered ceaselessly at the dangers implicit in Latimer's seizure. How many slave-catchers would now pour into Boston? Would

a former slave who had gained his freedom in another state be
protected? Would Massachusetts police, courts, and jails become
an appendage of Southern power? Bowditch induced Whittier
to write his poem, "Massachusetts to Virginia," its lines becoming the credo of the struggle:

> No slave hunt in our borders,—no pirate on our strand!
> No fetters in the Bay State,—no slave upon our land!

At meetings in Worcester, Lynn, and across the state, Bowditch
collected signatures for two petitions. The first was presented to
Congress by John Quincy Adams, the second to the Massachusetts
Legislature by his son, Charles Francis. This giant roll of paper
with 62,791 signers prayed the Legislature to forbid all state office-
holders from aiding in the arrest and detention of fugitive slaves
and prohibit the use of jails and other state property for their detention. It would soon have explosive results.

Meanwhile, Bowditch sent the Reverend Grimes to negotiate
with Gray, hoping to buy Latimer's freedom. When Gray kept
insisting on exorbitant sums, Bowditch conceived a desperate,
cloak-and-dagger plan for Latimer's escape. The plot was eventually exposed by Austin, Gray's lawyer, who publicly accused
Bowditch of attempting to bribe the jailers. ". . . Messrs. Gray
and Austin were the true bribers in this case," Bowditch retorted.
"They induced the jailers to do wrongly with public property
in order to gain a private end."

The charges and countercharges kept the columns of the
Boston Courier in fiery heat for days, Bowditch finally admitting
he had offered the jailer money to allow friends to reach Latimer's
cell and effect his escape. ". . . I GLORY IN THE DEED," he announced. "Lawyer, slaveholder, sheriff and jailer, all have combined to keep illegally a man in bondage."

Fearing that Gray might attempt to whisk Latimer out of the
state, Bowditch kept a group of Negroes on twenty-four-hour
watch outside the jail. Gray, too, was getting nervous. The threat
of escape and mounting costs of legal and agents' fees finally
forced him to reduce Latimer's price from fifteen hundred to four
hundred dollars. On November 17, the purchase was consum-

mated. Amidst a celebrating band of abolitionists, the courts decreed Latimer a free Negro.

The furor over Latimer's arrest now produced abolition's first
legislative triumph. The Senate and House of the Massachusetts
Legislature established a Joint Special Committee which reported,
"not only that the criminal processes of Massachusetts have been
outrageously perverted to the purposes of the slave-catchers, but
that a jail has been made the storehouse, and the officers of justice
have become voluntary instruments" to return Latimer to slavery.

Although most of the Boston delegation still backed the pro-
Southern textile interests, the rural vote lined up almost solidly
against slavery. On March 24, 1843, the Legislature passed a Personal Liberty Act, forbidding the state judiciary or any legal
officers to take part in the capture of fugitive slaves or use state
buildings to hold them. Despite the Prigg decision, affirming
Congressional jurisdiction over fugitive slaves, the states had
found a loophole. Their own magistrates could and would be
stopped from assisting the execution of federal law.

The Act was a landmark in the impact of abolition on the
Commonwealth. What is more, it became a model for similar acts
in Vermont, Rhode Island, Pennsylvania, and other Northern
states. There was good cause for Dr. Bowditch to write Mrs.
Chapman exuberantly, "the 'palmy' days of the cause are coming
and it is becoming fashionable to be considered an *Anti-slavery*
man."

THE RINGING denunciation of the Constitution by Phillips at the
Latimer meeting intensified the split that had long been growing
in abolition ranks. Since 1836 Garrison had been virtually operat-
ing as a separate entity from the American Antislavery Society,
which now claimed over a thousand state and local affiliates. Garrison had alienated many abolitionists through his highly personal
"heresies." They call him "a Fanny Wright man—an infidel—a
Sabbath-breaker—a bad and dangerous man promulgating the
doctrines of the French Jacobins," complained Mrs. Chapman, a
stanch ally. Above all, Garrison's critics were repelled by his

boundless egotism—"the belief that his mighty self was abolition incarnate," protested Reverend Torrey; the conviction he was "whip-master-general and supreme judge of all abolitionists," added Reverend Daniel Wise.

The real split, however, stemmed from the Garrisonian policy on nonresistance and dis-Union, equality for women in the movement, and his denunciation of the churches. Nonresistance to Garrison meant not only pacifism but the refusal to use any political weapon, even the ballot, in the abolition struggle. Although in 1835 he had run for the State Legislature, he soon vehemently insisted that a vote for any candidate only prolonged the political framework under which slavery flourished. Thus he came into bitter conflict with the political wing of abolition which founded the Liberty party in 1840. "Manufacturing political moonshine," he called it. But even his devoted friend, Samuel Sewall, who followed Garrison on all other issues, demanded political action, ran for Governor on the Liberty ticket, and was elected to the State Senate by the Free-Soil party in 1851.

Garrison unrelentingly placed his faith in the power of moral principle; the political wing insisted the struggle could be won, despite compromises and alliances of necessity, by electing abolition candidates. Forty years later, Frederick Douglass reconciled the cleavage: "They looked at slavery as a creature of law; we regarded it as a creature of public opinion. . . . The two were halves necessary to make the whole."

Dis-Union had been preached by Garrison in *The Liberator* as early as 1832. But it only became a formal plank of the Garrison wing when the Massachusetts Antislavery Society in 1843 passed its provocative resolution, "That the compact which exists between the North and the South is a covenant with death and an agreement with hell. . . ." Until the outbreak of war, *The Liberator* kept blazoned on its masthead the slogan, "NO UNION WITH SLAVEHOLDERS!" After the passage of the infamous Fugitive Slave Law of 1850, Garrison shocked many associates by burning a copy of the Constitution at a public meeting, crying "So perish all compromises with tyranny—and let the people say Amen!"

Although critics have accused Garrison of "clambering up the ladder of his wonderful life towards pure principles" while losing "the ground of the real world under his feet," it is significant that Francis Jackson, perhaps the toughest-minded abolitionist, remained a firm dis-Unionist. "The Constitution . . . is so utterly broken down by the influences and effects of slavery, so imbecile for the highest good of the nation and so powerful for evil," he wrote in 1846, "that I can give no voluntary assistance in holding it up any longer."

It was the woman question, however, that most disastrously split the abolitionists into brawling factions. The trouble started at the New England Antislavery meeting in 1838 when Garrison supported a resolution to give all female delegates voting rights. The dissenters, many from the clergy, resigned. By 1840 Garrison was certain he had the votes to secure feminine equality at the American Antislavery Society meeting in New York. His agents scurried ahead to Philadelphia and New York. His specially chartered steamboat carried four hundred and fifty New England delegates to the meeting. Francis Jackson immediately nominated Abby Kelley for the business committee, and she was elected 557 to 488. Amid cries of a "packed house," Garrison won the election of three more women to the executive committee.

When the Tappan brothers and other national leaders resigned and organized the American and Foreign Antislavery Society, the movement was irreconcilably split. Henceforth the Garrison wing would be known as "Old Org," the Tappan wing as "New Org."

But nothing was really settled. The woman question continued to plague abolitionists, particularly the clergy. "I will not sit at a meeting where the sorcery of woman's tongue is thrown around my heart," proclaimed one minister. ". . . I will not submit to petticoat government, here, nor anywhere."

The orthodox clergy was further infuriated by Garrison's ceaseless attack on the church, which he branded in 1835 the "stronghold of slavery." Boston ministers that year organized such unanimous opposition to abolition that Garrison could not secure one church, not even the Masonic Temple, for his meetings. Two years later, the Massachusetts Society was forced to hold its annual convention in a hotel stable, causing Garrison to remark in one of his rare humorous sallies that, "abolition today, as on every day, stands upon a stable foundation."

At that point, the only prominent minister in Boston giving abolition even hesitant support was Dr. Channing. And as a countermeasure, the orthodox Unitarians delegated the Reverend Lyman Beecher to purge liberal and abolition elements from their ranks.

While many ministers outside Boston soon supported abolition, they were often too intimidated by wealthy parishioners to attack slavery in their sermons. "I have never yet introduced it into my pulpit," admitted Dr. Samuel Osgood of Springfield. "If I had done so, I should have grieved away some of my best people." The clergy "respected a compromise more than a principle," Reverend May wrote bitterly, "and trusted to what seemed politic rather than to that which was self-evidently right."

The church hierarchy, above all, led this rigid opposition. In 1836, the General Conference of the Methodist Episcopal Church rejected "any right, wish or intention to interfere with the civil and political relations of master and slave." A year later the General Association of Massachusetts Congregational Churches warned against "strangers" contaminating its services with abolition theories. John Jay, a devout Episcopalian, branded his sect "a mute and careless spectator of this great conflict." By 1838, the issue had split the Presbyterians into two separate bodies; five years later the Old School General Assembly still tabled unread any antislavery memorial.

Although Free-Will Baptists were early opponents of slavery, the American Baptist Convention of 1836 refused to "intermeddle with the subject." When the American and Foreign Bible Society voted to furnish Bibles to all families in the nation, one elder, who asked whether that included slaves, was violently shouted down. The Unitarians as a group always comprised the backbone of abolition. But as late as 1845, the clergy were badly split. That year 153 ministers from New England signed an antislavery petition, 80 refused.

Even Quakers, of all sects most vigorously opposed to slavery, often compromised the issue. The Grimké sisters attacked their

Philadelphia brethren for supporting the Colonization Society and segregating Negroes in special seats. Visiting New Rochelle, New York, Mrs. Child was startled to find the Quakers "making such a fuss about colored people sitting on the same floor with them." Thomas P. Beach, a former Congregationalist minister, who was refused the floor at the Quaker Society in Lynn, Massachusetts, branded it a "Quaker Bastille."

Most New England churches ruthlessly opposed unsegregated worship. One wealthy Negro purchased a pew at Boston's Park Street Church. But after attending Sunday morning service with his family, he returned that afternoon to find the door of his pew nailed up and a constable on duty to prevent him from entering.

At the Warren Street Chapel, where Dr. Bowditch worshiped, a colored girl, who joined the Sunday school class, was forced to sit in a special pew. When Bowditch's protests failed to move the church board, he resigned, stating, "I saw slavery throwing its viper folds around us . . . yet no preacher dared to open his mouth but the fingers of the money-holders were thrust over it."

Even James G. Birney, although breaking with Garrison, was strongly anticlerical, labeling the churches, "The Bulwark of American Slavery."

Garrison, therefore, initiated the policy of purging the churches. His tactics were based on the Biblical admonition, "Come out of her, my people, that ye partake not of her sins, and that ye receive not of her plagues." Or as William Goodell put in the title of his book, *Come-Outerism—The Duty of Secession from a Corrupt Church.*

The abolitionists promptly seceded or *came out* of their churches, Bowditch, for example, attending services only twice in the two years following the Warren Street incident. A small band, led by Stephen S. Foster, however, not only seceded individually, but for the next few years invaded the churches each Sunday much like the seventeenth century Quakers in an effort to persuade the whole parish to boycott them. Labeled appropriately enough, the "Come-Outers," they soon turned the peaceful Sabbath into one of the most frantic and wildly comic propaganda forums that New England had ever witnessed. "It needed something to shake New

England and stun it into listening," Phillips said of Foster. "He
was the man and offered himself for the martyrdom."

On a crisp, fall Sunday in 1841, Stephen S. Foster quietly entered
the Old North Church in Concord, New Hampshire. He was New
Hampshire-born, the son of Colonel Asa Foster of the Continental
Army, a scraggly-bearded giant whose battered silk topper would
become the symbol of his private war. At the first lull in the service, Foster rose to his feet and plunged into a florid dissertation on
the horrors of slavery. The startled minister tried to interrupt him,
but Foster kept right on going. Finally three members of the congregation took him by the arms and led him out the door.

Ten minutes later, Foster returned, demanding that every good
Christian pay heed to "our two-and-a-half million brothers in
bondage." The minister ordered the choir to drown him out, but
Foster could outbellow a score of voices. Again he was dragged
out the door, this time more violently.

Foster arrived early for the afternoon service and began to address the half-filled pews. But his audience had lost patience. They
dragged him down the aisle by his hair, kicked him, and hurled him
down a flight of stairs. In future, Foster would be able to wave his
battered topper aloft, crying, "They smashed this in a *church!*"
Foster was forced to spend the next two weeks in bed recuperating.

Repeating his invasions in a dozen churches across New England
that winter and spring, Foster staged a return engagement at Concord in June, 1842. This time his target was the South Church. At
the morning service, he was thrown out by "main brute force," as
he recorded: in the afternoon, by "kicks, hair-pulling and other
indignities." Although Foster was a powerful man, neither he nor
any "Come-Outer" ever raised a finger in their own defense. Like
Garrison, they were dedicated to nonresistance, a policy which
often left them bruised and broken-boned. But it undoubtedly
saved them from frequent mobs which might have resorted to
lynching if Foster or his friends had fought back.

Nothing, however, could save Foster from the legal vengeance of the South Church parish which pressed civil damages against him before Judge Badger. Foster pleaded his defense passionately. What if your child were kidnaped? Would you not have the right to come into church and raise the alarm? When millions of our countrymen then have been kidnaped and sold into slavery, what law is violated by entering your church and calling for aid?

This logic, unfortunately, did not impress the judge who fined Foster five dollars and costs. Foster was virtually penniless; his friends from town had to empty their pockets, covering the table with coins. The sheriff, however, was impressed with the "Come-Outer" preachings. He not only remitted his fees and costs but drove Foster back to his lodgings.

Now Foster was joined by Thomas Beach, Jesse P. Harriman, Nathaniel P. Rogers, editor of New Hampshire's abolition paper, and Parker Pillsbury. Working as a wagoner, Pillsbury had earned tuition to put himself through Andover Theological Seminary but gave up the ministry when forced to choose between abolition and the church. He had a leonine voice, "tearing up words like trees by the roots," James Russell Lowell described it. Like Foster's battered topper, he prized his patched and shredded coat, man-handled by many Sunday congregations. Each man received a slim salary from the Anti-Slavery Society, at most four hundred dollars a year, and supplemented it with abolition lectures. Foster, his diary proudly noted, was thirty-seven cents ahead at the end of one week.

The "Come-Outers" often worked as a team, three of them invading Lynn, Massachusetts, on June 26, 1842. Foster took the Quaker meetinghouse, but they immediately "carried him out, passive as a log, and set him on the sidewalk." Undaunted, he returned for the afternoon service. This time three men caught him, "two of them by the shoulder, his face downward, and the other, a most conveniently short man as though gotten up for just that use, catching him by the ankles, as he might a wheelbarrow by the handles."

But before Foster had been "wheeled" down the aisle, several young Quakers rushed to his support. Surprisingly, Foster was allowed to return and address the congregation.

Pillsbury, who invaded the Baptist Church, was simply shoved into a closet and held prisoner until the end of the service.

Beach, who had already been jailed for three months as a "Come-Outer" in Newburyport, leaped the altar railing of the First Methodist Church during the last prayer, and started to address the congregation. He was promptly dragged off to a dark closet under the stairs and thrown among the lamps, oilcans, and other sanctuary utensils.

Carrying the invasion to nearby Danvers, the first Sunday in July, Beach was thrown headlong into the water trough outside the Baptist Church. But he emerged unwetted, for a sympathetic youth had pulled out the water plug. Harriman was finally jailed in Salem on September 24, ironically enough, because he had refused to assist the constables in locating Beach and taking him to jail. ". . . Through his prison bars," Pillsbury noted proudly, "he spoke to larger audiences and to better purpose than ever before."

After his release, Beach roused such furious mobs on Nantucket that he was forced to flee the island "to prevent the shedding of human blood." Foster went on to Hancock, New Hampshire. When he invaded the service that Sunday, parishioners clanged the church bell to drown him out, booed, hissed, and slammed books on the floor. Foster just shouted above the din. Finally the whole congregation walked out, Foster crying after them, "Did your fathers adjourn at Bunker Hill when fired upon by the enemies of freedom?"

At the end of the year in Portland, Maine, Foster was temporarily retired to an enforced vacation in bed when a particularly agile mob, shouting for the "blood of the damned scoundrel," beat him savagely around the face and head. Adding up his achievements, he recorded, "Four times have they opened up their dismal cells for my reception, twenty-four times have my countrymen dragged me from their temples of worship and twice have they thrown me with great violence from the second story of their buildings. . . . Once have they attempted to put me in irons. . . . Once in a mob of two thousand have they deliberately attempted to murder me. . . ."

Foster's volatile wife, Abby Kelley, promptly introduced at

the next Massachusetts Antislavery Society meeting the resolution, "That the sectarian organizations called churches are combinations of thieves, robbers, adulterers, pirates, and murderers. . . ." It was a grotesque hyperbole. But the "Come-Outers" had been scratching with their fingernails at the walls of clerical ostracism for too many years to worry about verbal niceties. Even worse, they had to face vehement and high-placed defenders of slavery in the New England churches themselves. Professor Moses Stuart of Andover Theological Seminary, for example, constantly wrote and preached the God-given right of white Americans to keep the Negro in chains. If the "Come-Outers" had been forced to use "a lamb's horn instead of a silver trumpet," as Garrison put it, "it was because thus only could the walls of our slave-holding Jericho be shaken to their overthrow."

At a time when few newspapers would open their columns to the Garrisonian faith, and the abolition journals had miniscule circulations, the "Come-Outers" created a unique method of communication which reached tens of thousands of churchgoers. They were flamboyant, even reckless, rather than persuasive. But their purpose was to startle the conscience of the slumbering parishes, to rivet attention on clerical responsibility in a moral crisis. In this they were amazingly successful, for the Presbyterians and Methodists soon took a firmer stand against slavery, and other denominations would follow. Pillsbury now was not indulging in exaggeration when he concluded, "Nothing like it or unlike it, before or since, so stirred the whole people until John Brown."

CHAPTER X

The Political Plunge—
Liberty and Free Soil Parties: 1840–1848

"CAN ANY MAN tell what increase of power, moral power, William Goodell would have to abolish slavery, if he were elected to the office of roadmaster in the ancient and honorable village of Whitesboro?" demanded one Garrisonian in January, 1840. His sarcasm was directed at the first abolition ticket, the Liberty party, which not only completed the abolition schism but transformed the movement into a turbulent political force.

Although the backbone of the Liberty party was "New Org" men, even devoted Garrisonians like Sewall had become convinced that moral power was no longer enough to halt the annexation of Texas or the spread of slavery into new territories. And Texas was now the core of the slavery struggle.

The organizing genius of the Liberty convention which met at Albany, New York, on April 1, 1840, was Gerrit Smith. A philanthropist whose wild enthusiasms ranged from peace to temperance, he owned hundreds of thousands of acres around Peterboro, New York, probably making him the nation's largest landholder. To the abolitionists and infant Liberty party he contributed huge sums. Later he would distribute hundreds of tracts to Negro farmers and provide a haven for John Brown and his family.

The Liberty candidate for President was a distinguished maverick, James G. Birney of Huntsville, Alabama. Born to social and political power, his father a wealthy Kentucky manufacturer, Birney owned plantations and slaves and practiced law and politics so successfully that he had wide support for high state office. But his religious convictions finally turned him against the Southern system. He freed his slaves and campaigned tirelessly against the institution, living in imminent danger until he was driven from home and fled to Cincinnati. There he published an abolition paper until his office was attacked by mobs and his press destroyed.

Birney ran poorly in 1840, polling only 7100 votes while William Henry Harrison swept the Whigs to their first victory over Van Buren in his bid for reelection. In the Massachusetts gubernatorial race two years later, however, Sewall carried ninety-five towns, blocking both Whig and Democratic candidates from a majority and throwing the election into the State Legislature. Henceforth, either the Liberty or future Free Soil party would hold the balance of power in Massachusetts.

By 1844, John Tyler, who had succeeded to the Presidency after Harrison's death, was determined to add Texas to the Union and submitted a treaty of annexation to the Senate. But he failed to secure the necessary two-thirds vote, and the Southern bloc was desperate. The campaign of 1844 would bring the issue to a boil.

The Democrats cleverly exploited the dream of Texas and "Manifest Destiny." Although John Quincy Adams railed at the "Texas plot," it captured the imagination of large segments of the North and West, bursting with unquenchable faith in the nation's growth and the dazzling image of boundaries stretching from coast to coast. Many sincere Northerners recognized the dangers of Southern expansion but considered it worth the cost. Many others were tantalized by the fortunes to be made in land and scrip speculation.

Birney was the only candidate unequivocally opposed to annexation. Van Buren dodged the question until pinned down just before the Democratic convention. Then he admitted opposing annexation, at least temporarily. His enemies exploited the issue. Although Van Buren had a majority of delegates, he could never muster the two-thirds quota. Backed by the Jackson wing of Southern planters and Western farmers, James K. Polk of Tennessee, an ardent annexationist, won the nomination.

Henry Clay, the Whig candidate, personally opposed immediate annexation. But his party and platform adroitly avoided any mention of Texas.

The Liberty party made startling gains. Birney received 62,300 votes nationally, 10,830 in Massachusetts alone. In western New

York, he took enough votes from Clay to give Polk the state.

Tyler considered Polk's election a mandate for annexation. He had already made John C. Calhoun, the flamboyant symbol of Southern expansion, his Secretary of State. On February 27, 1845, they maneuvered a joint resolution of annexation through Congress, which required only a majority vote. Three days before turning the Presidency over to Polk, Tyler signed the resolution and rushed it to Texas for acceptance.

The Massachusetts Legislature protested against admitting an independent state into the Union through joint resolution, proclaiming that "such an act of admission would have no binding force whatever on the people of Massachusetts." But the deed was done and Tyler had handed Polk an inescapable war.

MEANWHILE, another crisis heightened the tension between Massachusetts and the South. For years the Legislature had protested a provocative South Carolina law, aimed at free Negro sailors on ships out of Boston and other Northern ports. When Northern ships reached Charleston, the law provided that free Negroes must be jailed during their stay and the captain charged for their board and fees. If the captain sailed without them, or even failed to pay their fees, the Negroes were automatically sold into slavery.

Determined to test the law's constitutionality and carry it to the Supreme Court, the Massachusetts Legislature in 1844 empowered the governor to send legal counsel to Charleston. The choice for this ticklish assignment was Samuel Hoar of Concord, a distinguished, gray-haired, sixty-six-year-old lawyer and former Congressman. His family had gained prominence in the Revolution, his father and both grandfathers as well as three uncles fighting at Concord bridge in the Lincoln company.

Arriving at Charleston on November 28, Hoar was startled to find that the South Carolina Legislature had directed the governor to expel him. The leading paper branded him a "bold, insolent and officious abolition emissary."

When a mob gathered at Hoar's hotel, the manager, fearing destruction of his property, asked the city to force him to vacate. The sheriff arrived and, according to Hoar's account, warned, "You are in great danger and had better leave the city as soon as possible." Hoar was later accosted by a sheriff's officer who shook his cane at him, threatening, "If you stay here until tomorrow morning, you'll feel something you will not like, I'm thinking."

". . . Had not Mr. Hoar had a daughter with him," concluded the *United States Gazette*, "he would surely have been hung by Judge Lynch."

Hoar refused to leave, stating he was "too old to run and would not go back to Massachusetts without attempting to do his duty." Meanwhile, the mob had grown so unruly that James L. Pettigru, a prominent lawyer and stanch Union man (he remained in Charleston throughout the Civil War although openly opposed to secession), organized a few friends to protect Hoar in case of physical attack. The decisive blow, however, came from a delegation of seventy leading citizens, including bankers and doctors. A "legal mob," Hoar called them. Arriving at his hotel, they informed him that a carriage was waiting at the door to take him to the boat. Either he would enter it voluntarily, or they would drag him by force.

At this point, Hoar had no choice. He and his daughter walked to the carriage.

The insult to its counsel and the Commonwealth, as well as the challenge to the Constitution, stirred tempers throughout Massachusetts. As Hoar put it in his report, "Has the Constitution of the United States the least practical validity or binding force in South Carolina excepting where she thinks its operation favorable to her?" If South Carolina could arrest Massachusetts citizens on its soil, why should not Massachusetts arrest visitors from Charleston? The question roused the Legislature to such a fever that Charles Francis Adams introduced a resolution of retaliation, which was promptly passed. But in a few months the storm subsided, and except for its implications, the resolution was forgotten. "The final contest between the North and the South," concluded the Charleston correspondent of the New York *Tribune*, "has commenced. . . ."

THE TEXAS crisis inexorably hastened the formation of an anti-slavery political coalition. The first serious split in the Massachusetts Whigs took place at a mass meeting against annexation on July 4, 1845. Although Webster had always declaimed loudly against Texas, he suddenly retreated, and Sumner leaped into the breach, taking over leadership of the "Conscience" Whigs. Robert C. Winthrop, descendant of the first governor of the Bay Colony, Congressman from Boston, and Webster's heir, accentuated the split with his toast to unlimited territorial ambitions, "Our country, however bounded!"

Webster would secretly demand his pound of flesh. Always deep in debt and living in regal luxury, he welcomed a fifty-thousand-dollar subsidy from Boston's textile magnates. The Lawrence brothers refused to contribute, but many others, led by the Appletons, raised the money.

The Mexican government had continually made it clear that annexation meant war. It had never recognized Texas independence and still claimed a strip of territory along the Rio Grande. But Polk wasted no time on negotiations. As soon as he took office, he rushed United States troops to the disputed area and ordered General Zachary Taylor to occupy the East bank of the Rio Grande. On April 23, 1846, Mexico declared what it considered a defensive war. "A wicked contest," Theodore Parker called it, "Mexico clearly in the right, we notoriously in the wrong."

He was echoing the sentiments not only of abolitionists but many Whigs and Democrats. When Congress voted war on May 12, Winthrop could rally only half the Massachusetts delegation to support it. The Senate, however, succumbed completely to war fever, John Davis of Massachusetts casting one of only two votes against it with forty in favor.

The fall elections of 1846 heightened the Whig schism. The "Conscience" Whigs refused to support Winthrop for Congress and induced Dr. Samuel Gridley Howe to run against him. Although Howe lost as expected, the Liberty party made marked gains in Massachusetts and received seventy-four thousand votes throughout the country, its highest total.

In Congress that summer, a money bill to settle the Mexican

boundary question strained divided loyalties among the old parties even further. This time it was a radical Democrat who led the opposition. David Wilmot of Pennsylvania insisted on attaching a proviso to the bill, specifically prohibiting slavery in any territory acquired from Mexico.

The Wilmot Proviso achieved a stunning victory, passing the House on August 8 with only eighteen Northern Democrats and fourteen Northern Whigs voting against it. But it was blocked in the Senate by filibuster and adjournment. "Gentlemen, deceive not yourselves; you cannot deceive others," Congressman Robert Toombs of Georgia warned. "This is a pro-slavery government."

Yet the proviso was a portentous symbol of increasing determination in both parties. Despite his disdain for abolition, Webster always supported the proviso and even opposed the acquisition of California and New Mexico as a result of the Mexican War. "It is time," demanded Sumner, "that the lines be now distinctly drawn all over the United States."

BOSTON THAT fall was rocked by another fugitive slave case. A mulatto slave, known only as Joe, working on the docks at New Orleans, had hidden in the hold of a Boston ship, the *Ottoman*. When it reached Boston harbor on September 22, Captain Hannum discovered the stowaway and informed the owner, John H. Pierson, a wealthy merchant whose ships sailed regularly to Southern ports. Pierson decided to return the fugitive to New Orleans and held him under secret guard on an island in the bay. That night Joe escaped, reached South Boston, and enjoyed twenty-four hours of freedom. Pierson might well have considered that he had done his duty. Instead, despite the urgent pleas of prominent Bostonians like Dr. Howe, he hunted down the fugitive and dragged him back to the ship.

A wave of revulsion ran through the city. For in the Latimer case, a slaveholder had used the courts to recover his supposed property. Now a Boston merchant, acting on his own, with no court order and not even a claim from Joe's master, had assumed the authority of a slave-hunter. "I feel the irreparable shame to

Boston of this abduction," Emerson protested. ". . . I hope it is not only not to be sustained by the mercantile body but not even by the smallest portion of that class."

The protests throughout the city were proof how radically political lines had altered. A few years before, the abolitionists alone had defended Latimer. Now "Conscience" Whigs and independents formed a united front with abolitionists. Dr. Howe organized the huge protest meetings at Faneuil Hall. Whigs like Sumner, John A. Andrew, and Charles Francis Adams sat proudly beside Wendell Phillips and Edmund Quincy. "He was seized in our city, bound and carried into slavery," Howe told a wildly cheering audience, "by those who had no more right to do so than has the slave-trader to descend upon the coast of Guinea and carry off the inhabitants."

The climax of the meeting was the appearance of John Quincy Adams. The old man tottered to the platform. Near him on the walls of Faneuil Hall hung both his father's portrait and his own. His health had been failing rapidly, his voice hardly audible beyond the first few rows. But years later Higginson could still remember the hushed reverence of the audience when Adams announced that if he had but one more day to live, he would use it to take his stand with them. Two months later, Adams was dead.

All protests, however, failed to shake Pierson. The fugitive was carried back to New Orleans on his next ship. ". . . We have tried the 'let alone' system long enough," Dr. Howe told a few close friends. He called a meeting for the night of September 30 at Dr. Bowditch's home on Otis Place, attended by eighty Whigs, abolitionists, and independents. The time for debate and protests had passed. A secret association, the Vigilance Committee, was organized to oppose all slave-catchers. The committee members swore a secret compact that no further fugitives would be dragged from the city back to slavery.

ON FEBRUARY 2, 1848, Polk signed the treaty of peace with Mexico. A vast chunk of the old Mexican Empire, almost the size of the original thirteen colonies, from which would come California,

New Mexico, Arizona, and parts of Nevada and Colorado, was ceded to the United States.

The war brought the schisms in the two national parties to a crisis. In May, the Conscience Whigs caucused and demanded that the Presidential nomination go to an acknowledged anti-slavery candidate. The Whig convention ignored the ultimatum and selected General Taylor, attempting to hold Massachusetts by begging Abbott Lawrence to take the Vice-Presidential nomination. But he refused. "Massachusetts will spurn the bribe," announced the Boston *Whig*. The Conscience Whigs thereupon walked out of the convention.

One of the chief architects of the break was Francis W. Bird, a tall, gaunt, paper manufacturer from Walpole, a disciple of Theodore Parker's "natural religion," a reformer whose enthusiasms ranged from abolition to temperance. "My only drink is cold water as pure as I can get it," he liked to say. But Bird made up for abstention with his Lucullian Saturday afternoon dinners at the Cornhill Coffee House, and Parker's in Boston. The leading men of the Conscience Whigs and abolitionists, Sumner, Wilson, Andrew, and George L. Stearns, met regularly at his table. The "Bird Club," as it was called, soon became a Saturday tradition. Bird was an astute politician. With the old political lines crumbling, he was convinced that 1848 was the year to weld all dissident elements into a third party.

For the Democrats were torn by an even deeper rift than the Whigs. In New York, the radical wing or "Barnburners" (a satirical reference to their reformist zeal in burning down the whole barn to get out the rats) had broken with the conservative "Hunkers" (named for their "hankering" after political plums) over Van Buren's loss of the nomination in 1844. When the convention picked Senator Lewis Cass of Michigan over Van Buren on a platform designed to please the South, the Barnburners walked out and called a new convention in Buffalo on August 9. Under a huge canvas tent in the broiling sun, they were joined by dissidents and splinters of every party—a strange alliance pieced together under the slogan, "Free Soil, Free Speech, Free Labor and Free Men."

Van Buren himself, the candidate of the new Free Soil party, was hardly noted for his antislavery record. And ironically, Charles Francis Adams, who had led the Conscience Whigs to the convention to stop Van Buren's nomination, finally accepted the Vice-Presidency on his ticket.

A large segment of the Liberty party joined the coalition. "The Liberty party is not dead but TRANSLATED," Joshua Leavitt, a prominent Massachusetts abolitionist, announced to the cheering audience as he led his delegates into the alliance.

Free Soil not only inherited ready-made political organizations in key states like Massachusetts and New York. But by breaking out of the strait jacket of abolition, it appealed to a vast new audience—farmers and emigrants with visions of homesteads in the West, small businessmen, and even a few industrialists who grasped the possibilities of railroads and factories stretching across the Western plains. Here was a broadening political base that would be successfully transformed only eight years later into the Republican party. Above all, Free Soil offered the North a decisive stand against Southern expansion. It had drawn the line with Texas; no future state would be opened to slavery.

Van Buren made a remarkable showing, running second in three states and polling almost three hundred thousand votes. Nine Free Soil Representatives were elected to the House. In New York, Van Buren won one hundred twenty thousand votes; in Massachusetts, where he swept Worcester and twenty-nine towns, thirty-eight thousand. His inroads into Democratic strength in New York gave the state to Taylor, and sent the General to the White House.

The slavery struggle had finally broken party lines. Even Garrison, who abhorred political abolition and political deals in particular, wrote his wife that the Free Soil movement marked "the beginning of the end."

ON THE NIGHT of April 13, 1848, Washington glowed with festive bonfires. Torchlight processions snaked through the streets. The White House and all public buildings blazed with light. For the capital was celebrating the expulsion of Louis Philippe and the establishment of the French Republic. Ironically, while Senator Henry Foote of Mississippi extolled the rights of man from the speaker's platform, dark-skinned figures were slipping away from the crowds and disappearing into streets and alleys that led to White Horse wharf. There under a high bank of the Potomac, Captain Daniel Drayton of New Jersey had moored the *Pearl*, a small sloop on which he had promised to carry seventy-four slaves to freedom.

At 10 P.M., Drayton and Sayres, the sloop's owner, cast off. Delayed that night by an incoming tide, they did not reach the mouth of the Potomac until sunset the next day. Then the wind changed and they had to anchor in a small cove. It was after midnight when Drayton was awakened by a steamer pulling along-side. "I knew at once that we were taken," Drayton wrote later. The Negroes offered to fight but the sloop carried no weapons.

They were boarded by a heavily armed posse which almost shot Drayton on the spot. Taken back to Washington, the captives were marched in manacles up Pennsylvania Avenue, followed by a screaming mob that demanded lynching. The escape had been betrayed by a Negro hack driver who had carried some of the fugitives to the sloop.

Drayton was charged by the District Attorney with slave-running and the intention of selling his cargo in the West Indies. Under Maryland law, which operated in the capital, the penalty was death. At Faneuil Hall in Boston on April 25, a mass meeting raised money for Drayton's defense. The Committee, headed by Dr. Howe, was convinced that only one lawyer had the stature and skill to save him, Congressman Horace Mann.

Before entering politics, Mann had been the most influential educator in New England. As Secretary of the Massachusetts Board of Education, he had revolutionized the school system, established the first normal school in the nation, and raised the standards of free public education to a level that attracted observers from all over the world.

After John Quincy Adams's death, he had been elected to the House from the Quincy district and reelected in 1848 on both the

Whig and Free Soil tickets, one of the first beneficiaries of the new coalitions. In his maiden speech in the House, Mann had struck at slavery with stinging words that Sumner exulted "will gladden thousands of hearts throughout the country." Yet now, ironically, his name would be blazoned in every headline not for his work in Congress or the classroom but in the courtrooms of the capital. For four broiling weeks, he struggled to save Drayton's life. The trial gripped the city, packing the court with a boisterously hostile audience which laughed and shouted without admonition from the judge. It was like a fiesta, the noisy throng gathering each day in celebration of the expected verdict of hanging. Many spectators played with revolvers while they listened, punctuating Mann's words with the ominous snapping of hammerlocks.

Mann fought to defeat the slave-running indictment, which carried the death penalty, and limit the charge to abetting an escape. And after two trials, he gained his object. Drayton was fined $10,060, Sayres, $7,400. Since neither the abolitionists nor defendants could raise the money, they were held in jail over four years until Fillmore granted a Presidential pardon.

Overnight Mann was lionized throughout the North, and the Free Soil party jubilantly swept him back to office in 1850, one of the nucleus of new leaders like Sumner and Dr. Palfrey who had emerged from the breakup of the old parties. Mann never received a fee for the Drayton defense, and it took all Dr. Howe's efforts to get even his expenses paid. "I feel in this case," Mann wrote his wife uncomplainingly, "as tho' I were not working for Drayton and Sayres only but for the whole colored race."

CHAPTER XI

Parker's "Law" and the Crisis of 1850

THE DAY AFTER Christmas, 1848, a young planter, accompanied by his Negro valet, left Macon, Georgia, to seek medical treatment in Philadelphia for his crippling arthritis. Under any circumstances, the constant change of train and steamship made it a tedious trip. But this was a uniquely agonizing ordeal. For the travelers were William and Ellen Craft, fugitive slaves in disguise, who had embarked on one of the most daring unassisted escapes of the fugitive epoch.

The plot had been scrupulously planned for over a year. William, whose family had been auctioned on the slave block, and long scattered to distant parts of the South, was a skilled cabinetmaker. His wife, Ellen, taken from her mother as a child, was "a delicate, almost-white quadroon girl with simple, lady-like manners . . . evidently tinged with some high blood of the South," noted Dr. Bowditch. All these factors were brilliantly exploited. For William, rented out by his master for two hundred dollars a year, was allowed to keep anything above that sum he made from carpentering. Stealthily and piece by piece, he had purchased the high felt hat, cape, and other accoutrements of a gentleman. These would be worn by Ellen whose fair skin enabled her to take the disguise of an aristocratic planter.

At Christmas, William and Ellen were given a few days off, thus preventing their disappearance from being immediately noticed. Ellen cut her hair short, swathed her jaws in a muffler which would be explained as the result of a toothache but would actually hide her lack of beard, and carried her "arthritic" right arm in a sling to eliminate the signing of a hotel register in her untutored writing. She wore green glasses to complete the disguise and planned deafness as an excuse for not using her voice.

The first crisis came at the railroad station when a Mr. Gray, who had just dined at her master's home the night before, took the seat next to Ellen on the Savannah train. Three times he spoke to her, but she feigned deafness, bowing and smiling graciously at his conversation.

At Savannah, they took the boat for Charleston. William made himself a model servant, constantly warming flannels for his master's arthritis and bringing them to Ellen's stateroom. Ellen's regal clothes clearly marked her elevated station, and the Captain seated her beside him at dinner. William hovered around solicitously, cutting her meat to save her painful arm. At the Charleston customhouse, when Ellen was asked to register before purchasing tickets to Philadelphia, the Captain gallantly explained the infirmity and signed for her, "William Johnson and slave."

The final crisis came at the Baltimore railroad station. The Crafts had not known of the regulation requiring any master traveling with a slave to have proof that the slave was his property. They were taken to the depot office where the stationmaster lectured Ellen on the danger of slave escapes. William explained they had left Macon hurriedly, that his young master was too ill to wait in Baltimore for the necessary papers. The train bell sounded. Suddenly relenting, the stationmaster allowed them to board the train. The next morning they reached the free soil of Philadelphia, welcomed by friendly Quakers.

The Crafts finally settled in Boston, William securing a job as a carpenter, Ellen as a seamstress. They became active members of Theodore Parker's congregation, one of the few welcoming Negroes. For over a year, nothing disturbed their freedom. Then on September 18, 1850, President Fillmore signed the Fugitive Slave Bill, part of the Compromise of 1850, which gave the South almost unlimited power to pursue a fugitive in the free states and immediately unleashed the most furious slave hunt in the nation's history.

At least six hundred escaped slaves lived in Boston. A fugitive had little choice but to go into hiding. "Asleep or awake, at work or at rest, he was liable to surprise or capture," wrote Frederick Douglass. Lewis Hayden kept dozens of fugitives at his home and two kegs of powder in his cellar, which he planned to explode rather than surrender to slave hunters. The Vigilance Committee, revived and strengthened since 1846, patroled the streets and hotels to watch for the arrival of Southern agents. "I must not let a fugitive slave be taken from Boston, cost what it may justly cost," wrote Theodore Parker, chairman of the Vigilance Committee's executive committee. Parker would soon be put to the test. On October 25, the jailer of Macon, Georgia, named Hughes, and John Knight, who had worked in the carpenter's shop with William Craft, arrived at the United States Hotel. They had warrants to arrest the Crafts and take them back to slavery.

When Parker returned from Plymouth that afternoon, he found Dr. Howe waiting to take him to the Vigilance Committee. "Gentlemen," Parker told them bluntly, "this committee can appoint me to no duty I will not perform." Later he wrote in his journal, "I am not a man who loves violence; I respect the sacredness of human life; but this I say, solemnly, that I will do all in my power to rescue any fugitive slave from the hands of any officer who attempts to return him to bondage."

Craft was immediately hidden by the Committee in a South Boston home. "Mr. _____ took him up in a coach," Parker noted, not trusting names to his personal journal. "Ellen is tonight at _____ in _____ street." Parker first checked William's arms, "a good revolver with six caps on a large pistol, and small ones, a large dirk and a short one," he wrote.

The Vigilance Committee assigned two men to watch Hughes and Knight, trailing them in the streets, keeping guard near their hotel rooms. Posters describing the agents were distributed by the Committee throughout the city. Each time they left their hotel, crowds gathered and jeered them. As Hughes entered his carriage one morning on the way to the sheriff's office, a Negro smashed its window and was about to attack the agent when a Vigilance Committee member stopped him. "I'll have them [the Crafts] if I have to stay here to all eternity," Knight swore, "and if there are not men enough in Massachusetts to take them, I will bring them some from the South."

But these threats were pointless while the Crafts remained

hidden. Ellen had been moved to Ellis G. Loring's Brookline home. William, now hidden at Lewis Hayden's, begged to see her that Sunday, and Dr. Bowditch drove him out. "I will carry my pistol and revolver and will certainly use then if necessary," William promised. The Committee decided it was safer to keep alternating the hiding places. Ellen was moved to Parker's home on Exeter Place, where the minister constantly kept a loaded pistol on his desk. "This is a pretty state of things," he wrote in his journal, "that I am liable to be fined a 1000 dollars and goaled for six months for sheltering one of my own parishioners who has violated no law of God and only took possession of herself."

It was a city gripped by tension and split by divided loyalties, for most businessmen and "respectable citizens," as the conservative Whig papers liked to call them, supported the Fugitive Slave Bill. When the treasurer of the United States Hotel told Francis Jackson, "he would carry out the law if it was to apply to his own daughter," Parker commented wryly in his journal, "No doubt; but suppose it came to his dividends?"

The tension reached a peak on October 30th. "Talk in the newspapers," Parker noted, "about the President sending us 600 or 700 soldiers to dragoon us into keeping the Fugitive Slave Law." The Vigilance Committee appointed sixty members under Parker to visit the slave hunters at their hotel. They arrived at six in the morning, some patroling the lobby, others the stairs, Parker posting himself in front of Room 44. The minister informed Hughes and Knight that "they were not safe in Boston another night." It was, of course, a polite form of intimidation. The agents blustered and bargained for time. But Parker insisted the crowds around the hotel were getting out of hand, that the Vigilance Committee could no longer be responsible for maintaining order. The bluff worked. That afternoon, Hughes and Knight left Boston for New York on the 2:30 train.

A week later Parker officiated at a moving ceremony. Since Southern law prohibited legal marriage between slaves, William and Ellen had asked the minister to unite them under Massachusetts law. Parker put a Bible in William's right hand and "charged him," as he wrote later, "to use it for the noble truths for the salvation of his own soul and his wife's soul." Then he placed a bowie knife in William's other hand and "charged him to use it only in the last extremity. . . . Nay, if you cannot use the sword in defense of your wife's liberty without hating the man you strike, then your action will not be without sin."

It was obvious, however, that the Crafts were still not out of danger. Their escape had stirred a fury of protests among Southern Congressmen, who swore that the United States Marshal's office in Boston would be reinforced and the fugitives captured. The Vigilance Committee promptly bought passage, and on November 11, the Crafts were placed on board a ship to England. Ten days later, Parker wrote President Fillmore, "I must say I would rather lie all my life in jail, and starve there, than refuse to protect one of these parishioners of mine. Do not call me a fanatic; I am a cool and sober man: but I must reverence the laws of God, come of that what will come. . . . You cannot think that I am to stand by and see my own church carried off to slavery and do nothing to hinder such a wrong."

In this letter, as in all instances when opposing the Fugitive Slave Law, Parker based his defense on the "higher law" principle which would now become the foundation of abolitionism. Garrison, too, vehemently expounded the "higher law." But although he supported the Vigilance Committee and did not oppose the use of violence by others, his own nonresistant philosophy prevented him from joining Parker and the Committee in using physical force against the Fugitive Slave Bill.

Parker had no such scruples. "I am no non-resistant," he announced. "That nonsense never went down with me . . . I am not very careful of my reputation; but I dare not violate the eternal law of God."

Parker also differed from Garrison on dis-Union. While he admitted it might become a temporary necessity, he insisted that by holding the Union together, abolitionists could maintain contact with the slaves and continually expand assistance to fugitives through the Underground Railroad. He refused to limit his actions in any way. He worked through the Vigilance Committee, churches, and political parties. He would accept all allies as long as they were unreservedly opposed to slavery.

The "higher law" was a curious and explosive doctrine. "When rulers have inverted their functions," Parker defined it after passage of the Fugitive Bill, "and enacted wickedness into a law which treads down the inalienable rights of man to such a degree as this, then I know no ruler but God, no law but natural Justice."

"Nothing can truly become *law, real law*," stated Dr. Howe in his interpretation, "that contravenes the eternal principles of right."

A Vermont editorial writer, describing the "higher law" as "printed by the finger of God on the heart of man," proclaimed like dozens of similar abolition writers that, "Our first duties are not to the government. We belong first to God and next to humanity."

The "higher law" goes many steps beyond freedom of conscience, beyond the religious rebels who fled the Puritan oligarchy in Massachusetts to follow their own forms of worship in Rhode Island. Rather than opposing authority, they sought freedom elsewhere, a pattern followed later by the Mormons. We might find a closer parallel in the Boston Tea Party. Yet even here, the revolt was based on political rights rather than natural rights; its justification stemmed from man-made laws of taxation without representation.

Many historians have ridiculed this doctrine, Charles and Mary Beard, for example, calling it "one of the prime curiosities in the annals of logic." But there is little point in measuring the "higher law" with logic. Its only basis is belief and transcendental optimism. Its only authority is the human spirit and its grasp of the eternal laws of God. Parker and his followers are thus the natural heirs of the creators of the Declaration of Independence. For such principles in the Declaration as "all men are created equal" can no more be logically proved than the abolitionist's belief in the evil of slavery.

The "higher law" applies only to the highest levels of human conduct, and few appeals have been made to it in our history. The

Quaker or pacifist who refuses military service is one of the rare
examples which fit the definition. The religious sect which refuses
to swear allegiance to the government but only to God is another.
By contrast, the nullification of the tariff by South Carolina in
1832 must rank not as a recourse to "higher law" but only as a
protest against economic and political controls.

Above all, the "higher law" is an instrument not of governments but individuals. Never once did the Commonwealth of
Massachusetts, much as the Legislature may have detested it, violate the Fugitive Slave Law. Rather it was Parker, Dr. Bowditch,
and hundreds of individuals, often acting in groups like the Vigilance Committee, who openly resisted Federal authority and used
force when necessary to prevent a slave from capture.

This is the crucial difference, this individual act of revolt, that
separates Parker from the citizens of Little Rock, Arkansas, who
fought the segregation decision of the Supreme Court in 1957. For
their policy was state policy, the implementation of the legal,
moral, and physical actions of Governor Faubus and the Arkansas
Legislature.

But what of the night-riders of the Ku Klux Klan? Were they
not individuals pursuing their standard of justice under the "higher
law"? Could this private vigilante group claim as much right to
the use of force as Parker and the Vigilance Committee who
virtually threatened the agents from Macon at their hotel and
drove them from Boston?

Here is the critical dilemma of the "higher law" philosophy.
For its only sanction is the validity of the cause. And the only
test of validity is the intuition of the human conscience.

While the abolitionist considered slavery an indefensible sin
against God, the planter considered it a way of life. Both were
right in their own minds. Yet in the progress of ethical history,
only the abolitionist is right, and his rightness is written deep in
the conscience of civilization.

No MAN better than Theodore Parker, by 1850 virtually the
militant and moral leader of the movement, expresses the sweep

and tumult of this decade. His roots deep in the Puritan past, grandson of Captain John Parker of the Lexington "Minute Men," no man was more determined to fulfill his Revolutionary heritage.

An early prototype of the American legend of self-made success, Parker had six generations of Lexington farmers behind him. As a boy, he often worked eighteen hours a day at hard physical labor. He was the eleventh child, and the family had little savings for education. He put himself through Harvard, always ranking high, although he had to drop out of class for long stretches to make money at odd jobs.

Dr. Howe would call him "the foremost man of this continent" and Higginson, "the most variously learned of living Americans," but there was an earthiness about Parker that always separated him from the aristocracy. His figure had a heavy clumsiness. He was short, stocky, and prematurely bald with a head that seemed a bit large for his body. The poet, Lowell, thought he looked "more like a ploughman than a priest."

At the Harvard Divinity School between 1834 and 1836, Parker soon demonstrated his almost fanatical obsession with knowledge. He mastered Hebrew, Latin, Greek, and all the prime modern languages as a student. He would go on to Syriac, Coptic, Icelandic and many of the African dialects. Eventually he knew between twenty and thirty languages. After taking the small parish of West Roxbury outside Boston, he regularly studied fifteen to seventeen hours a day in his insatiable hunger to encompass everything significant that had been written.

His library of over sixteen thousand volumes was the largest private collection in New England. When he moved to 1 Exeter Place in Boston, a house adjacent to that of Wendell Phillips, a friend described the library's growth. "These shelves gradually crept over the door, the window and the chimney places, thence into little adjoining rooms, and finally stepped boldly down the stairs, one flight at a time for three flights, colonizing every room by the way, including the large parlor in the second story, and finally only paused at the dining room close to the front door."

Parker was a unique combination of pedant and practical reformer. His *Discourse on Religion,* published when he was only thirty-two, was a monument of learning. Yet no amount of study could keep him from public controversy. Emerson called him the "Savonarola of Transcendentalists." When Abner Kneeland, a former Universalist minister turned freethinker, was indicted for blasphemy, Parker was one of the few New England liberals along with Emerson and George Ripley who defended him. Kneeland had to go to jail, but no man since in Massachusetts has ever been convicted of blasphemy.

The most important preacher of his time, Parker shattered the idols of the past and revolutionized Unitarianism, a "corpse-cold" religion, Emerson had called it. After his sermon on "The Transient and Permanent in Christianity," set off the "Unitarian controversy," Boston flocked to hear him at the Masonic Temple, and when his audience overflowed it, the larger Melodeon Hall. His parish of seven thousand became the largest in the city. Eventually he had to move to the Music Hall whose three thousand seats were almost always filled.

But his parish was actually the nation. He traveled continuously, speaking one year to eighty thousand people in every Northern state from Maine to Wisconsin. Wendell Phillips said he had "the Rocky Mountains for a sounding board and the hearts of every hopeful and oppressed man for an audience."

His revolt against orthodoxy brought him under attack from fellow ministers and newspapers as a "heretic" and "blasphemer." When his friend, Convers Francis, who was in line for a theological professorship at Harvard, suggested an exchange of pulpits with him one Sunday, the University authorities warned Francis to cancel it. By 1845 almost every church in the Boston area was closed to him. Even ten years later during a religious revival, one conservative minister asked the people to pray for Parker at 1 P.M. each day. ". . . Oh, Lord," the minister pleaded from the pulpit, "put a hook in his jaws so that he may not be able to speak!"

The Boston Association, made up of leading orthodox ministers, accused Parker in 1843 of deserting Christianity because he denied the validity of miracles, and abandoning Unitarianism because he denied the divinity of Christ. They could force him out of the association, Parker retorted, but "I will not withdraw voluntarily while I consider rights of conscience at issue."

What Parker had left, after virtually removing Christ and the Bible from his church, he called "natural religion." All ritual and dogma was eliminated, all vestiges of Calvinism and original sin. The heart of his system was the application of transcendental philosophy to religion. God spoke, not through Christ or the church, but through man's constantly intensified drive toward the ultimate good. Parker expected Boston to set the moral tone for the nation, and the nation to follow his concept of perfectionism. His assault on slavery was the logical result of making religion the highest expression of man's growth.

He was also the radical voice of middle-class reform, protesting the excesses of industrial exploitation, demanding "the application of religion to social life." He attacked the perverted use of money and monopoly, the false gods of State Street. "Everything must yield to money," he charged. Applying transcendental ideals to politics, he scourged the Whig party where "there is no Absolute Right, no Absolute Wrong. . . . There is Expediency and Inexpediency." At least half a century before his ideas penetrated the economic system, Parker envisioned the purest of industrial democracies, an age of plenty that would bring equal benefits to every class of society.

He would have preferred a life of contemplation. He loved to sit and write fifteen hours at a stretch at his old, roll-top desk, a bowl of wild flowers at his elbow. He was devoted to his wife, Lydia, but childless themselves, they made their home a playground for neighboring boys and girls. Once when his wife had to take a week's trip, he complained to a friend, "I cannot sleep or eat or work or live without her. . . . I want someone always in the arms of my heart to caress or comfort. . . ."

Yet from the moment of the Fugitive Slave Bill, he was committed to action, even violence. "I call upon all men who love law," he proclaimed immediately, "to violate and break the Fugitive Slave Bill; to do it 'peaceably if they can; forcibly if they must.'" Within a year he admitted to Sumner, perhaps with a touch of pride, ". . . I am possibly the most unpopular man in the land, certainly the most hated of anyone in it." But despite his prodigious labors against slavery, superimposed on an already grueling schedule, he fretted in his journal, "As I lie awake in the night, I feel as if I had done nothing." By 1853, the pace was taking its toll, and he admitted, "The last three years have made great alterations in my health and vigor." At the end he tried to recoup his health in Italy but he died there in 1860, exhausted, less than fifty years old, but as his friend Higginson lamented, "looking seventy."

JEFFERSON'S prediction that the Compromise of 1820 was "a reprieve only" would have its tragic fulfillment in the Compromise of 1850. When Clay had steered the earlier Compromise through Congress, he had been hailed as the "great peace-maker." Now at seventy-three, wracked by fits of coughing, the bones protruding sharply from his gaunt face, he would struggle once more to hold the Union together. Although he represented a slave state, he had no liking for the institution, and his cousin Cassius would even run for governor of Kentucky that fall on an anti-slavery platform. Clay had outlived his chance for the Presidency and buried his ambitions. He loved the Union, and wanted this Compromise to be his final monument.

At least three explosive issues tormented Congress. California had organized itself as a state the previous year, adopting a constitution that prohibited slavery. President Taylor wanted it admitted immediately as a free state, but the South saw the chance to link its admission with the territorial status of New Mexico and Utah, insisting on a "squatter sovereignty" that would permit settlers to bring in their slaves. Further, Texas was quarreling with New Mexico over the upper Rio Grande Valley. Taylor said it belonged to New Mexico, and wanted it and California admitted together as free states.

Angered by the President's stand, Southern extremists introduced a completely unrelated bill to redress their grievances, the drastic Fugitive Slave Law. Its harsh provisions, which gave the South almost unlimited power to pursue and capture a fugitive within the free states, were certain to provoke even moderate Northerners.

Although the Constitution provided a jury trial in common law suits exceeding twenty dollars, there would be no jury for a fugitive slave. The accused was allowed no hearing; his testimony would not be admitted. All that a slaveholder needed to reclaim his supposed property was an affidavit of identity. Nor did he have to appear before a judge, only before specially appointed Federal Commissioners, who could immediately return the fugitive to his master without chance of stay or appeal. An even more blatant provision was the payment of ten dollars to the Commissioner for each slave returned to a claimant, but only five dollars if he were set free.

The penalties were equally severe. A marshal or deputy refusing to make an arrest could be fined one thousand dollars. Any person concealing or rescuing a fugitive could be fined one thousand dollars, imprisoned for six months, and assessed additional civil damages of one thousand dollars for each slave lost.

The Bill not only made "every vessel, sea, lake and river a hunting ground for the kidnapper," as Parker Pillsbury put it, but it virtually made every citizen of a free state a slave-catcher since Comissioners were authorized to call bystanders, or *posse comitatus*, in legal terminology, to their aid.

In his eagerness to avoid a disastrous clash between extremists of both sides, Clay combined all issues, including the Fugitive Bill, into one Omnibus Bill and convinced Webster to throw his influence behind it. On March 7, before a crowded Senate, Webster came out for the Compromise, speaking for "the preservation of the Union" and pleading with the North to "conquer their prejudices."

Webster had been the idol of New England, even Parker, dazzled by his grandeur, exclaiming, "What a brow it was! What eyes! Like a charcoal fire in the bottom of a deep, dark well." Only a few years before Webster had committed himself irrevocably against the expansion of slavery and called the Wilmot Proviso his "thunder." Now, claiming to put the Union above all other issues, he had drastically reversed himself. Shocked and angered, Massachusetts abolitionists and radicals accused him of "elaborate treason," as Sumner put it. His enemies may have exaggerated Webster's gamble to appease the South. But there is little doubt his rampant ambitions, frustrated by loss of the Presidential nomination in 1848, had driven him to placate the Southern Whigs to get their support in 1852. "Fallen, fallen, fallen from his high estate," moaned Longfellow.

Sewall lamented, "It is not pleasant to have the god we worshipped thus metamorphosed into a common mortal." Horace Mann proclaimed, "Webster is a fallen star! Lucifer descended from Heaven." And Whittier mourned the great defection in his ode:

> All else is gone; from those great eyes
> The soul has fled;
> When faith is lost, when honor dies,
> The man is dead!

Clay, who had launched "Save-the-Union" meetings throughout the nation, pressed his efforts to rally moderates of both major parties behind the Compromise. His objective was simplified to a great extent by the death on March 31 of Calhoun, who less than a month previous had insisted, "As things now stand, the Southern states cannot with safety remain within the Union." Then on July 9, President Taylor, who had consistently opposed the Compromise, succumbed to typhoid fever after taking sick at a public reception. Millard Fillmore, his successor, a New York Whig and Unitarian who had opposed slavery while serving in the House, now allied himself unreservedly with Clay and Webster. Seward, the wiry, intense spokesman of the free-soil radicals and confidant of the late President, was dropped from the inner circle. The cabinet was completely revamped, Webster installed as Secretary of State. To compensate for Webster's claim of a crippling loss of income from his legal practice, Boston Whigs put together for him a twenty-thousand-dollar purse.

When a vote was finally reached in August, the Omnibus Bill was dropped and its integral parts taken up, one by one. The Texas boundary settlement was passed on August 9, Texas receiving a large slice of territory that New Mexico had vigorously claimed. California was admitted as a free state on August 13, and a day later the New Mexico-Utah territory organized under the inflammable "squatter sovereignty" provision.

Finally, on August 19, the bitterly-debated Fugitive Slave Bill passed the House 109 to 75, with the vote on engrossment of the bill in the Senate, 27 to 12. The only favorable House vote from Massachusetts was that of Samuel A. Eliot of Boston. Although free state Representatives outnumbered the South 141 to 91, many Northerners, both Democrats and Whigs, either supported the bill or evaded their responsibility by absence. All twelve Senate votes against the bill were from the North. But of twenty absent Senators, fifteen represented free states!

The business centers of the North breathed easier. Clay was cheered lustily on his trip through Baltimore, Philadelphia, and New York. A hundred-gun salute greeted the passage of the bill in Boston where Webster was the hero of the hour. Over 3,000 citizens signed their names for a mass rally at Faneuil Hall in support of the Fugitive Law. *The Daily Evening Transcript*, calling them "the moral worth, intelligence and patriotism of Boston," boasted that "a weightier or more influential list of names was never appended to any document ever issued in New England." In New York, 10,000 businessmen pledged themselves to aid in the rendition of fugitive slaves, and those who refused to sign were blacklisted. Attacking the abolitionists at a Castle Garden rally, James W. Gerard insisted, "We must root them up as poisonous weeds. . . ."

In the enthusiasm of the moment, even Senator Stephen A. Douglas, a devoted supporter of the Compromise, was convinced that the conflict had been settled, telling the Senate, ". . . I have determined never to make another speech on the slavery question."

Yet tragedy was imminent, not only for the Fugitive Bill but its chief protagonist. Webster would make his last frantic bid for the Presidency in the spring of 1852. Wrapping himself in the patriotic mantle of Compromise so insistently that Emerson snapped, "The word liberty in the mouth of Mr. Webster sounds like the word love in the mouth of a courtesan," he sought his reward at the Whig convention and found himself ignored. A colorless, uncommitted candidate was needed, and the Whigs chose General Winfield Scott. Webster was cast aside not only by New England, which gave him only six delegate votes, but by the Southern planters, who gave him none.

". . . After having done my duty to my Southern brethren," Webster complained bitterly, "they had neither the courage nor kindness to place me on the record of that convention. I do not say I did not want the nomination, but I would rather have had *their record* than the nomination."

Gaunt, exhausted, and badly shaken after being thrown from his carriage, Webster died only a few months after the convention on October 24. Bells tolled throughout New England, and Parker called the fallen colossus, "the saddest sight in all the Western world." Thousands of men and women who crowded Faneuil Hall at the memorial service wept for the grandeur of the past and the ignominy of his last years. Clay had died in June. With its two leaders gone, nothing could save the Whigs from breaking apart.

CHAPTER XII

Black Squall Over Boston—
The Vigilance Committee and Shadrach Rescue: 1851

"WHEN WEBSTER made his great speech on the 7th of March, 1850, supporting the Fugitive Slave Law, and endorsing all the compromises by which we surrendered to the slaveowners," wrote John Murray Forbes, "the scales fell from my eyes, and I gave up the Whig party and acted in my quiet way with the Republicans, then called the 'Free Soilers.'" Forbes was not alone among prominent men shocked into action. Amos Lawrence, already alienated from the "Cotton" Whigs, took the final step with his financial support of the Vigilance Committee. Francis G. Shaw, one of Boston's wealthiest merchants, and George R. Russell, mayor of West Roxbury, also contributed generously. Emerson furiously branded the law, "a filthy enactment," and joined the militant opposition, announcing, "I will not obey it by God!"

No other single factor, not even Texas, had so jarred and revolted increasingly large segments of the North. For the Fugitive Law was a constant and agonizing reminder that the South could now reach into any corner of the free states. Congressman Toombs of Georgia only intensified the bitterness by announcing that he would soon read his list of slaves in the shadow of Bunker Hill. When a friend of Maria Child's sheltered a fugitive at Medford, the town fire company, previously aloof to the struggle, "sent for the man chattel," as Mrs. Child described it, "elected him a member of their company, and promised at a given signal to rally for his defense in case he was pursued and to stand by him to the death, one and all."

Through the Personal Liberty Law of 1843, the Massachusetts Legislature had already erected legal barriers against employment of state buildings or personnel in the hunting of fugitive slaves. Revulsion against the Fugitive Bill now stirred almost every Northern state to pass similar laws. Eight states even provided that the accused should be defended at public expense.

Politically, the Fugitive Bill had sweeping repercussions at the polls. In Massachusetts that fall, the Free Soilers, already incorporating the Conscience Whigs, allied themselves with the Democrats to carry the state. George S. Boutwell, an antislavery Democrat, was elected Governor by the Legislature in 1851 and again in 1852. The same coalition sent Sumner to the Senate in 1851. Another antislavery Whig, Benjamin Wade, was elected to the Senate from Ohio. In New York, where the Whig schism ran deep, Gerrit Smith scored a startling upset in 1852 by winning election for Congress on the Liberty party ticket.

Nothing before had roused moderates of both parties to such strenuous opposition. Richard Henry Dana, Jr., the aristocratic Boston lawyer, author of *Two Years Before the Mast,* and previously a moderate Whig, introduced the resolution at the protest meeting at Faneuil Hall on October 14, 1850, which labeled the Fugitive Slave Law unconstitutional. "Law or no law," Dana insisted, "not a slave should be taken back from Massachusetts."

"The Stamp Act could not be executed here," cried Sumner. "Can the Fugitive Slave Bill?" Almost four thousand men and women in the audience roared back, "Never!" And Sumner concluded, "The public conscience will not allow a man, who has trodden our streets as a free man, to be dragged away as a slave."

It was the Vigilance Committee, however, which carried out the detailed strategy of opposition. The Committee, which quickly enlisted over two hundred members, embarked on a vigorous fund-raising campaign. Its account book, kept by Francis Jackson and still in the possession of the Bostonian Society, is a remarkable record of distinguished contributors ranging from George W. Bond, the merchant, Francis W. Bird, James Russell Lowell, and Palfrey to the anonymous donor of a dollar, listed only as "Webster Whig." Special appeals were made to the clergy for two church collections which brought in over two thousand dollars. Jackson, of course, was taking a sizable risk by even recording these names, for any participant in the Committee was subject to heavy fines and imprisonment under the Fugitive Law.

The account book also presents a graphic record of the Committee's scope. In November, 1850, it paid out three dollars for "posting 300 bills describing the personal appearance of Slave Hunters." By November 16, it was already employing Henry Highland Garnet and Lewis Hayden to harbor fugitive slaves. Amos Cummings was paid $6.25 for a barrel of flour to feed fugitives. Eight dollars was given John Thomas, his wife, and two children, a family of escaped slaves, who were sent on their way to Canada. A large share of the Committee's funds went to the Underground Railroad, both to fugitives and "station operators." When John H. Walker had his leg crushed by a railroad car in Delaware during his escape, the Committee purchased for him an artificial leg. One particularly significant payment of $24.50 was made to Samuel Clemens to bring him "from Missouri penitentiary to Boston—he having been imprisoned there two years for aiding fugitives to escape."

The most active agent of the Committee was Austin Bearse, a brawny, ruddy-faced sea captain from Cape Cod who had been one of the first "Come-Outers" and now carried secret messages for the Committee, guarded the door during meetings, and collected money from the outlying towns. But it was as captain of his schooner, *Moby Dick*, that Bearse became virtually a one-man rescue force. The Committee kept informants in the United States Marshal's office and along the waterfronts of major ports like Boston, New Bedford, and Salem to bring word in case fugitives had been discovered on incoming ships. Ostensibly Bearse used his schooner for fishing, but more often he was patroling the harbors and coast.

Once Bearse was tipped off that a fugitive slave had been discovered on the brig *Florence* from Wilmington, North Carolina. Taking three or four associates on his schooner, he surprised the brig in the harbor and "said roughly to the mate, 'I want him damn quick'—and I started for him," as he wrote later. The startled mate turned over the fugitive without resistance. That night Bearse hid him at a Brookline home and then sent him on to Worcester and Canada through the Underground Railroad.

Another time, Bearse forged papers representing him as the legal claimant of a fugitive who had been discovered on a ship in Boston harbor. Presenting them to the captain with due ceremony, he sailed off five minutes later with the slave safely aboard the *Moby Dick*.

But when Bearse tried to board the *Sally Ann* by force to seize another fugitive, its captain and crew drove him off with iron bars and spikes. He returned to Boston for reinforcements but could find no one but his brother. Since the night was still dark, they collected a dozen fishermen's hats and coats and nailed them on wooden frames along the rail of the schooner. This time they returned and brusquely informed the *Sally Ann* they were attacking with superior numbers. Fooled by the ruse, the captain turned over the fugitive without a struggle. The next day he was escorted to Worcester and then on to Canada.

The Boston Vigilance Committee kept close liaison with committees in other cities. Theodore Parker's journal for March 15, 1851, records the dispatch of two couriers who left Boston for New Bedford at midnight, covering the sixty miles in four and a half hours, half by horse, half by railroad. Parker had been warned that Deputy United States Marshal William Russell had left Charleston by ship with an armed force to seize a fugitive. Nathaniel P. Borden's house was a key center for the Underground Railroad on the Cape. By 5 A.M. the bell on Liberty Hall was tolling its warning, and New Bedford was in an uproar. Hundreds of Negroes met with leading citizens of the city at the Hall. By the time a mysterious ship appeared in the harbor, all fugitives were in hiding.

Another Vigilance Committee courier raced by train and horse from Boston to Manchester, Vermont, to warn a fugitive, now the town barber, that Southern agents were on their way to seize him. While some members of the local committee shadowed the agents from the moment of arrival, others raised a purse and quickly sent the barber to safety in Canada.

Reverend Samuel May's home at Brooklyn, Connecticut, was a key "station" on the Underground Railroad for fugitives coming up the Connecticut River Valley. May, who had been called the "Lord's chore boy" by Bronson Alcott, his brother-in-law, carried the fugitives on to Effingham L. Capron at Uxbridge, Massachusetts. He, in turn, delivered them to Stephen Foster and Abby Kelley at their Worcester farm. Higginson also frequently drove escaped slaves to the Fosters from where the route led through New Hampshire or Vermont to Canada.

At Natick, Massachusetts, Edward Walcott constructed a brick escape tunnel from his cellar to the nearby tracks of the Boston & Albany Railroad. Walcott delivered his fugitives to Israel H. Brown at South Sudbury, who carried them in the straw-bedded false bottom of his market wagon. Together they aided the escape of over a hundred slaves. Richard Plummer of Newburyport transported fugitives under the piled-up bags of grain in his wagon. Once he was pursued so closely by Deputy Marshals he had to hide his passengers in the high corn along the road while they searched his wagon.

The Worcester Vigilance Committee, a stronghold of abolition, once had to protect a Southern agent rather than a slave. The hotel managers of the city, united against the Fugitive Law, had refused to lodge the agent on their premises. When he was surrounded on the street by an angry crowd, threatening to tar and feather him, he had to be rushed out of town for his own safety under escort from the local committee.

THE Fugitive Slave Law not only heightened tension between the South and abolitionist areas of the North; it accentuated the schism in Boston itself. The hardening of antislavery opinion throughout the Commonwealth in the previous decade had remarkably little impact on the city. The conservative Whig vote held fast.

Boston's prosperity kept it a bastion of Toryism. The Commonwealth's manufactures rose from $86 million in 1837 to almost $300 million in 1855, much of it controlled from State Street, particularly by one closely knit group. "Boston is become the focus of all the Union for capital . . . ," wrote John Murray

Forbes, the financier, in 1847. The fifteen families, comprising the core of the "Boston Associates," held by 1850 two fifths of the city's banking capital, a third of the State's railroad mileage, two fifths of the State's insurance capital, and a fifth of all the cotton spindles in the nation.

The city's population had risen as sharply as its wealth. In 1830, Boston was little more than an overgrown town of sixty thousand. By 1855, it boasted one hundred sixty thousand residents.

Through all this growth, Whig policy remained astonishingly rigid. Its leading spokesmen like Nathan Appleton relentlessly pursued the same comfortable ends despite disintegration in their own national party. Appleton, who was largely responsible for developing the textile centers of Lowell and Lawrence, and represented the Boston interests in the Massachusetts Legislature and Congress, clung stubbornly to his faith in a tariff, which would protect New England textiles, and a pact of friendship with Southern planters, which would unite all Whigs in blissful harmony.

But if Appleton represents the inflexible component in Boston society, Forbes represents the decisive variable, a limited group of progressive Whig businessmen who shifted their allegiance to Free Soil and Republicanism. The two groups are separated not only by a political but by a broad economic gulf. While Appleton was bound to the South, Forbes looked westward. After making a fortune in China by the time he was twenty-four with the family firm, Russell & Co., he ignored the textile industry and concentrated his investing talents in the railroads and natural resources of Pennsylvania, Michigan, Kansas, and the Mississippi Valley. In 1846, he gained control of the Michigan Central Railroad, developed another line from Hannibal to St. Joseph, and set out systematically to purchase Western lands. "I think that with a Million of Dollars I could show such a development of Coal and Iron as would change the whole Iron trade of this country!" he wrote his brother in 1848. "Then I want a couple of Millions more to help join Boston to the Mississippi River."

It takes no special cynicism to conclude that Forbes profited handsomely from his vision. And when he, the Lawrence brothers, and their associates contributed to the Kansas Emigrant Aid Society and the free-soil settlers of that state, they were supporting not only a principle but their private investments. At the same time, they were devoted men, stanchly opposed to slavery. By aligning themselves with Free Soil, they widened the base of the movement, gave it immeasurable prestige, attracted a large following of small businessmen, and eventually hastened its transformation into the Republican party.

DEFEATED once in the Crafts' case, the South wasted little time employing the Federal law a second time against Boston. In early February, 1851, John De Bere of Norfolk, Virginia, dispatched his agent, John Caphart, to seize the fugitive, Frederick Wilkins, commonly known as Shadrach. For almost a year, Shadrach had been employed as a waiter at Taft's Cornhill Coffee House near the courthouse. It was there that Caphart captured him early on the morning of Saturday, February 15. Taking no chance of intervention by the Vigilance Committee, he used nine United States Deputy Marshals. The Coffee House was surrounded quickly and with complete surprise.

"Mr. Warren and myself went immediately into the dining hall of the coffee house," Deputy Marshall Patrick Riley testified later, "and to avoid suspicion, ordered some coffee. . . . In the passageway between the bar-room and the hall, Mr. Sawin and Mr. Byrne came up and each took the Negro by an arm and walked him out of the back passageway. . . ."

Shadrach was carried the few blocks to the courthouse, and Riley immediately notified Mayor John P. Bigelow and City Marshal Francis Tukey. At 10:30 the prisoner was brought before the United States Commissioner, Judge George T. Curtis.

A Vigilance Committee informant rushed the news to Dana, whose office was directly opposite the courthouse. Dana immediately hurried to the Marshal's office where he prepared a writ *de homine replegniando* and a petition of *habeas corpus* for Chief Justice Lemuel Shaw. "The Chief Justice read the petition," Dana reported, "and said in a most ungracious manner, 'This won't do.

I can't do anything on this.'" Dana, testing for the first time traditional Massachusetts statutes for the protection of the accused against the harsh provision of the Fugitive Slave Law, was convinced Shaw "attempted to bluff me off" and "that all these objections were frivolous and invalid."

Dana was soon joined by four other lawyers, Charles G. Davis, Charles List, Ellis G. Loring, and Samuel Sewall, all members of the Vigilance Committee. Sewall requested a delay until Tuesday, and Commissioner Curtis granted it.

It was now about noon, and Riley attempted to clear the courtroom, "making the most absurd exhibition of pomposity," as Dana described it. ". . . Mr. C. [Curtis], dressed in a little brief authority, was swelling into the dignity of an arbiter of life and death with a pomposity as ludicrous as that of R."

Prohibited from placing Shadrach in the city jail because of the state's Personal Liberty Law, Riley sent a message to the Charleston Navy Yard, requesting a Federal cell. For some reason, the Navy Yard could not comply; Riley, therefore, had to convert the courtroom into a prison.

About 1 P.M. he sent a message to the marshal for more guards, and posted his deputy marshals at the door. The courtroom had now been "cleared of all save some fifteen officers being all the reliable men whom we had been able to collect, the counsel and some newspaper reporters," Riley testified later. ". . . At about 2 o'clock, all the counsel had left except Mr. Charles G. Davis, and a reporter who I learned was Elizur Wright, one of the editors of the Commonwealth."

What Riley did not know, although he should have heard the din, was that a crowd of Negroes, estimated by the Boston *Transcript* at between one hundred and one hundred fifty, had gathered at the courtroom door. They had rushed from their homes and jobs on Beacon Hill, notified of Shadrach's arrest by a member of the Vigilance Committee, probably Lewis Hayden.

The officers at the door now opened it to allow Davis, Wright, and the Reverend Grimes (whom Riley later remembered had also remained behind) to leave the court. The Federal prosecutors eventually claimed their delay was part of a carefully conceived plot. The officers allowed the door to open only a few feet. But in those few seconds, an explosion shook the room.

". . . The negroes without, who had filled the passageway on the outside, took hold of the edges of the door as it opened," Riley testified. "I was at the table when I heard a cry that they were rushing in—the cry came from the officers. . . . I immediately rushed to the door—some officers were between the green door and the outer door—just then it cracked, the perpendicular piece was broken. I pushed as hard as I could with one of my feet against the judge's desk; I was there some three minutes; some one or two officers were outside pulling the green door towards them."

". . . A stream of men began to rush in, Patrick Riley being snugly squeezed behind the door, a place of semi-concealment and safety which he seemed loath to leave," Wright testified.

"As he [Wright] was passing the threshold, he raised his arm and exclaimed, 'Come in! Now! Now!'—and those outside immediately rushed in," United States Deputy Marshal Frederick D. Byrnes related. "We succeeded in closing the inner door, but it was immediately forced open. . . . When it was forced open a second time, in came Mr. Wright and a tall negro close by him."

Dozens of feet and arms jammed inside the door, and at least twenty men swept into the room. "One of the mob seized the Marshal's sword, which usually stands by his desk, and carried it away," reported the Boston *Daily Advertiser*, "but it has since been returned." The guards seemed to have been too startled or cowed to fight back, Wright stating, "Not an officer was struck or menaced there. . . . Neither did an officer that we saw offer any resistance to the egress of Shadrach with his friends."

The intruders lifted Shadrach high in the air, virtually carrying him from the room on their shoulders, half passing him, half flinging him down the stairs. The most remarkable factor of the abduction was its speed. "All done in ten seconds, I should think," related Henry Horner, a Municipal Court clerk, standing on the stairs above the courtroom level. "Never saw anything done so quickly before. Saw two men take hold of Shadrach and fetch him out, about twenty other men following. . . . They kind of threw him down the stairs. . . . Shadrach was very much frightened,—did not seem to know whether he had got among his friends or enemies."

From his office across the street, Dana heard the commotion and rushed to the window. ". . . Down the steps came two huge Negroes bearing the prisoner between them with his clothes half torn off, and so stupified by the sudden rescue and the violence of his dragging off that he sat almost dumb, and I thought he had fainted," Dana related, "but the men seized him, and being power-ful fellows, hurried him through the square into Court Street, where he found the use of his feet, and they went off towards Cambridge like a black squall, the crowd driving along with them and cheering as they went."

A few blocks up Court Street, the rescuers placed Shadrach in a waiting carriage, one indication that some plans had been made. In minutes Shadrach was gone, the whole abduction, in fact, taking place with such efficiency that the marshals could not organize a pursuit.

The abolition press was exultant. "Massachusetts Safe Yet! The Higher Law Still Respected," the *Commonwealth* announced. "That rescue will be cited fifty years hence, yes twenty years hence, as one of the chief glories of Boston," Warrington pro-claimed in the *Lowell American*. Theodore Parker called it in his journal, "the most noble deed done in Boston since the destruction of the tea in 1773. I thank God for it." When Parker gave the news to his congregation the Sunday morning after the rescue, "one spontaneous shout of applause reechoed through the building," an associate recalled.

The conservative press, however, attacked the rescue angrily. "An outrage!" cried the Boston *Daily Advertiser*, demanding "protection of life and property which we put in jeopardy by such an exhibition of the impotence of civil authorities." The Boston *Transcript* branded it, "the triumph of mob law"; the New York *Express*, "an outrage upon the country and a deep stain upon the city of Boston."

In Washington, Webster labeled the rescue an act of "treason."

Clay demanded "whether government of white men is to be yielded to a government of blacks." A few days later, President Fillmore announced his intention to "enforce the law at all riskes in every state of the Union" and ordered "prosecution to be commenced against all . . . aiders and abettors of this flagitious offense."

Pressure from Washington and Boston Whig leaders quickly brought a reversal in the city's attitude toward enforcement of the Fugitive Law. While state law prevented city officers from aiding the arrest or detention of a slave, did it prevent them from dispersing a mob seeking to rescue the slave? The mayor and city marshal may have thought so. U.S. Marshal Riley complained in the Shadrach investigation that neither "has appeared, nor has a single officer under their direction appeared or sided in attempting to disperse the mob. . . ." The Boston *Courier* commented acidly that forty police in the city marshal's office down the hall from the court did not lift a finger to halt the rescue. Now, however, the mayor specifically instructed the city marshal to aid agents of the Federal government when obstructed by a mob.

On February 17, Davis, Morris, and Wright, and James Scott, a Negro who had forced his way into the courtroom, were arrested for their roles in the Shadrach escape. The Vigilance Committee raised thirteen hundred dollars to defend them. While the District Attorney set out to prove that the rescue was a carefully premeditated plot, Dana for the defense insisted it was "unexpected and only successful because unexpected," the momentary inspiration of Shadrach's friends who had gathered at the door. "Three men outside the door could have prevented the rescue," Dana argued. "Mr. Riley did not suspect it, Mr. Wright did not suspect it, nobody suspected it. . . . No premeditations! No plan! Counsel knew nothing about it. Nobody suspected it and the whole thing was over in a minute."

After a trial of three weeks, the jury could reach no verdict. In the case of each defendant, the vote was either deadlocked, or one juryman held out stubbornly against conviction. The judge finally dismissed the case.

Many years after the Civil War, Dana was vacationing in the White Mountains, according to an account given the Massachusetts Historical Society, when his coach driver remarked that he was the juryman who disagreed. Why had he opposed conviction, asked Dana? "I was one of the men who helped him [Shadrach] escape," the driver replied.

The authenticity of this account has no more substantiation than the origins of the Shadrach rescue itself. While it is doubtful the Vigilance Committee, except for Hayden's notification of the Beacon Hill Negroes, could have had time for an organized plot, there is reasonable evidence the abduction was not a momentary whim. Higginson attributes the leadership to "a colored man of great energy and character," probably the same man mentioned by Dr. Bowditch in his diary as rushing off from his employer, John L. Emmons, to go to the courthouse. At the stairs, he asked the Negroes assembled there, "Will you follow me and rescue him?" He led the charge up the stairs, and after forcing his way into the courtroom, seized the Marshal's sword, later returning it to a nearby shop and asking the proprietor "to allow it to remain until called for by its rightful owner."

That there was at least a modicum of planning is proved by another witness who, while the courtroom was being cleared, "saw a man standing behind the rail, who was disinclined to leave. . . . He reached his hand over to the prisoner, and I believe, calling him 'Fred' said—'We will stand by you to the death.' "

But from the moment Shadrach was swept into a waiting carriage, the Vigilance Committee took charge of the flight from Boston. The drivers of the carriage were later identified as Lewis Hayden and Samuel Crocker of Lawrence, a paper manufacturer and deacon of the Baptist Church. Shadrach was rushed to the Watertown home of William S. White, who in turn drove him to the home of Mrs. Mary M. Brooks in Concord. Her friends late that night conducted Shadrach to Leominster where he was sheltered at the home of Jonathan Drake.

Oddly enough, an antislavery convention was being held in Leominster that Sunday. Disguised as a woman, Shadrach was taken by his friends to the meeting where he listened with no visible emotion to the chairman's description of his own escape twenty-four hours before. The next night, Shadrach was escorted to Fitchburg, Ashburnham, and finally freedom in Canada.

Excluded previous chapter

"A Top Eye Open"—
Uncle Tom and the Capture of
Thomas Sims: 1851–1852

THE FUROR over the Fugitive Slave Law and the Shadrach escape was still shaking the country when a professor's wife in Brunswick, Maine, describing herself as "somewhat more than forty, about as thin and dry as a pinch of snuff," sat down to write the first installments of a magazine serial which appeared on June 5, 1851, in the *National Era*. Published in book form the following March, Harriet Beecher Stowe's *Uncle Tom's Cabin* was an immediate literary phenomenon. Ten thousand copies were sold in a few days, three hundred thousand within a year, and at least a million and a half more throughout Great Britain and her colonies. It was translated not only into French, Spanish, Italian, and Russian but Arabic, Armenian, Bohemian, Wallachian, and Welsh, a total of thirty-seven languages and a handful of dialects. Seventy-five editions were run off in German alone, and no one has even tried to compute the total sales in translation.

Its impact was vastly enlarged a year later when the novel was converted into a play. In New York, where audiences were accustomed to a change of bill every few nights, it played eighteen shows a week, the cast hastily munching sandwiches between performances. In both London and Paris, two theaters presented it concurrently to overflow audiences. Uncle Tom's "cabins" appeared all over Europe as restaurants and shops, and Topsy and Eva soon became legendary figures as far away as Siam.

As a work of propaganda, *Uncle Tom's Cabin* has never been equaled. Most families read it aloud at night around the fire and passed their copies to neighbors. It undoubtedly reached almost every literate family in the North, avidly read by children, many of whom would be the voters and soldiers of 1861. It was even read by Queen Victoria and Prince Albert, who were said to be profoundly impressed, a factor of no little importance since Canada was considering closing its borders to fugitive slaves. Mrs. Stowe herself was greeted like royalty on her trips to Britain, crowds turning out at every railroad station as she toured the countryside in triumphal procession, peers of the realm from the Dukes of Sutherland and Argyll to Lords Palmerston and Shaftesbury flocking to meet her at London receptions.

The only discordant note was that the book was placed on the Vatican Index as being subversive of established authority. But Dr. Oliver Wendell Holmes better gauged Mrs. Stowe's contribution. In a poetic tribute on her seventieth birthday, he wrote:

> She moved the earth! Its thunders pealed,
> Its mountains shook, its temples reeled.

And President Lincoln paid his own special tribute although our only authority for his statement is Mrs. Stowe's daughter. When the authoress visited the White House, Lincoln seized her hands, drew her to a seat by the window, and said, "Is this the little woman who made the great war?"

The President's habit of wry exaggeration always covered a strong core of truth. Although Mrs. Stowe hardly made the war, what she accomplished brilliantly was to give it moral sanction. To a great extent she was able to convince the great mass of people in the free states that God was on the side of the North. Largely unmoved by moral issues, they had become increasingly perturbed by the threat of Southern expansion in Texas, the opening of Kansas and Nebraska to squatter sovereignty and the invasion of free soil under the Fugitive Slave Law. But these were political and economic aspects of the section struggle. It was Mrs. Stowe's mission to weld them together with her moral fury so that the plight of the individual slave, not just the political crisis, personally threatened the lives of millions never reached by Garrison or Theodore Parker.

Uncle Tom's Cabin, one of the most convincing documents ever written, translated the Puritan absorption with sin into the popular vernacular. At a time when the North fearfully faced the blowup of one more Compromise, Mrs. Stowe virtually bathed it in sin and the promise of cleansing righteousness. It was the great exorcism in which all could partake. It was the final witch-burning of the devils of slavery. And although today we are apt to consider the novel overstuffed with virtuous sentimentality, *Uncle Tom* swept its readers up the golden road simply because, as Hilaire Belloc noted, "there was in it more genuine faith than in any book."

There is considerable irony in the fact that although Garrison's critics considered slavery a purely political struggle after 1840, Mrs. Stowe made the nation face its crisis on moral grounds. For *Uncle Tom* is infused with abolition spirit. Yet Mrs. Stowe was no abolitionist; her father, Dr. Lyman Beecher, had even tangled with Theodore Weld and his followers when he was director of Lane Seminary.

The final irony is that Mrs. Stowe resorted to fiction to do the work of the Lord. As a girl, she had been diligently protected from novels by her father, who only unbended enough to let her sample Sir Walter Scott. The novel, in fact, had been virtually ignored as an instrument against slavery. Whittier and Lowell had effectively utilized poetry. Two plays, *The Branded Hand* in 1845, and *Warren: A Tragedy* in 1850, had caused a small stir. But the only previous novel of any standing was *The Slave: or, Memoirs of Archy Moore* in 1834 by Richard Hildreth, the historian and editor. And Hildreth, unable to secure a reputable publisher because of antagonism toward abolition, brought the book out without a publisher's name on the title page, complaining later that "no review or magazine or hardly a newspaper took any notice of it. . . ."

Uncle Tom was a passionate outburst that had its roots in the rugged past of Calvinist New England. Born in the hills of Litchfield, Connecticut, only a few miles from the birthplace of John Brown eleven years before, Harriet was reared in the shadow of Jonathan Edwards and the agonizing search for salvation. "I am beset behind and before, and my sins take away all my happiness," she confessed to one brother at fourteen. Almost all her youth she would be wracked by doubt and morbid introspection, and her struggle, in a sense, was never resolved until she made *Uncle Tom* her testament of faith.

Old Dr. Beecher, called from Litchfield to Boston in 1826 to battle the rising tide of liberal Unitarianism, transplanted the Puritan fury to his children. Seven sons became ministers, and Parker called him, "the father of more brains than any other man in America." Edward was a close associate of Lovejoy's in Illinois. Henry Ward Beecher would make his Brooklyn parish one of the most influential in the country, and John Hay considered him "the greatest preacher the world has seen since St. Paul preached on Mars Hill." Harriet's grandson, Lyman Beecher Stowe, wrote later that, "One might as hopefully have tried to keep a fish from swimming as a Beecher from preaching." And Harriet's father undoubtedly regretted losing even one child to the cause, for he remarked shortly after her birth, "I would give a hundred dollars if she was a boy."

And yet quite logically, Harriet turned out to be the greatest preacher of them all. Submerged by pots and pans, sick and dying children, and a bumbling husband, Professor Calvin Stowe, who rarely emerged from his world of Greek, Arabic, and Hebrew, she blended her personal torment with the horrors of slavery and reached a vaster audience in a few months than all the Beechers could reach from their pulpits in a lifetime.

Uncle Tom was the immediate product of the Fugitive Slave Law which Mrs. Stowe called, "This horror, this nightmare abomination!" Years later she confessed to one son, "I remember many a night weeping over you as you lay sleeping beside me, and I thought of the slave mothers whose babes were torn from them." When Mrs. Edward Beecher suggested that Harriet attack the law through a book, she decided, "I would write something that would make this whole nation feel what an accursed thing slavery is." And then she added, "God helping me, I will write something." From that moment on, she was certain she and God were in partnership.

"She always spoke and behaved," her official biographer noted, "as if she recognized herself to be an instrument breathed upon by the Divine spirit." She wrote the book at breakneck speed, dashing off the chapter on Uncle Tom's death in one sitting, hardly making a correction later in the original manuscript. When she read it to her children, they broke out sobbing. As the book progressed, the Beecher household became a torrent of tears, and a good part of the nation would soon follow their briny example. Mrs. Stowe was convinced that "Eternal right and justice are with me. . . ." She was producing "a work of religion." Before too many years, she would tell a complete stranger, "The Lord himself wrote it, and I was but the humblest of instruments in His hands."

In this sense of Divine mission, in her unshakable belief that she had been specially chosen by God as His spokesman, Mrs. Stowe represented the culmination of two hundred years of Puritan fervor. She was determined to make over the nation in the Puritan image, and to a great extent, she succeeded. Her timing, of course, was perfect. In the crisis of the Fugitive Slave Law and Kansas, people needed faith and a guarantee of moral righteousness, and she was able to supply them in the human and personal terms that the abolitionists could never equal. After the death of her son, Henry, by drowning, an old woman, a former slave, comforted her, "Bear up, dear soul. You must bear it, for the Lord loves ye." Mrs. Stowe convinced the North that the Lord loved them also.

THE Fugitive Slave Bill was a frenzied symbol for the South of such proportions that the Georgia convention, accepting the Compromise of 1850, could proclaim, "That it is the deliberate opinion of this convention that upon the faithful execution of the Fugitive Slave Bill by the proper authorities depends the preservation of our much-loved Union." In the first six years, the South at best recovered one hundred thousand dollars in human property. But since expenses to the slaveholders and Federal government certainly equaled and probably exceeded this figure, it was hardly a question of mathematics that equated the recovery of fugitives with the preservation of the Union.

The law's Northern supporters were no less frantic in their demands for compliance. Webster made frequent trips to abolition centers, angrily warning his audience in Syracuse, New York, for example, that "Those persons in this city who mean to oppose the execution of the Fugitive Slave Law are traitors! traitors! traitors!" In Boston, the Reverend Orville Dewey told his congregation, "I would consent that my own brother, my own son, should go, *ten times rather* would I go myself into slavery, than that this Union should be sacrificed."

The tragedy was that the South had created a symbol that was more a test of passions than a bulwark to its system. But if it would take Federal troops to enforce it, the slaveholders welcomed the test. Above all, they wanted it in Boston, and conveniently enough, less than two months after Shadrach's escape, a seventeen-year-old fugitive named Thomas Sims was arrested there.

Sims, claimed by James Potter of Chatham, Georgia, had stowed away on the brig, *M. & J. C. Gilmore*, at Savannah and arrived in Boston harbor on March 7, 1851. But the mate had discovered him, and expecting a reward, locked him in the cabin overnight. Sims promptly unscrewed the door hinges, stole a boat and escaped to South Boston. At Long Wharf, he was recognized by crew members and taken back to the *Gilmore*. Again he escaped, and for almost a month, lived quietly in Boston, working as a waiter.

About 9 P.M. on the night of April 3 Sims was walking with another fugitive on Richmond Street when he was seized by two officers employed by U.S. Deputy Marshal Byrnes. They pretended he was wanted for theft, but after a few minutes Sims got suspicious, tried to break free, and was finally overpowered by the arrival of more officers. The other fugitive escaped.

At the massive, three-story courthouse, Sims was locked up on the third floor. A special guard of sixty-five men, armed with "straight, double-edged, pointed Roman swords," Dr. Bowditch noted, patrolled outside the building. The entire regular police force, and an added contingent from the Watch Department, was stationed at the doors. In addition, a heavy iron chain, a virtual barricade against any crowd, was stretched around the court-house four feet from the ground. "Our temple of justice is a slave pen," Dana commented.

Despite the Personal Liberty Law, most of the guard were municipal officers under direct orders from Mayor Bigelow. They had not arrested Sims and were not his immediate jailers. But under the guise of preserving the peace of the city, the mayor was doing his best to implement the Fugitive Slave Law.

The Vigilance Committee recognized this in the posters, addressed to the colored population, with which it plastered the city:

> You are hereby respectfully *cautioned* and advised to avoid conversing with the WATCHMEN AND POLICE OFFICERS OF BOSTON. For since the recent *order of the Mayor and Aldermen*, they are empowered to act as KIDNAPPERS and SLAVE CATCHERS. . . . KEEP A SHARP LOOKOUT FOR KIDNAPPERS, and have a TOP EYE open.

The Committee sent Samuel Sewall rushing to the courthouse where he met Deputy Marshal Riley and asked where Sims was being held. Riley refused to say. "You must tell me," Sewall insisted, according to his diary. "I have a right to know; I am his attorney." When Sewall persisted, Riley angrily called an officer of the Watch and ordered him arrested. Although the Captain of the Watch had sense enough to release him immediately, it was obvious that the authorities would use their power ruthlessly.

Sewall was quickly joined as defense counsel by Dana, Charles G. Loring, and Robert Rantoul, Jr., the tense, witty, Harvard-educated politician who had risen rapidly in the State Legislature, served as Collector of the Port, and had just been elected to Congress as an antislavery Democrat in the Democratic-Free Soil coalition. Heavily guarded, they were admitted to Sims. The prisoner begged them, "Give me a knife and when the Commissioner declares me a slave, I will stab myself to the heart. . . ."

On Friday morning, April 4, Sims was brought before United States Commissioner George T. Curtis. Rantoul asked for a delay, and Curtis grudgingly gave the defense until next morning.

On Saturday at 10 A.M., John B. Bacon, a Southern agent, testified he had seen Sims "last on the 21st of February. . . . Have not the shadow of a doubt as to the identity of the prisoner as Potter's slave." Edmund Barrett, another agent, stated he had known Sims as a bricklayer for ten months, "worked on the same scaffold with him last August, also September." The defense staked its case on the fact that Sims was really a free Negro. Sewall presented an affidavit that Sims, alias Joseph Santinna, had been born in St. Augustine, Florida, that his free papers, which had been obtained in St. Augustine by his father, a Spaniard, had been left many years ago with Morris Potter of Savannah.

All through Saturday and the following week, the defense attempted a series of legal maneuvers. After a writ of *habeas corpus* was turned down by the State Supreme Court, the defense brought charges against Sims for attacking an officer at the time of his arrest in order to transfer his case to State jurisdiction. Rantoul applied for a *habeas corpus* from the United States Circuit Court, but was again turned down. Sumner entered the case and demanded the same writ from another judge. He too was turned down.

In the midst of this frantic skirmishing, crowds packed Court House Square, held back by the cordon of guards and ring of heavy chain, which Longfellow called "the last form of degradation." Many shops in the square closed and shuttered their windows. Dana proudly refused to stoop under the chain when he entered the court. "I either jump over it or go round to the end and have the rope removed," he noted in his diary. But when Judge Shaw humbled himself by stooping, Theodore Parker wrote gleefully, "Think of old, stiff-necked Lemuel visibly going under the chains. That was a spectacle!"

On Tuesday, the Vigilance Committee called a mass meeting of protest on the Common. Many churches tolled their bells in Boston and in Worcester, Lynn, and New Bedford where other meetings convened. At night another protest was staged in Tremont Temple with Horace Mann presiding and Wendell Phillips rousing a cheering audience with what the *Evening Transcript* called "an epileptic pitch of froth and fury."

But Phillips's eloquence only cloaked increasing tension in the Vigilance Committee. Higginson, along with Parker, the leading exponent of militant action, was hastily summoned from Newburyport. Higginson assured the Committee that Boston's Negroes had "proved their mettle and would doubtless do it again." Hayden said, "Of course, they will." Later he admitted to Higginson privately that the Shadrach prosecution had forced hundreds to flee the city and that the remainder could not be counted on for a rescue plot. The meeting broke up without any plan of action, and Higginson worriedly wrote Samuel J. May, ". . . There is neither organization, resolution, plan nor popular sentiment—the Negroes are cowed and the Abolitionists irresolute and hopeless, with nothing better to do on Saturday than send off circulars to the clergymen!"

Surveying the courthouse, Higginson found that the permanent guard of at least a thousand armed police would allow no one but defense lawyers and authorized personnel to enter the building. Sims's cell door was fastened by iron bars and guarded by fifteen to twenty officers. When Sims was brought to court, he was handcuffed and surrounded by seven burly policemen. A frontal attack was obviously impossible.

But there was one weak link, and around it Higginson formed his plot. The windows of Sims's cell were unbarred. It was on the third floor, the top floor, and certainly a dangerous distance to the ground. But if the street below was well padded with mattresses, a man might jump without critical injuries.

Higginson prepared a signal, which he would give from the street, and transmitted it to Sims through the Reverend Grimes, who was authorized to visit the cell. He had the mattresses hidden nearby, and arranged for a coach and fast horses, which would wait a few hundred feet away. Above all, the plot depended on twelve men who could attack and hold off the guards on the street while Sims made his leap. The twelve included Dr. Bowditch, who had been "living in a fiendish state of existence," he noted in his diary; Parker, "that Martin Luther of our times"; and Higginson himself, "our general wit and bold leader."

All was ready that Wednesday night when Higginson made a last survey of the courthouse. Then disaster! In the dim light Higginson could see workmen attaching bars to the window of the cell. Either the marshals had grown cautious, or someone had betrayed the plot.

There was nothing left now but desperate legal maneuvering. On Friday, Sewall demanded more time to secure Sims's free papers from Savannah. But Commissioner Curtis refused, and issued Bacon the certificate to remove Sims to Georgia. That night, Sumner secured a warrant from Richard Hildreth, conveniently enough a Justice of the Peace as well as a devoted abolitionist, to arrest Sims for stealing a boat from the *Gilmore*. Sumner insisted that "the right of the State to enforce her criminal laws against a fugitive slave was higher than the right of the owner to recover his slave," but Sheriff John Eveleth refused to yield the prisoner to the State.

The Vigilance Committee had issued a call to the Commonwealth to "come by the thousands." All Friday, Court Square was filled with milling throngs from Lynn, Worcester, and New Bedford. Most merchants, however, had already made it plain they were standing behind the Fugitive Slave Law. Fifteen hundred signed a petition that they would take arms themselves to escort Sims to the boat which would carry him to Georgia. Later, Sims's owner in a public letter of appreciation called them "conspicuous in their efforts to serve us."

In final contradiction of the Personal Liberty Law, Mayor Bigelow ordered three companies of city militia to aid the Federal marshals. Boston police were even equipped with United States arms. "I know that I am violating the State Law as well as you know it," City Marshal Tukey told a Massachusetts Senate committee later. ". . . I am acting under orders, and it is the Mayor and the Aldermen who are responsible."

About 4 A.M. that Saturday, April 12, a hundred police with swords began marching and countermarching before the courthouse, driving the gathering crowds back into the side streets.

At 4:15 A.M. three hundred soldiers and police formed a hollow, double-filed, close-locked square. Lines of militia were stationed along the street to Long Wharf. At Charleston Navy Yard, two hundred fifty United States troops were held in readiness.

"It was a horrible thing, that hollow square," Higginson stated. ". . . Massachusetts ceased to exist, and we seemed to stand in Vienna." Dr. Bowditch described the guard as a combination of "a volunteer corps of the young aristocrats of the city" and "a set of hired wretches."

At 4:30, United States Marshal Charles Devens and City Marshal Tukey with their deputies escorted Sims from the courthouse to the center of the hollow square. Mayor Bigelow, prim and fussing, joined the escort. The order was given; the inexorable tramp of six hundred feet echoed down Court Street. From dozens of throats in the crowd along the sidewalk came the cry, "Shame! Shame!"

The Vigilance Committee, carrying a symbolic black-draped coffin, the word "Liberty" printed large on its top, followed behind the procession.

The hollow square turned into State Street, marching over the spot where Attucks, the Negro hero, had fallen on March 5, 1770, "sacrilegiously desecrating by this act this martyr stand of the Revolution," Dr. Bowditch noted. At Long Wharf, Sims was taken on the brig, *Acorn*, by six United States Deputy Marshals who would escort him to Savannah. Hundreds of watchers broke into a mournful dirge, the Reverend Daniel Foster leading them in prayer, "In mercy, Heavenly Father, do thou destroy the wicked power which rules us."

Quickly, the flying jib was hoisted, a waiting steamboat escorted the *Acorn* downstream. It was all over, the first fugitive dragged back to slavery from Boston. ". . . The whole police force of the city was laid at the feet of the Slave Power, *against law*," protested the *Commonwealth*. "For eight days the criminal law of Massachusetts [Personal Liberty Law] was paralyzed by the claim of a Georgia slaveholder to his 'property.' . . . It is a combination of the money and the Websterism of Boston which is responsible," accused the *Lowell-American*. "This Boston, yes,

that same old Boston, world renowned as the Cradle of Liberty,"
mourned the Ohio *Star*, "has been turned into a military despot-
ism."

Less than two weeks later on April 24, some small measure of
shame was erased by the election of Sumner to the United States
Senate. All over New England, bonfires were lit, church bells
carried the tidings. A hundred-gun salute was fired on Boston
Common. "The papers are ringing with Sumner! Sumner! and
guns are thundering out their triumph," Longfellow recorded.

But for Sims in Georgia, there was only jail and brutal lashing
that almost killed him. When he regained his health, he was
shipped to the New Orleans slave market and sold to a Vicksburg
brickmason. The Vigilance Committee sought to buy him back,
and in 1860 his owner set a price of eighteen hundred dollars.
Lydia Maria Child finally raised the money, probably from
Marshal Devens, who had long regretted the extradition. The
outbreak of war, however, prevented the sale.

During the seige of Vicksburg, Sims escaped to the Federal
lines and reached Boston where he was aided by Devens and Mrs.
Child. When Devens became United States Attorney General in
1877, he hired Sims as a clerk. The Department of Justice, indeed,
was a logical end to a tortuous journey.

IT WAS no accidental gesture that the Vigilance Committee summoned Thomas Wentworth Higginson from Newburyport at
the height of the Sims crisis. Like Parker, Higginson was a Unitarian minister. And ironically, they were the two most militant
members of the Committee. At twenty-eight, lean, hard-muscled,
towering well over six feet tall, Higginson had committed himself
to a policy of force against the Fugitive Slave Law. "Tough,
swart-minded Higginson," the poet, Stephen Vincent Benét,
later described him. Far more than a cleric, he resembled a
cavalier of the Jacobean court, dashing, slightly reckless, a touch
of the buccaneer about him. He described his "unfailing, animal
spirits" in one letter. Even when contemplating the ministry, he

wrote, "I cannot in action any more than in thought bear confinement— How then can I settle down into the quiet though noble duties of a minister. . . . I crave action." And he admitted later, "Never did I hear of anything dare-devil without wishing to leave all else and do it."

It was certainly tradition in part which drew him into the church. The first member of his family in America was the Reverend Francis Higginson who landed at Salem in 1629. More recent generations became shipowners and merchants, Higginson's grandfather reputedly making seventy thousand dollars as a privateer during the Revolution and amassing five hundred thousand dollars, a considerable fortune then, by 1800. He was a member of the Continental Congress, and in 1798, there being no official Secretary of the Navy, virtually performed the duties without title.

Higginson's mother descended from two of New Hampshire's most distinguished families. Among the earlier Appletons was the colony's first Royal Governor. And the Wentworths were closely linked to the English crown, so closely, in fact, that one local wit observed they only spoke of Queen Elizabeth I as "Cousin Betsy Tudor." Appropriately enough, Higginson's maternal grandfather was the flamboyant Captain Thomas Storrow of the British Army who was captured at sea by an American privateer and brought to Portsmouth, New Hampshire, where despite the impediments of war and family protests, he wooed and won Anne Appleton.

Higginson's father had been a prosperous merchant and shipowner, entertaining regally at his Mt. Vernon Street mansion, until Jefferson's embargo closed down his business. He secured the post of Bursar, or steward, at Harvard where he organized the Divinity School and planted the finest trees in the College Yard. He was hardly a scholar, once insisting that a new shipment of Hebrew Bibles be returned to the printer because the title pages were at the wrong end. Higginson was the youngest of ten children by his father's second wife. His father died when he was nine, leaving the family a commodious house on "Professor's Row" and little else but a heritage of impoverished gentility.

Unlike Garrison and many of the abolitionists who had been reared in the harsh Calvinist struggle for salvation, Higginson's boyhood, as he noted, "escaped almost absolutely all those rigors of the old New England theology which leaves darkened the lives of so many." He was eminently happy and strikingly precocious, his mother recording that he "read a good many books" at the age of four. He was only thirteen when he entered Harvard, the youngest boy in his class. At sixteen, he was admitted to Phi Beta Kappa. He was graduated the next year, second in his class.

Already he had established a pattern of nonconformity, taking part in one student uprising as an undergraduate, and at Divinity School leading an open protest against the dismissal of a fellow student for his belief in spiritualism. At a time when Higginson described "the whole feeling of the college strongly opposed to the abolition movement," he collected petitions against the annexation of Texas, and preached opposition by the Commonwealth to its quota of troops for the Mexican War.

Ordained in 1847 as minister of the First Religious Society at Newburyport, Higginson became the prototype of the intellectual as a man of action. He invited Parker to his pulpit and Emerson to the local Lyceum, the twin devils of atheism and anarchy as far as his conservative parishioners were concerned. He supported the Kossuth uprising and demanded American intervention in Hungary. Worst of all, in strongly Whig Newburyport, allied to the South through its shipowners and shipbuilders, he damned slavery unceasingly and condemned his congregation for supporting a slaveholder, General Taylor, for the Presidency. It is little wonder that Higginson quickly "preached himself out of his pulpit," as he remarked.

He continued living at Newburyport, however, running unsuccessfully for Congress in 1850 on the Free Soil ticket in a boisterous campaign. Although most abolitionists ignored the ferment of labor organization among the textile towns and Boston immigrants, Higginson had joined the Social Reform Association while still at Harvard and worked on a railroad construction gang for a dollar a day. Now he declared himself "at least a halfway socialist for life" and established a school at Newburyport for the workers from surrounding factories.

Eventually he found a parish tailored to his radicalism, the Free Church of Worcester, modeled after Parker's Boston congregation. He quickly turned it into a hotbed of abolition, labeling his followers "Jerusalem wildcats."

For Higginson, principles were not enough. They demanded the responsibility of action. Unlike other intellectual leaders, even as bold as Emerson, who feared to commit themselves to conflicts that might mar an idealistic concept, Higginson welcomed any chance to make a stand. If it involved physical danger, so much the better. He plunged into it almost gaily.

When the fugitive slave, Anthony Burns, was captured in 1854, he would lead a storming party against the Boston courthouse in an attempt to rescue him, suffering a clubbed head and a saber slash across his face in the process. He hastened to Kansas when the territory was overrun with "border ruffians" from the South and formulated the policy of arming free-state settlers. He became a confidant of John Brown and a key member of the secret committee which supplied the arms and money for the attack on Harpers Ferry. Thus his fervent principles would make him almost a party to treason. But instead of running for cover after his indictment, he would engineer even one further plot—an amazingly daring attempt to rescue Brown and part of his band from their Virginia jail.

It was obvious that no pulpit could hold Higginson long. When war broke out, he threw off his clerical robes, trained a Massachusetts regiment, and finally became Colonel of the first Union regiment of former slaves, the 1st South Carolina Volunteers.

"Will not Uncle Wentworth be in bliss!" one of his uninhibited nieces exclaimed when she heard the news. "A thousand men, every one as black as coal." And a Boston wit celebrated his unquenchable enthusiasm for Negro troops with the limerick:

There was a young curate of Worcester
Who could have a command if he'd chose ter,

But he said each recruit
Must be blacker than soot
Or else he'd go preach where he used ter.

He had kept himself in remarkable physical condition through an outdoor life of swimming, skating, and hiking. He had never really been a scholar, never worn himself down with seventeen hours at his desk day after day like Parker. At Newburyport, he had cut a sharp figure, even something of a dandy, sporting a specially-tailored gray, clerical garb instead of the usual black. "A young man of singular beauty," a French visitor described him. Now he wore an elegantly bushy beard, and with his deep piercing eyes and the flashing gold of his Colonel's uniform, assumed almost heroic proportions to his Negro troops. They adored him both for his fairness and courage which he demonstrated continually during the South Carolina campaign. Once, for example, when it was urgent to reconnoiter Confederate positions on the opposite river bank, he quickly removed his uniform, dove into the river and swam stealthily up and down the bank under the guns of rebel sentries.

But for all his tough-fibered impetuosity, Higginson was remarkably tender, "the sweetest saint I ever knew," a young Newburyport farmer called him. He once admitted, "there is really no sentimental school-girl whose demand for being loved is greater or more comprehensive than mine—it makes me uncomfortable to be for five minutes in the room with a strange child without winning it to love me." At nineteen he became engaged to his second cousin, Mary Channing, sister of William Ellery Channing, the Concord poet. But he insisted on postponing marriage for four years until he had the means to support her. She was invalided a good part of her life, and when she died in 1877, he married Mary P. Thacher who bore him two daughters. Thus he could fuss proudly over his first children when almost sixty and grandchildren when over eighty.

His enthusiasm for the Women's Rights movement almost equaled that for the Negro. After 1865, when he became a prominent author, probably New England's most resplendent representative of literary gentility, his desk was always crowded with letters from feminine admirers and requests for advice. One shy poetess, describing herself, "small like the wren . . . my eyes like the sherry in the glass that the guest leaves," frequently sent him copies of her work whose haunting beauty he quickly recognized. Although considering it unorthodox, he struggled unsuccessfully to lure her to the literary pomp of Boston. She wrote her mentor regularly for twenty-four years, but it was not until 1870 that Higginson finally journeyed to Amherst, Massachusetts, to meet Emily Dickinson. "A remarkable experience," he enthused, but privately called her, "my eccentric poetess." Mary Higginson, often ruffled, although perhaps secretly pleased by the reformers and eccentrics who swarmed around him, complained, "Why do the insane always come to you!"

Mary Higginson might have been less querulous if she had known him in front of the Boston courthouse in 1854. Higginson was undoubtedly the only Harvard Phi Beta Kappa, Unitarian minister, and master of seven languages who had led a storming party against a Federal bastion with a battering ram in his hands.

CHAPTER XIV

Sumner and Kansas—
New England Battleground: 1853–1856

THE NEW President, Franklin Pierce of New Hampshire, complacently assured the nation in 1853 that the slavery issue was "at rest." The Democrats, with the planters firmly in control, had swept all but four states. The dominant cabinet members, Jefferson Davis of Mississippi, Secretary of War, and Caleb Cushing of Massachusetts, the Attorney General, one a Southern extremist, the other pledged to Southern policy, expected little trouble keeping an irresolute President in line. The Whigs had been almost decimated as a national party, the Free Soilers reduced to a splinter. Cushing quickly set out to crush his major resistance, the Democratic-Free Soil coalition in Massachusetts. With the President's authority, a letter known as "Cushing's Ukase," he threatened to purge any Democrat cooperating with "the dangerous element of Abolitionism."

In less than a year, however, Pierce's promise of tranquillity was rudely destroyed. On January 4, 1854, Stephen A. Douglas, the stocky, pugnacious Democratic Senator from Illinois, introduced his revised Kansas-Nebraska Bill, and set off not only the most bitter storm of sectional antagonism up to this time, but a bloody conflict on the Western plains.

Since 1820, the compromise line of 36° 30′ had become the bedrock of national policy. Not even Webster in the Compromise debates of 1850 had dared suggest a change. Now in one stroke, Douglas opened to slavery under the principle of "squatter sovereignty," allowing settlers themselves to decide whether their new state would be slave or free, a vast territory larger than the original thirteen states. With Missouri across the border, slaveholders could inundate the area. They could block free settlers from the Northwest. And they could be reasonably certain of attaching New Mexico and the whole Southwest to the planter system.

Even Douglas at first may not have appreciated the extent of his holocaust. His shrewd, willful and often unscrupulous mind had focused on the White House. And he was arrogantly sure he had found the formula for Southern support where Webster had failed.

The Kansas Bill was bait for the South. It was essentially a manufactured issue, for the territory was almost empty of white settlers. By opening Kansas to slavery, Douglas expected to win the South both for his railroad from Chicago to Oregon and his Presidential ambitions.

The land values along his railroad would be immeasurably increased by a flood of new settlers. For the South, there was a glorious vista—an alliance between cotton and corn that would make the Mississippi Valley a Southern domain and virtually guarantee that the Northwest would be developed by the planters.

Once Douglas had committed himself, he was swept forward by the Southern extremists. And the President, only partly grasping the Bill's implications, falteringly accepted the strategy.

On every front, the extremists maneuvered for expansion. The Gadsden purchase in 1853, an extensive strip south of New Mexico, opened a prime Southern route for a transcontinental railroad. And when Pierce allowed John Slidell and the ambassadors to Spain, France, and England ruthlessly to pursue the annexation of Cuba with their shoddy Ostend Manifesto and threats of American force, it was obvious the extremists wanted not only the Caribbean but Central America.

Even the hard core of Southern allegiance in Boston was horrified by the Kansas Bill. Despite a driving snowstorm on February 23, 1854, over three thousand businessmen, mainly the die-hard group which had supported the 1850 Compromise, crowded Faneuil Hall for a protest meeting. Samuel Eliot, the only Massachusetts Representative to vote for the 1850 Compromise, presided. Robert C. Winthrop, high priest of ultraconservatism, led the attack on the Bill.

The New England clergy, which despite denials had never united even against the 1850 Compromise, now formed an almost unbroken front in a petition to Congress against the Bill signed by 3050 ministers.

In Washington, Sumner and Chase, joined by a handful of Free Soil Representatives, branded the Kansas Bill "a criminal betrayal of sacred rights." But when the vote was taken on March 4 after Douglas had harangued the Senate until almost daybreak, the Kansas Bill passed 37 to 14. Only one Southern Democrat and one Southern Whig opposed it while fourteen Northern Democrats supported it.

In the House the Kansas Bill passed 113 to 100, the South almost solidly behind it. Again the crucial margin of support came from 44 Northern Democrats.

The day after the passage of the Bill, thirty House members from all parties held an emergency meeting and decided on the organization of the new Republican party, taking its name from a small rebel group that had previously met in Wisconsin. The Kansas Bill had inexorably forced the dissolution of the Whigs and the division of the Democrats into increasingly antagonistic sections. Sumner unerringly prophesied that the Bill "annuls all past compromises with slavery and makes all future compromises impossible."

SUMNER was the ultimate symbol of inflexible morality, the Puritan prophet transplanted to politics. When he took office in 1851, Parker begged him to be "the Senator with a conscience." He did far more than that. He sought to impose the New England conscience on the Senate, on the nation itself. Garrison and Phillips may have been the public gadflies of this conscience; Parker, its pulpit voice; Harriet Beecher Stowe, its literary oracle. But with Sumner, New England at last produced its representative man of politics, its incorruptible angel hurling moral fury through the corridors of Washington.

Sumner not only refused compromise; he hardly understood the word. While any supposedly respectable politician accepted two sides of a question, he saw only one. "For myself if two evils are presented to me," he proclaimed, "I will take neither." When associates tried to convince him that a minor point on slavery had been settled, he retorted furiously, "*Nothing, sir, can be settled which is not right*. Nothing can be settled which is against freedom."

Relentlessly, he opposed every concession to the South, writing the Republican State Committee, "In the name of Liberty, I supplicate you not to let her take any backward step—*not an inch, not a hair's breadth*." He was just as severe when it came to his own political advancement. In month after month of balloting in 1851, Sumner lacked only a few votes of election to the Senate by the Massachusetts Legislature. But when leaders of the Democratic-Free Soil coalition begged him to temper his anti-slavery stand to win over a few recalcitrant legislators, he curtly refused. "The slave of principles," he announced, "I call no party master."

His inflexible morality would not yield even to friendship. Sumner, a lonely man who never married until fifty-five and then was divorced shortly afterward, cherished his friends. Yet when Cornelius Felton, professor and later president of Harvard and an intimate of many years, supported the Fugitive Slave Bill, Sumner immediately broke with him. The rift was not healed until 1856 when Felton visited the Senator, then seriously ill after being caned over the head by a Southern Congressman.

When Representative Winthrop, a boyhood friend and school-mate at Boston Latin, supported the Mexican War bill, Sumner condemned him bitterly, "Blood! blood! is on the hands of the representative from Boston." Winthrop thought the criticism might have been made with less personal vitriol. Sumner insisted it was a matter of principle, and the two men never spoke for twenty years.

If Sumner often seems less than human, the striking contradictions of his personality soften the harshness. Prude he may have been, one classmate recalling that as a youth he "rarely indulged in expletives"; another, that "his good taste, if nothing else, kept him from the company of fast young men. . . ." At a dinner party at Sumner's home, when one guest began a story, "I suppose I can tell this, there being no ladies present," the Senator interrupted, "But there are gentlemen present."

Yet his radiant charm and magnificent bearing drew people to him immediately. His head and brow had a massive nobility. He looked the perfect Senator. His eyes were deep blue and warm. Although Dr. Oliver Wendell Holmes complained he had "little imagination, wit or sense of humor," he laughed easily and heartily. One friend described "his strangely winning smile, half bright, half full of sadness." His rich mass of brown hair, soon streaked with gray, hung loosely down the back of his neck. He stood an impressive six feet, four inches. Although gangly and awkward even at Law School, weighing only a hundred and twenty pounds, his broad shoulders filled out quickly, and he kept himself in such physical trim that he became one of the few men, according to Higginson, to swim the Niagara River just below the Falls. Judge Hoar was particularly impressed by the "grace of his motions."

His cultured manners gave him quick entree to the highest social circles. When he visited Philadelphia at twenty-three, an aristocratic young lady reported that the company was "utterly routed by the wonderful charm of his conversation." A few years later Sumner traveled through Europe and virtually became the lion of the season. The greatest homes of England were opened to him. He was welcomed by leading authors, jurists, and peers from Macaulay and Wordsworth to the Duchess of Sutherland. Perhaps his final conquest was riding to hounds without disaster, for Lady Wharncliffe gushed, "I never knew an American who had the degree of social success he had. . . ."

Many associates complained of Sumner's pride. Carl Schurz, who worked with him closely in Republican politics, described his "high opinion of himself" and his quest of praise "with a child-like relish." He was remote, even haughty. Few men would have dared slap him on the back. Yet he adored close friends like Howe and Longfellow almost to the point of dependence. When he left Boston for the Senate, he wept openly during his farewells. And Longfellow wrote Sumner wistfully, "We ate our dinner somewhat silently by ourselves, and talked of you far off, looking at your empty chair. . . ."

What often appeared as pride actually shielded a retiring and scholarly mind. For Sumner, who had never sought the Senate, would have preferred devoting himself to writing and history. He read prodigiously even in the busiest Senate sessions and was so deeply versed in the classics that his speeches overflowed with ancient references and quotations. As a result, they were often pedantic and ornate, "smelling of the lamp," as one critic put it.

There were contradictions even in Sumner's ambitions. He craved acceptance at first by the cultured Whig aristocracy that centered around the salon of George Ticknor. When he was finally welcomed, however, his plunge into political radicalism automatically made him an outcast.

He came from old Puritan stock, his paternal grandfather having left Harvard to join the Continental Army where he rose to the rank of major. He was obviously a respected man, for Vice President John Adams and Secretary of War Henry Knox attended his funeral. Sumner's father studied at Phillips Academy, Andover, and Harvard. As a Democratic wheel horse, he achieved minor eminence as Sheriff of Suffolk County, leaving his family at death a house on Hancock Street and a fifty-thousand-dollar estate.

Sumner, who with a twin sister was the oldest of nine children, went to Harvard and Harvard Law School, and quickly made his mark as a legal scholar. But he disliked the tedium of daily practice, and left Boston in 1837 for Europe. The success of his reception abroad preceded him home. His family had never been wealthy enough to get past the social fringes. And his father's Democratic alliance was hardly an asset in the Whig citadel. But now Sumner was embraced as a conquering hero and his law practice temporarily blossomed.

He had, in fact, so impressed the city fathers that they selected him to deliver the official oration on July 4, 1845. The audience was resplendent, the highest ranking officers from nearby Federal garrisons and State and local militia, glittering in their braid and swords. Quite unexpectedly, since Sumner had shown scant in-

Above. An artist's drawing from *Gleason's Pictorial Magazine* showing U. S. Marshal's guard patrolling the Boston Court House where fugitive slave Thomas Sims was imprisoned. The chain around the building is to ward off attack by crowds which, said lawyer Richard H. Dana, Jr., made "our temple of justice . . . a slave pen." *Left.* Pages from treasurer's book of Vigilance Committee listing contributions for defense of Shadrach, fugitive slave arrested February 15, 1851. Francis Jackson took grave risks keeping such records. Contributors were subject to severe fines and imprisonment under the Fugitive Slave Law *(From original at Bostonian Society, Old State House)*

Above, left. Harriet Beecher Stowe, author of *Uncle Tom's Cabin* (*Widener Library, Harvard*). *Above, right.* Charles Sumner, Massachusetts Senator, violently beaten on the Senate floor for his anti-slavery speech in May, 1856 (*Widener Library, Harvard*) *Below, left.* Thomas Wentworth Higginson, Unitarian minister who led attack on Boston Court House in 1854 (*Courtesy Houghton Mifflin Co.*). *Below, right.* John Brown, who led the attack on Harper's Ferry (*Widener Library, Harvard*)

terest in political affairs outside of subscribing to the *Liberator*, he launched a bitter attack on war in general and the armed forces in particular. His audience sat sullen and shocked. Within hours, the oration became the talk of Boston. When Sumner soon after turned on Congressman Winthrop for supporting the Mexican War, Ticknor officially pronounced him "outside the pale of society."

Sumner, who was subject to wide swings of elation and despair, had only recently gone through his most severe depression, writing Howe, "For me there is no future of either usefulness or happiness." Now for the first time his life had found real direction. The Conscience Whigs welcomed him as an influential spokesman. With the emergence of the Free Soil party in 1848, he agreed to be its candidate for Congress against Winthrop although he faced inevitable defeat in a strong Whig district.

Sumner then argued the case against segregated Negro schools before the State Supreme Court. Although he lost the decision, his speeches and articles prepared the way for the removal of educational discrimination by legislation a few years later. Again he took the Free Soil candidacy for Congress against Samuel A. Eliot and lost as expected. But his brilliant campaigning made him the logical choice for the Senate on the Free Soil ticket in 1850.

Sumner had joined with Henry Wilson to build the Democratic-Free Soil coalition which swept the state, winning 21 Senate seats against 11 for the Whigs, and 220 seats in the House against 176. Under the terms of the coalition, a Democrat, George S. Boutwell, would get the Governor's seat, and he was duly elected by the Legislature. But many Democratic representatives now reneged on their agreement. For three dreary months, the House took ballot after ballot, Sumner always falling a few votes short of election. Not till a few key towns forced their representatives in special meetings to vote for Sumner was he finally elected on the twenty-sixth ballot on April 24, 1851.

"I feel heartsick here," he wrote Longfellow not long after taking his seat. "The Senate is a lone place, with few men who are capable of yielding any true sympathy to me." Outside of Chase, Hale and Benjamin Wade of Ohio, Sumner was a solitary rebel those first years. He stayed above the crowd, mixing little with other Senators. He was like an archangel of righteousness in temporary residence. During one slavery debate, a Southern Senator demanded if Sumner would return a fugitive to his owner under the terms of the Fugitive Slave Law. Sumner unhesitatingly said he would not, making him probably the first lawmaker who calmly refused to obey one of the laws he had sworn to uphold. The Senate turned on him furiously, threatening a resolution of expulsion. Sumner doggedly refused to see why he should follow the "higher law" in Boston and deny it in Washington.

If Sumner's morality seems unrelenting, and often a trifle unbelievable, his constituents rejoiced in such perfectibility and would return him to the Senate for the rest of his life with resounding majorities. The Commonwealth had raised up a unique prophet, the final product of the Puritan quest. "May God keep Charles Sumner's garments spotless," pleaded Lydia Maria Child. "He is the only one of our representatives in whose integrity I have implicit trust. If he falls from his pedestal, I shall never set up another idol."

IF SOUTHERN extremists had planned an easy conquest in Kansas, they had badly misjudged New England resourcefulness. The Bill's proponents expected thousands of Missourians to pour into the area and quickly take control of the territorial government. But a month before its passage, a young Massachusetts educator and politician, Eli Thayer of Worcester, had already conceived the Massachusetts Emigrant Aid Company, whose objective was to keep Kansas and Nebraska as free soil. Thayer was convinced that if a Missourian could come a hundred miles to stake his plot for slavery, the rugged farmers and mechanics from New England would be willing to trek a thousand. The Emigrant Aid Company would raise money to send groups at reduced travel rates. It would finance the construction of schools, hotels, churches, gristmills, sawmills, virtually complete bastions of free-dom.

Thayer realized he faced staggering odds. Even the Massachusetts Legislative committee to which he brought the plan considered it "impracticable and utterly futile," but finally voted a charter for the company.

Fortunately, Thayer was a tough and inexhaustible campaigner. Born almost in poverty, in a proud family that claimed direct descent from John and Priscilla Alden, he had to work his way through Brown University. Ranked high as a scholar, he was soon appointed principal of Worcester Academy and, at thirty, founded the Oread Collegiate Institute, one of the first schools providing higher education for women. On a vehement anti-slavery platform, he was sent to the Massachusetts Legislature in 1854; two years later he would win election to Congress.

While the Emigrant Aid Company was primarily philanthropic, Thayer organized it as a stock corporation in the hope that investors would eventually reap dividends from Kansas. But Thayer was a visionary in finance. The primary investors never expected, and never received, a penny in return. Thayer was far more practical in forming his board of directors. Dr. Samuel Cabot, John Lowell, Le Baron Russell and Amos A. Lawrence came from the wealthiest strata of the old Whig aristocracy. The Kansas Bill had now convinced them that freedom in the territory transcended all past allegiances.

Lawrence, whose courage and financial acumen would steer the company through perpetual crises, was the son of Amos Lawrence who, with his brother Abbott, had founded one of New England's great textile fortunes. Amos A. Lawrence married Sarah Appleton, thus linking two textile dynasties. He cheerfully confessed always remaining a "Hunker" Whig. But he had the courage to desert the party frequently. In 1850, he attacked Webster and the Compromise. And although he opposed Sumner's candidacy, he praised the Senator's stand on the Kansas Bill and fought it vigorously himself. On May 24, 1854, when the fugitive, Anthony Burns, was captured and imprisoned in the Boston courthouse, Lawrence told the mayor he would "prefer to see the court house razed rather than that the fugitive now confined there should be returned to slavery"—incendiary words, indeed, for an incorrigible conservative.

Lawrence would make constant private donations to the New England communities in Kansas, particularly the town of Wakarusa, and later the University of Kansas. When the people of Wakarusa voted to change the town's name to Lawrence, he insisted, "it would give my future efforts the appearance of promoting my own celebrity. . . ." They went ahead, however, despite his protests.

The first Emigrant Aid party set out from Boston in June, 1854, twenty-nine settlers gathering at the railroad station under the leadership of Charles Branscomb. A brass band played lustily and thousands of Bostonians turned out to cheer. On July 17, Thayer instructed Branscomb by letter, "Take this colony through the Shawnee reservation and locate them on the South bank of the Kansas, on the first good town site you find west of the reservation." The party picked up recruits, doubling its size as it moved westward. On August 1, they established a site as instructed. Six more parties were dispatched during the summer, and by late fall, Wakarusa, or Lawrence, could boast six hundred fifty settlers.

On December 5, the second colony, Topeka, was founded by two flamboyant Emigrant Aid Company agents, Dr. Charles Robinson of Fitchburg, Massachusetts, and Samuel C. Pomeroy of Southampton. Robinson, who had whetted his appetite for adventure in the California gold fields in 1849, would eventually become Governor of Kansas, and Pomeroy, a United States Senator. New parties went out from Boston under the leadership of Dr. Calvin Cutter and Martin Stowell, a close Worcester associate of Higginson's, to found Plymouth, Lexington, and Concord, and colonies at Osawatomie, Pottawatomie, Manhattan, and Hampden followed in quick order. In many cases, the Emigrant Aid Company simply furnished the nucleus, one group, for example, that left Boston in 1856 with a hundred settlers expanding to 384 by the time it reached Iowa.

That first winter was dreary and often desperate. Amasa Soule, who had come from Maine to join the second Emigrant Aid party out of Boston, wrote back that Lawrence was hardly a cluster of log huts, covered by turf or grass. Meals were supplied at a central "mess" where settlers paid $2.50 a week, mainly for bread, molasses, and beef. Corn could be planted only by chipping holes in the sod with an axe, dropping the seed, and stamping the hole closed with heavy boots. On many days, families had to stay in bed to keep from freezing. "Frequently the girls, who slept in the loft of the cabin," one of Soule's descendants wrote, "awoke in the morning to find several inches of snow on the bed."

Such hardships, however, were almost minor compared to the danger of attack by armed bands of Missourians, known as "Border Ruffians," who swarmed into Kansas to drive out the free-state settlers. In June, 1854, even before the first New Englanders arrived, the *Platte County Argus* demanded that Missourians "meet and repel them even at the point of the bayonet." That fall, one thousand seven hundred Missourians crossed the border to cast illegal ballots in the first election and take forcible control of the government. Soon they would attempt to wipe out Lawrence itself, and resort to burning, pillage, and murder.

There was obviously little point for the company, now known as the New England Emigrant Aid Company, to pour its money into transportation, schools, and gristmills if the settlers could not protect their homes or lives. On April 2, 1855, Dr. Robinson wrote Thayer, begging for two hundred Sharps rifles. In July, he warned even more urgently, "We are in the midst of a revolution."

In an emergency session, the company officers agreed to establish a special rifle committee under Dr. Cabot. But the use of arms was complicated by the fact that Federal authorities and army units in Kansas frequently sided with the Missourians, and Amos A. Lawrence particularly insisted that no weapon be used against the Government. Legally, therefore, the rifle committee was kept detached from the company. But it was little more than pretense. Cabot and other officers not only raised most of the money for arms but took charge of their shipment.

Cabot's committee immediately ordered a hundred breech-loading Sharps rifles which fired ten shots a minute, and although free-state settlers would always be outnumbered, this continually gave them superior firepower. Lawrence, whose prudence never stood in the way of radical action in a crisis, personally ordered a hundred more. Shipped as books or hardware, they became known in popular lingo as "Sharps Rights of the People."

The drastic shift in Boston opinion had now made strange bedfellows on the list of donors. Cabot and other stalwarts like John Murray Forbes, Gerrit Smith, and Wendell Phillips, who quickly overcame his nonresistance principles, gave sizable sums. But remarkably enough, two of the principal contributors were notorious "Cotton" Whigs, former Congressman Samuel A. Eliot and the archconservative Theodore Lyman, son of Boston's mayor during the 1835 Garrison riot. "A small but mixed company of hunkers, republicans and abolitionists," Lawrence's son described them.

In the spring of 1856, Thayer helped organize the Connecticut Kansas colony and raised money for sixty-three rifles. A few days before their departure, Dr. Henry Ward Beecher praised the rifles as "a truly moral agency" and personally promised $625 if his congregation would match the amount. Yale students gave a special rifle to the group's leader, C. F. Lines. With each rifle, Beecher presented a Bible, and henceforth the Sharpses were known as "Beecher's Bibles."

Cabot's report reveals another $4,947 raised for two hundred Sharpses consigned to the National Kansas Committee and shipped to Tabor, Iowa. These eventually came into possession of John Brown at Harpers Ferry. Frederick Law Olmsted, known for his incisive books on plantation life, and later landscape architect of New York's Central Park, personally raised the money for a howitzer. All told, Cabot's committee and the Massachusetts State Kansas Committee, headed by Higginson and George Stearns, raised almost fifty thousand dollars to arm the Kansas settlers.

The most serious obstacle was not the purchase of rifles but their shipment. After many crates, despite ingenious camouflage, were intercepted near the Kansas border, David Starr Hoyt of Deerfield, Massachusetts, volunteered to escort a hundred Sharpses personally. He reached St. Louis without mishap and stowed his cargo on board the Missouri River steamboat, *Arabia*. But from shipboard, he foolishly wrote his family, describing the progress of his mission. The letter was opened by the captain who handed it to a group of passengers from Missouri. When the *Arabia* docked at Lexington, Hoyt was surrounded by a furious mob, demanding that he sign over the rifles to them and threatening him with death. Hoyt refused, and the mob seized the rifles. But they proved useless since Dr. Cutter had wisely carried the breechblocks to Kansas by a different route!

Returning to St. Louis unhurt, Hoyt brought suit against the *Arabia's* owners and collected full value for the rifles. In a lengthier court action, the Emigrant Aid Company finally recovered its shipment. But Hoyt himself was never able to deliver it. He went into Kansas a few weeks after his ill-fated boat trip and was killed by "Border Ruffians" near Fort Saunders.

Even the officials back home were obviously taking severe risks. For when a Congressional investigating committee linked Brown's rifles to the Emigrant Aid Company after the Harpers Ferry raid, Higginson, Howe, Stearns, and others were indicted. Thayer swore that the company had never sent arms to Kansas. He was technically correct, of course. But he had to shave the point exceedingly fine since the company secretary had negotiated for the rifles over his signature.

Lawrence himself stoutly defended his gunrunning role in a blunt letter to the President on July 15, 1855: "Up to this time the government has kept so far aloof as to force the settlers to the conclusion that if they would be safe, they must defend *themselves*; and therefore many persons here who have refused at first (myself included) have rendered them assistance, by furnishing the means of defense."

Higginson, always eager for militant action, was appointed an agent of the National Kansas Committee and escorted a group of one hundred fifty settlers, arms, and supplies to the territory in the fall of 1856. Since the "Ruffians" had closed the Missouri River, his party had to take the northern route through Iowa, making the last hundred miles by foot. "Emigrants must toil week after week beneath a burning sun, over the parched and endless 'rolling prairie,' " he wrote, "sometimes seeing no house for a day or two together, camping often without wood, and sometimes without water, and obliged to carry with them every eatable they use."

When Higginson finally reached Topeka, he was taken into temporary custody by a troop of United States Cavalry and escorted to Lecompton for questioning. "If they had had wit to discover the Sharps rifles and cannon we brought in with us," he wrote, "we should all have been arrested. . . ." Instead, his closest escape came at Leavenworth, where he overheard a band of Missourians cursing the parson from Massachusetts whom they intended to lynch when they found him. Higginson gave supplies and clothing to James H. Lane, a swashbuckling soldier of fortune, now Major General of the "Army of the North." Lane promptly reciprocated by appointing Higginson a "Briga-dier General."

"It is precisely like waking up some morning and stepping out on the Battle of Bunker Hill. . . . The same persons whom you saw a year ago in Boston, indolent and timid, are here trans-formed to heroes," Higginson described that turbulent autumn in Kansas. After Lawrence was sacked by the Missourians, the settlers told him, "We are scattered, starving, hunted, half-naked, but we are not conquered yet."

Higginson, of course, was unrestrainedly partial to the exploits of the New England emigrants. And Thayer, too, would later claim that his company had almost single-handedly built a free state, transporting thirty thousand settlers to Kansas. Even if Thayer included settlers who joined his parties en route, his figure is still a wild exaggeration. The New Englanders in those first crucial years probably never exceeded three thousand, the majority of emigrants coming from the Ohio Valley and sur-rounding states.

Still, the Emigrant Aid Company was the decisive factor in saving Kansas. It was New England, half a continent away, that stirred the first resistance to the "Border Ruffians" who could reach reinforcements and supplies in a matter of hours. It was

New England that established strongholds like Lawrence and Topeka, provided the most astute and responsible leaders, and infused the movement with Puritan fury and tenacity. "I have in my house no meat, no flour, no meal, no potatoes, no money to buy them, no prospect of a dollar," one settler told Higginson, "but I'll live or die in Kansas!"

Above all, it was New Englanders like Amos A. Lawrence who poured a fortune into schools, mills, and arms long before New York and Chicago had formed their own committees; New Englanders like Thayer and Higginson who saw that the settlers and supplies got through. A few years later, Governor Robinson, the state's first elected Governor, wrote Lawrence, "I am very much mistaken in my estimate of the influences that have contributed to the freedom of Kansas if we are not far more indebted to you than to any other man for our success."

CHAPTER XV

The Reverend Storms the Court House, Boston: May 24, 1854

THE CITY already rumbled angrily at the news of passage of the Kansas Bill by the House of Representatives on May 22. A few days later Boston would be in a state of siege and close to rebellion. "It was like the firing on Fort Sumter," Higginson wrote, "a proof that war had really begun."

It was certainly no accident that Colonel Charles F. Suttle of Alexandria, Virginia, had chosen this moment to seize a fugitive in Boston. The Democratic alliance with the planters was riding high in Washington. Kansas and Nebraska seemed within easy plucking. While Cushing demolished the Democratic-Free Soil coalition in Massachusetts, the Administration determined to make a final object lesson of Boston resistance to the Fugitive Law. The temper of the city had altered radically since fifteen hundred merchants volunteered to escort Sims back to slavery in 1851. "There was never, in fact, in the history of Northern sentiment," noted Dr. Bowditch, "such an entire change as has occurred since the passage of the Nebraska Bill. . . ."

"But the most remarkable exhibition is from the Whigs, the Hunker Whigs, the Compromise men of 1850," Richard H. Dana, Jr. stated. "Men who would not speak to me in 1850 or 1851, and who enrolled themselves as special policemen in the Sims affair, stop me in the street and talk treason." And he added that, "The 'Webster Whigs,' if anything, feel worse than the others. They feel to blame. They feel that they have been deceived by the South and that they have misled others."

It would take overwhelming force now to carry out the Fugitive Law, but President Pierce was ready. "Incur any expense," he wired United States Marshal Watson Freeman and promised

Army reinforcements from New York if necessary. Soon two thousand troops would patrol the city; blood would flow on the courthouse steps and the streets to the wharf; and Theodore Parker would tell an infuriated populace, "Yes, we are the vassals of Virginia."

A little after 6 P.M. on May 24, Anthony Burns, a fugitive now employed in a clothing store on Brattle Street, was arrested by United States Deputy Marshal Asa O. Butman and six assistants on the pretense that he was wanted for robbery. Burns, a tall husky man who would have resisted violently if he had suspected the ruse, was hustled quickly to the courthouse, so quickly that no one on the street noticed the arrest, and it was not until 9 the next morning that the Vigilance Committee was alerted.

Twenty minutes after Burns was locked up in the United States jury room on the third floor, leased from Suffolk County by the Federal government, the Marshal confronted him with Colonel Suttle. Burns, finally realizing he had been arrested as a fugitive, greeted him quietly according to later trial evidence, "How do you do, Master Charles."

"Why did you run away from me?" Suttle demanded.

"I fell asleep on board the vessel where I worked," Burns replied, "and before I woke up, she set sail and carried me off."

When Suttle asked if he had ever whipped him, Burns shook his head. But when the Colonel inquired if he had not always given him enough money, the prisoner replied laconically, "Twelve-and-a-half cents once a year."

Innocent as these questions appeared at the time, they became the crucial proof at the trial in establishing the past relationship between Suttle and Burns. Even after Suttle left, the seven deputies plied him with questions during the night between periods of heavy concentration on their well-stocked liquor supply.

In the morning Burns was led, handcuffed, before United States Commissioner Edward G. Loring, who had issued the warrant for his arrest. Dana, notified by a friend in the court-house, hurried to Burns. "I spoke to him and offered my services," he testified later. "He said it would be of no use; that they had got him and if he protracted the matter and made any delay, it would be worse for him when he got back to Virginia." Burns seemed "stupified with fear" but finally agreed to let Dana represent him. The examination was adjourned until Monday, May 29, the interval being used by the deputy marshals to force further admissions from him that might be used in court.

The Vigilance Committee sent an urgent message to Higginson at Worcester and he rushed to Boston with Martin Stowell. Sixty members of the committee met secretly that Thursday afternoon. They agreed unanimously that Burns's return to slavery must be stopped at any cost, and assigned a detail of men to watch the courthouse twenty-four hours a day so that the prisoner could not be removed in secret. But there was a sharp division of opinion as to a plan of rescue. The moderates favored a delay until Commissioner Loring had given his decision. The militants, led by Higginson, demanded an immediate attack on the courthouse. Nothing was settled except the calling of a mass meeting at Faneuil Hall at 7 the next evening.

Twenty militants remained behind after adjournment and chose Higginson chairman of a special rescue committee. Stowell proposed a plan to use the momentum of the Faneuil Hall meeting for an attack on the courthouse. The twenty would be hidden nearby with axes and crowbars and make the first assault. The crowd at Faneuil Hall, roused to the necessity of rescue by one of the speakers, would then be notified of the assault and come swarming to the courthouse. The plan was approved by vote. But when Higginson asked each of the twenty to sign a compact binding them to the plan, only seven gave their signatures.

It was an angry, determined crowd that overflowed Faneuil Hall the next evening, probably the largest crowd ever assembled there. Reporters noted that men and women filled every inch of the main floor, standing in an almost solid phalanx. The galleries, the stairs and the entrance halls were packed solid. Hundreds more clustered outside the doors. And no longer was the assemblage limited to radicals and abolitionists. That very morning Amos A. Lawrence and his friends had pledged money for an eminent Whig lawyer to defend Burns, "determined it should be known," Dana noted, "that it was not the Free-Soilers only who were in favor of the liberation of the slaves, but the conservative, compromise men."

It was the very size and temper of the crowd, however, that proved the greatest obstacle to rescue. Higginson's seven associates were to meet in the anteroom of the hall before the meeting for final instructions; most of them never fought their way through the jam. And Higginson never established decisive liaison between his group and the Vigilance Committee leaders on the platform. Howe and Parker admitted later they had only partial knowledge of the plan. Dr. Bowditch, secretary of the meeting, confessed, "I knew nothing save in general of the proposed attack. . . ." Phillips could not be found. Higginson, therefore, hurried to the square to organize the assault, leaving a messenger to coordinate the timing with the Vigilance Committee.

The meeting was in chaos from the moment that George R. Russell, former mayor of Roxbury, pounded his gavel for order. Phillips, his voice thundering over the hall, had the audience in an uproar with his warning, "If that man [Burns] leaves the city of Boston, Massachusetts is a conquered state!"

When Parker rose to speak, he called his listeners "Fellow-subjects of Virginia!" They shouted back, "No! *No!*" Parker insisted, "There was a Boston once. Now there is a north suburb to the city of Alexandria."

He whipped the audience to a fury, reminding them that their ancestors had not submitted to the Stamp Act. "I say there are two great laws in the country. One is the slave law: that is the law of the President of the United States. . . . There is another law. . . . It is the law of the people when they are sure they are right and determined to go ahead!"

Then Parker, who obviously had not been reached by Higginson's messenger, proposed that the meeting should adjourn to Court House Square at nine the next morning. But someone in the audience shouted, "Let's go tonight!" And the crowd picked up the chant, "Tonight! *Tonight!*"

Parker could not control them. Phillips rose again, pleading for order, promising "If I thought it would be done tonight, I would go first to the Court House or the Revere House [where

Colonel Suttle lodged]. . . . The zeal that will not keep till to-morrow never will free a slave."

Phillips seemed to have quieted the audience when suddenly a man near the door shouted, "Mr. Chairman, I am just informed that a mob of negroes is in Court Square attempting to rescue Burns. I move that we adjourn to Court Square!"

There was almost panic now, people screaming "Forward! *Forward!*" The massive crowd pushed and fought its way through the narrow doors in an angry, jostling wave. This was the critical moment, for the leaders on the platform should have been able to reach the square first to control and direct the crowd. But Faneuil Hall then had no separate entrance to the platform, "no more communication with the platform," as Higginson wrote, "than if the Atlantic Ocean rolled between." And thus, not only was Higginson's assault made too soon, but those who arrived first in the square were mainly casual bystanders at the periphery of the meeting who had come more for excitement than disciplined action.

An hour before, Higginson had met his small band, Stowell, Hayden, Kemp—we have no record of the other names. They carried revolvers, axes that Higginson had brought from Worcester, and butchers' cleavers concealed in bags. In an alleyway nearby, they had hidden a heavy beam for a battering ram. Since there was still time to get new recruits, they made a final search and returned in half an hour, the assault force increased to almost twenty-five, ten of them Negroes brought by Hayden.

The Supreme Court was in session that night; the attackers, therefore, aroused no particular suspicions. Higginson had chosen the west door, entering almost directly on the stairs, for the assault. He knew that Marshal Freeman had appointed fifty "specials" that afternoon, armed with cutlasses, in addition to the marshal's "guard" already posted in the massive, granite court-house. The two-section doors were heavy oak, closed by locks and a row of iron bolts.

A few minutes after nine, Higginson heard the first rumble of feet from the direction of Faneuil Hall, then "a rush of running figures like the sweep of a wave came round the corner of Court

Square," he wrote. He gave the order to attack. They carried the battering ram quickly to the west door and began smashing it open. In a few minutes, one panel had been broken, another panel partially forced back on its hinges.

A Negro member of the assault team fought his way through the door, followed by Higginson who was immediately driven against the wall of the entrance hall by six or eight guards, slashing at his head with cutlasses. Then Higginson remembered hearing a shot. A moment later, one of the guards, a drayman named James Batchelder who had braced himself against the door, cried out in pain. He was carried by other guards to the marshal's office and died within minutes.

At the coroner's inquest later, the cause of Batchelder's death was diagnosed as a wound in the lower part of the abdomen which had severed a vital artery. The coroner believed it had been inflicted by a knife stroke from one of the attackers. No one, however, was ever indicted. The shot Higginson heard may have been purely coincidental, but many years after, it was revealed that Stowell carried a pistol that night.

Higginson now had been badly battered on the head by clubs, his chin slashed by a saber, giving him a scar he would always carry. "Meanwhile," he described the action, "the Deputy Marshals retreated to the stairway over which we could see their pistols pointing, the whole hall between us and them very brightly lighted." Only a handful of attackers had fought their way inside the entrance hall, and he shouted to the others, "You cowards, will you desert us now?" Higginson did not know that eight or nine of his associates had already been captured by the police, summoned by the frantic clanging of the courthouse bell.

This was the moment when proper coordination with the Faneuil Hall meeting would have ensured Higginson's success. For a massive assault now on the half-battered doors could have carried the building. But neither Parker nor any of the Vigilance Committee had reached the square yet. "We had the froth and scum of the meeting, the fringe of idlers on its edge," Higginson wrote. And without proper leadership, they quickly retreated before the police.

One lone figure, the venerable Amos Bronson Alcott, founder of the Fruitlands community, transcendentalist, father of Louisa May, walked unhurriedly up the courthouse stairs, his cane tapping on the stones. At the top he turned and asked, "Why are we not within?" No one followed him. A shot rang out, but missed its target. He stood for a moment, then walked slowly down the stairs.

Higginson had now been driven from the entrance hall, his chin bleeding profusely. Oddly enough, he had carried an umbrella to the square and hung it from the railing of the courthouse steps. Someone returned it, casually remarking, "Mister, I guess you've left your rumberill." Higginson, seeing the futility of waiting for arrest, melted into the crowd and made his way to William F. Channing's house where his wound was dressed.

Mayor J. V. C. Smith arrived with two companies of artillery which were stationed at the courthouse and at City Hall. One company of Marines hurried from Fort Warren, a second from Charleston Navy Yard. What was left of the Faneuil Hall crowd drifted into the side streets; the city returned to its troubled calm.

Later, as bold an abolitionist as Dr. Bowditch would criticize "the too ardent and premature movements of Higginson and his party, for I suppose I do them no dishonor in thus writing the truth." And Edmund Quincy would call the assault "a gallant and generous attempt but ill-advised and injudicious under the circumstances."

But Higginson always insisted, "It was one of the best plots that ever failed." And he was probably right. Its strategy was excellent; any delay would have given the authorities more time to improve the courthouse defenses. Marshal Freeman's successor later quoted him as admitting, "the surprise was complete and that thirty resolute men could have carried off Burns."

THE Vigilance Committee's lawyers now served a writ of personal replevin on Marshal Freeman, an ancient English writ incorporated into the Commonwealth's statutes in 1786, abolished in 1836 but restored the following year. It would have removed

Burns from Commissioner Loring's court and guaranteed him trial by jury under the state courts. The marshal, however, refused to give him up. Coroner Charles Smith told the committee he would serve the writ by force if Governor Emory Washburn supported him with the state militia. Samuel Sewall and Dr. Bowditch called on the governor, who made protestations of sympathy but insisted he could not call out the militia except for threatened violence or breach of peace. "Cold as an icicle though coming from Worcester!" Bowditch described him.

Colonel Suttle, obviously shaken by the attempted rescue, moved his room from a lower floor to the attic of his hotel, kept the door barricaded, and hired four armed guards to protect him around the clock. By Saturday, he was determined to get out of Boston as quickly as possible and informed Reverend Grimes he would sell Burns for twelve hundred dollars.

Grimes agreed to have the money by ten that night. He hurriedly collected the requisite pledges, and at 10:30 P.M. met with Suttle's lawyer at Commissioner Loring's office to draw up the bill of sale. But United States District Attorney Benjamin Hallett suddenly raised a barrage of objections. Hallett had followed a devious course since his early support of Garrison almost twenty years before. A crony of Caleb Cushing's and chairman of the Democratic national committee in 1852, he had helped guide President Pierce's Southern policy and had become one of slavery's most vehement defenders. Now he pointed to the spot where Batchelder had been killed and insisted, "That blood must be avenged." He was obviously determined the extradition of Burns must be turned into a pageant of Democratic strength. "The United States Attorney acted under orders from the Cabinet at Washington, with whom he was in constant communication by telegraph," Dana reported. By Monday, Hallett had convinced Suttle to revoke his pledge and refuse the sale of Burns.

The trial began on Monday, May 29, in an atmosphere of feverish excitement. The courthouse looked like a fortress, two companies of United States Artillery and a corps of Marines forming a cordon around the building and stationed at every floor and window. Marshal Freeman had sworn in 124 additional deputies whom Parker described as "pimps, gamblers, fighters, drunkards, public brawlers and convicts." The former city jailer told Dana that forty-five had served prison terms, including an indictment for murder.

All entrances to the courthouse were closed except one guarded by a strong police force. As a result, the State Supreme Court and other courts suspended operations for a week. Even Colonel Suttle had his own élite bodyguard, a group of young Southern students at Harvard. The courtroom itself bristled with weapons. Charles M. Ellis, one of the defense counsels, repeatedly protested against Suttle's lawyer carrying a pistol. Although Dana was widely known as senior defense counsel, he was stopped constantly at the door by soldiers with fixed bayonets and not passed without the marshal's approval.

The defense based its case on two weak links in Suttle's claim. First, since Suttle had leased Burns to a neighbor named Milspaugh, only Milspaugh could take legal steps for his extradition. Second, Suttle's chief witness, a Richmond grocer named William Brent, testified falsely that he had seen Burns last in Virginia on March 20 and, therefore, the prisoner could not be the fugitive in question.

The defense produced witness after witness to prove that Burns had actually been in Boston on that date. One testified he had been employed with Burns at the Mattapan Works on March 1. The Mattapan bookkeeper confirmed Burns's employment then from his records. A member of the City Council swore he had seen Burns in Boston on March 8 or 9. Altogether nine witnesses refuted Brent's testimony.

When Commissioner Loring rendered his decision on Friday morning, June 2, he admitted this conflict and then ignored it as evidence. The irrefutable proof that Burns was the fugitive claimed by Suttle, he insisted, was the conversation between them that evening after Burns's arrest which had been recorded by the marshal's deputies. The *Boston Atlas* considered this "no legal evidence." And Dana protested Burns had been "convicted on an *ex parte* record, against the actual evidence, and on his own admission made at the moment of arrest to his alleged master!"

Hallett, who had virtually assumed control of the Federal troops and the marshal's deputies and guard, was so confident of Loring's decision that he had arranged for extradition that very morning. Mayor Smith—"a poor shoat, a physician of a timid, conceited, scatter-brain character, raised by accident to a mayoralty," Dana called him—weakly accepted Hallett's orders. Although prohibited by state law from helping the extradition of Burns, he turned over most of his power to Major General Benjamin F. Edmands, a druggist in civilian life, who commanded the 1st Division of Volunteer Militia.

That morning the Police Chief called in his captains, gave them maps of the areas to be cleared, and informed them they would be supported by militia who had orders to fire on any resisting crowd. When Captain Joseph K. Hayes suggested the city was directly helping the extradition, his protests were brushed aside. He immediately handed in his resignation.

By 8:30 that morning, General Edmands had made Boston an occupied city. On the Common, he paraded twenty companies of militia and two troops of cavalry. Supported in the next few hours by United States troops from nearby garrisons, they made a total of at least two thousand soldiers, probably the largest security force since the Revolution.

Angry crowds swarmed to the city; many came from outlying textile mills and machine shops, seven hundred from Worcester alone, carrying a banner inscribed "Worcester Freedom Club." Church bells tolled all morning. Dozens of buildings around the courthouse were draped in black. From a window opposite the Old State House was suspended a black coffin. One merchant had stretched a rope across State Street from which he hung the American flag draped in mourning with the Union down. ". . . Even John H. Pierson is aroused and has labored very much in his [Burns's] behalf," wrote Dr. Bowditch. "The enslaver of Sims is now a hater of slavery."

It was a sweltering June morning under a cloudless sky. At eleven o'clock, Edmands marched his troops from the Common to Court and State Streets. The soldiers, each equipped with eleven rounds of powder and ball, loaded their arms. The merchants in Court Square were ordered to close their shops, and the militia swept the square of people, pushing the crowds back into the side streets. "Men were arrested and imprisoned for merely making observations to each other which the ruling powers considered dangerous," wrote Lydia Maria Child.

In the square, Marshal Freeman had assembled five companies of United States troops and cannon from the Charleston Navy Yard. Deputy Marshal Riley went to the prison room and ordered Burns handcuffed. Burns protested the indignity and promised to go quietly, but insisted he would resist with all his strength if handcuffed. The marshal finally accepted his promise.

The proceedings were delayed from 1 to 2 P.M. while Edmands struggled to clear the streets along the one-third mile route to the wharf. "It seemed as if the whole population of the city had been concentrated upon this narrow space," wrote one reporter. The militia could force only a narrow lane, jamming the crowds back on the sidewalk. Spectators filled every window and balcony. The newspapers estimated over fifty thousand people lined the route.

At two o'clock, Edmands formed his column, first the United States artillery detachment, then the Marines, followed by the marshal's armed guard, and more Marines and cannon at the rear. From the courthouse, Burns was led through a line of soldiers to the center of the column. Marshal Freeman had promised Dana and the Reverend Grimes they could walk with Burns, but at the last minute retracted his pledge.

There was almost no sound except the heavy tramp of boots on the pavements, punctuated by hisses from the crowd and cries of, "Shame!" Occasionally a spectator recognized an officer and cried his name disdainfully to the assemblage. The column went past the Old State House, past the spot where Attucks fell. A fire alarm rang just after the column started and the engines tried to wedge their way down State Street. Whenever spectators were forced into the street by pressure from behind, lancers charged at them with drawn sabers. "Twice I saw the troops charge bayonet," reported Dr. Bowditch, "and once (in Parisian style) the cavalry charged with drawn swords." One spectator was wounded by a sword, a second had his head slashed by a saber, a third was knocked down and so badly pummeled by muskets he would always remain an invalid. Returning home later that evening, Dana himself would be beaten over the head by two members of the marshal's guard and almost blinded.

Dr. Howe stood in the crowd with tears running down his face. Higginson, his head bandaged, watched with his Worcester contingent. Thomas Garrett was there from Wilmington, Delaware, the devoted Quaker, now gray and stooped, who had helped hundreds of fugitives escape through the Underground Railroad. George S. Hillard, stanch Hunker Whig, watched from his office and later wrote, "I put my face in my hands and wept. I could do nothing less."

When the column reached Long Wharf, Burns was placed on board a small steamer which would take him to the revenue cutter, *Morris*, sent specially to Boston by the President. The total cost of the extradition was later estimated at close to one hundred thousand dollars.

But the nation would pay a far higher price to prove that Boston could still be humbled before the Fugitive Slave Law. The law had been executed, but almost at the cost of rebellion. ". . . It was nothing but the clearing of the streets previously and the immense display of military that prevented the total destruction of the United States marshal and his hired assistants," Amos A. Lawrence wrote his brother.

"No law can stand another such strain," proclaimed Chief Justice Shaw of the Massachusetts Supreme Court.

Even the *Richmond Enquirer* admitted that "a few more such victories and the South is undone."

"There was a lot of folks to see a colored man walk down the street," Burns remarked at the end.

ON JUNE 7, Higginson, Parker, Phillips, Stowell, and three others were indicted for aiding the assault on the courthouse. Higginson was arrested three days later, but when Deputy Marshal Butman came to Worcester to gather evidence, he was surrounded by angry crowds, knocked down by a stone, and saved from serious injury by the intervention of Higginson, George Frisbie Hoar, later a United States Senator, and other abolitionists. They rushed him out of town in a wagon, fighting off the demonstrators who clung to the spokes of the wheels, then transferred him to a hack which the city marshal drove all the way to Boston. Butman refused to enter the city until after dark, and remained hidden overnight at a hotel instead of going to his home. "There was a sort of dramatic perfection about this: the entire disappearance of Butman's own friends leaving him to be literally and absolutely saved by abolitionists," Higginson noted.

Through technical defects, however, the indictments were quashed and no case ever came to trial. Hallett wrote Parker caustically, "You have crept through a knot-hole this time." The minister retorted, "I will knock a bigger hole next time."

Meanwhile, Burns had reached Virginia and Colonel Suttle delivered him to Lumpkin's jail at Richmond where he was kept in a cell without bed or chair for four months. He was handcuffed at all times. His feet were fettered. He could remove his clothes neither day nor night, and the cell soon became a cesspool. Finally, he was sold to David McDaniel of Rocky Mount, North Carolina, for nine hundred five dollars although Suttle had turned down twelve hundred dollars in Boston. A local clergyman wrote Reverend Grimes that Burns could probably be purchased now for thirteen hundred dollars, and Grimes quickly raised the money, met McDaniel in Baltimore and completed the sale. Burns returned to Boston a free man, greeted in triumph by a packed meeting at Tremont Temple. Phineas Barnum immediately offered him a large salary to appear for five weeks at his museum, but Burns turned down the offer, remarking, "He wants to show me like a monkey." Awarded a scholarship at Oberlin College, he began his studies for the Baptist clergy.

All the fury roused in Boston by the Burns case, and the Fugitive Law was now directed at Commissioner Loring. "I have lost all pride in Massachusetts 'till she redeems herself from the second day of June," Phillips announced. "Let us roll up a petition a hundred thousand strong for the removal of Judge Loring."

Loring's butcher refused to sell him meat. The women of Wo-
burn sent him thirty pieces of silver. And at Harvard, where his
appointment as Lecturer at the Law School was up for renewal,
he came under even more bitter attack. A two-thirds vote of the
Board of Overseers, which included the Governor and Lieutenant
Governor of the State, the President of the State Senate and other
prominent officials, turned down his appointment. Two former
Governors, a Whig and a Democrat, both voted against him.

Only three times before had judges in the Commonwealth been
removed by petition. Loring, a Probate Judge in the State Courts,
now became the target of the antislavery revulsion sweeping New
England. The Senate voted 27 to 11 for his removal, the House,
206 to 111. Governor Henry J. Gardner vetoed the measure, but
it was passed three more times and vetoed each time. Finally in
1858 with Banks as Governor, the Legislature voted removal
again, and no veto saved Loring.

An even more important result of the Burns case was the passage in 1855 of a strengthened Personal Liberty Law which
virtually made the Fugitive Law unexecutable in Massachusetts.
President Pierce was well aware that an army of fifty thousand
men would have trouble removing a slave from Boston now, and
neither he nor Buchanan dared to take the risk again. "The people
are now more ripe than ever for revolution," predicted Dr.
Bowditch. "Peaceful I believe it may be, but bloody I fear it
will be."

CHAPTER XVI

Senate Blood and Ruffian Blood: 1856

No SOONER had the Free Soil-Democratic coalition fallen apart than a new movement, the American party or Know-Nothings, swept furiously over the old parties and obscured the slavery issue in new complexities.

A castoff Whig named Henry J. Gardner was hardly taken seriously when he ran for Governor of Massachusetts in 1854. Yet he was elected by eighty-one thousand votes. The Know-Nothings elected all members of Congress, and all but two members of the State Legislature. It was easily the most remarkable landslide in Massachusetts history.

That same fall, they carried Delaware, and through Whig coalition, Pennsylvania, and sent seventy-five Representatives to Washington. A year later, they added Connecticut, New Hampshire, and Rhode Island to their New England bloc, Kentucky and Maryland among the border states, and claimed the election of nine governors. By 1856, they confidently expected to elect the President.

In the North, particularly New England, the Know-Nothing phenomenon was a rebellion not only against Catholic immigration but slavery. For bitterness against the old parties and an almost paralytic fear of dis-Union seems to have driven the electorate to lump together Catholicism and slavery as the twin evils besetting the nation.

The best that can be claimed for the American party is that it completed the destruction of the Whigs and Democrats in New England and many parts of the North. And this was a bitter accomplishment balanced against the religious and racial hatreds it invoked! At worst, the Know-Nothings deflected attention from Kansas and slavery. But there is little justification for considering it a Southern plot. The inexorable necessity of a broadly based Republican party, representing all Northern and Western interests, was only temporarily blocked. For despite confident claims, the Know-Nothing candidate in 1856 polled only 20 per cent of the popular vote against 45 per cent for the winner, Buchanan, and an astonishingly high 33 per cent for Frémont, the Republican.

The Republican party was hastily built on a grab bag of issues. In each state, the party organized independently and baited its platform for a specific vote—in Pennsylvania and New Jersey for the businessman; in Massachusetts and the West for the small farmer; in most of New England for the abolitionist.

Neither in 1856, nor even 1860, would the cautious national platform even whisper the possibility of abolition in the existent slave states. And in the desperate winter and spring of compromise in 1860 and 1861, Seward, already Lincoln's Secretary-of-State-designate, would propose that future territories be organized without conditions as to freedom or slavery—a virtual retreat to the terms of the hated Kansas Bill!

The nearest the Republicans came to an abolition candidate was the momentary support of Sumner for the Vice Presidency in 1856. Radicals like Representative Owen Lovejoy of Illinois, who tried to make the Republicans see that "if slavery is right in Virginia, it is right in Kansas," were a minority. Nationally, the Republicans simply cloaked the economic aims of farmers and businessmen in the humanitarianism of New England and offered the nation a *status quo* for slavery that it hoped would placate the South.

"WE ARE now in Civil War," Theodore Parker described the Kansas struggle in 1856. He was hardly exaggerating the crisis. Former Senator David Atchison had led his "Platte County Rifles" across the border. Colonel Jefferson Buford sold his Alabama plantation and used the proceeds to finance his band of three hundred Ruffians. Other units came from Georgia and

South Carolina. By March, 1856, officials of Lafayette County, Missouri, estimated they had spent over one hundred thousand dollars to drive the free-state emigrants out of Kansas.

"Kansas today is the Crimea of liberty," warned James S. Pike, correspondent of the *New York Tribune*, "and if it falls, no man can tell when the tide of invasion will be rolled back."

The Ruffians not only had proximity of their Missouri base but the Federal Administration, to a large extent, on their side. Although no controls had been established, not even standards for residence, Andrew Reeder, the first Governor appointed by Pierce, insisted on an election for territorial delegate to Congress in November, 1854. The Ruffians came from Missouri in droves and captured the election, but at least half the ballots later proved illegal.

The same process was repeated in the election of a Legislature in March, 1855. Almost five thousand of a total of about six thousand three hundred votes were cast by residents of Missouri. The Ruffians thus took control of the government which legally should have been in Free State hands.

The so-called "Missouri" Legislature hastened to consolidate its power with a series of crushing laws—a ruthless Slave Code, the limitation of public office to sworn proslavery men, and imposition of the death penalty for even circulating a book or newspaper that might incite slave escapes. One Southern Senator considered the laws so drastic he doubted John C. Calhoun would have been safe from prison. Shocked into coping with the travesty he had helped create, Governor Reeder repudiated the legislation and insisted on immediate residence standards and election controls.

The "Missouri" Legislature, however, fitted the President's intentions perfectly. He therefore removed Reeder from office, and replaced him with the compliant Wilson Shannon. Two Southern extremists, Sterling Cato and Samuel D. Lecompte, were appointed to the judiciary.

The Free State settlers quickly acted to establish a legitimate government under free elections. On October 23, they called a convention at Topeka, and drew up a new constitution which outlawed slavery. For all intents and purposes, Kansas would henceforth have two governments.

Under the guise of emergency service in the Kansas militia, the "Missouri" Legislature summoned a thousand Ruffians to march on Lawrence and its neighboring towns in a campaign that has become known as the Wakarusa "war."

Lawrence, however, was better prepared than the Missourians expected. It had five forts manned by six hundred defenders; two hundred Sharps rifles had just arrived from Massachusetts. In addition, the Committee of Public Safety had recently appointed as captain a tall, gaunt man named John Brown with blue, almost metal-hard eyes and features seemingly chiseled from stone. Brown's four oldest sons had arrived in Kansas the previous winter and Brown, following shortly after, had seen the necessity of organizing his own armed band, highly trained in mobile guerrilla warfare. The Ruffians first pillaged settlements along the Wakarusa River, but after testing the strength of Lawrence's defenses, quickly withdrew.

On January 5, 1856, the Free State settlers called an election under the Topeka constitution and chose Robinson as Governor. In March, Lane and Reeder were elected Senators-designate. Robinson appealed to the President to use Federal troops to end the border raids. But in his message of January 24, Pierce brusquely responded that troops could be summoned only by the territorial government, which meant the "Missouri" Legislature.

"Kansas stands today, bound hand and foot by the Administration, who will not let her go free," protested the *New York Tribune*, "and she is to be sacrificed and turned over to slaverry. . . ."

Judge Lecompte now made himself a shoddy accomplice of the final attack on Lawrence. He charged a grand jury to issue warrants for treason against Lane, Reeder, Robinson, and other Free State leaders. Under the excuse of arresting them, Federal Marshal J. B. Donaldson summoned a "posse" of almost seven hundred men, who conveniently turned out to be Atchison's and Buford's Ruffians supported by four cannon. Lane and Reeder escaped, but Robinson was taken prisoner in Missouri on May 12. Still, the "posse" converged on Lawrence whose citizens had agreed not to resist Federal authority. The marshal entered the town, went through the perfunctory motions of carrying out his warrant, and retired. Then his "posse" sacked the town, bombarding the Free State Hotel and shops with cannon, wrecking two newspaper offices, and leaving dozens of homes, including Robinson's, in smoldering ruins. Through the tragic duplicity of a Federal Court and its marshal, most of the equipment, supplies, and money the New England Emigrant Aid Company had brought to Kansas were wiped out within hours.

A few days later, the *New York Daily Times* headlines proclaimed: "THE WAR BEGUN. LAWRENCE DESTROYED." But at the very moment on May 19 when the Ruffians were marching on Lawrence, Charles Sumner rose in the Senate to deliver the most crucial speech of his career, "The Crime Against Kansas."

WASHINGTON was broiling in a 90-degree heat that day, but the announcement that Sumner would speak had brought almost every Senator to his seat. The galleries were jammed with government officials and their wives. When space ran out, the Senate anteroom was opened to the ladies. Sumner, who had been working on his speech for weeks, told Parker he intended it to be "the most thorough philippic ever uttered in a legislative body." When an associate, who had seen Sumner's notes, begged him to moderate his vitriolic tone, the Senator insisted, "The whole arsenal of God is ours, and I will not remove one of the weapons,—not one!"

For two days Sumner struck and slashed at what he called "the rape of a virgin territory." The speech was a strange combination of classical oratory, studded with quotations from the English poets and Greek and Roman historians, and biting invective against many Senators and Missourians in Kansas. Douglas and Senator Andrew P. Butler of South Carolina were his particular targets—the Don Quixote and Sancho Panza of slavery, he branded them. Butler had chosen the "harlot, slavery" as his

"mistress." Douglas was slavery's "squire." The verbiage was almost excessive, the rhetoric often ornamental. But in its massive
detail, its grasp of every devious twist of Administration policy,
the speech was a masterpiece of scholarship. Angry, scathing,
majestic as Webster in his prime, Sumner seemed to represent the
total fury of the Puritan past as he scourged the nation of its sins
and demanded justice for Kansas.

Longfellow called the speech, reprinted by the thousands
throughout the North, "the greatest voice on the greatest subject
that has ever been uttered since we became a nation." Whittier
considered it, "a grand and terrible philippic."

But the reaction of the Southern bloc was instant and bitter,
one Senator telling the correspondent of the *New York Tribune*
that, "if he could have his way, he would hang Sumner on the
spot." Cass of Michigan called the speech, "the most un-American
and un-patriotic" ever made in the Senate. The resulting debate,
in fact, far surpassed Sumner's oratory in acid vehemence. Douglas attacked Sumner's allusions for their "lasciviousness and ob-
scenity." Sumner compared the Illinois Senator to a "noisome,
squat and nameless animal." Mason of Virginia, in turn, called
Sumner, "a cunning artificer or forger." Referring to Butler,
Sumner criticized "the loose expectoration of his speech." Clay
of Alabama brought the charges and countercharges to a climax
by labeling Sumner "a sneaking, sinuous, snake-like poltroon."

The Senate's mood had taken an ugly turn, and Henry Wilson
was concerned enough to insist on escorting Sumner home. But
Sumner would have none of it. By the following day, May 22,
tempers seemed to have cooled. The Senate adjourned early at
12:45 P.M., and Sumner stayed on the floor writing letters, his
long legs stretched under his desk.

Representative Preston Brooks of South Carolina, who was the
son of Senator Butler's cousin, entered the Senate and, taking a
seat near Sumner, waited for the floor to clear. Brooks was a
powerful man, over six feet tall. At thirty-six, he had served less
than three years in the House and still retained a ramrod military
bearing from his brief enlistment in the Mexican War. When
Wilson had finished his work and left the floor, Brooks asked a

puzzled attendant if he could speed the departure of a feminine visitor.

Then Brooks approached Sumner. The Senator did not recognize him, and hardly glanced up from his writing. "I have read your speech twice over carefully," Brooks told him. "It is a libel on South Carolina and on Mr. Butler, who is a relative of mine—"

Brooks instantly raised the heavy gutta-percha cane he was carrying and began to rain blows on Sumner's head. They were crunching blows from a man of considerable strength, "very rapid and as hard as he could hit," Senator Toombs of Georgia, a witness, testified later.

Brooks would admit he first considered using a heavy whip but feared that Sumner, who certainly equaled him in strength, might wrest it from him. Ironically enough, Brooks had introduced a resolution only two years before which would have banned concealed weapons in the House.

The first blows stunned Sumner immediately. "I saw no longer my assailant nor any other person or object in the room," he testified later. Instinctively he struggled to get to his feet, but his legs were pinioned firmly under the desk, which was fastened by screws to an iron plate, which in turn was bolted to the floor. All he could do was thrash his arms about to ward off the blows. In blind, desperate strength, he finally wrenched the desk clear off the floor and staggered to his feet.

Even then, Brooks seized him by the collar with his left hand and continued pounding him on the head until the cane broke in pieces. Witnesses estimated that from twelve to thirty blows had been struck.

Only a few feet away stood Representative Lawrence M. Keitt of South Carolina, who had approved the attack and accompanied Brooks to the Senate. A *New York Daily Times* correspondent, talking nearby, reported that Keitt cried, "Give it to him!" Keitt, also carrying a heavy cane, shook it threateningly at two New York Congressmen about fifty feet away, and shouted, "Let them alone!" Then he warned off Senator John J. Crittenden of Kentucky, who had rushed to stop the attack. One witness later reported Keitt even placed his hand on the pistol he carried.

Only one Senate officer, the doorkeeper, made any move to interfere, and at least six Senators within calling distance simply ignored the struggle. Senator Iverson of Georgia never left his seat. "As for rendering Mr. Sumner any assistance," Toombs stated tersely, "I did not do it."

Sumner finally collapsed unconscious on the floor, Representative Edwin B. Morgan of New York reaching him in time to prevent a heavy fall. He had bled profusely, and his clothes were drenched with blood. Two deep gashes on the back of his head had cut to the bone, laying it bare. The thickness of Sumner's hair, which dulled the blows, probably averted a serious fracture. After a doctor arrived and sewed up the wounds, Sumner was taken home by Wilson and other friends.

The attack raised cries of horror throughout the North. "Atrocious cowardice!" Cassius Clay called it. "An outrage of the decencies of civilized life," the Massachusetts Legislature branded it in a resolution. "O Southern 'chivalry'! O _____!" Longfellow wrote in his diary. "We have dropped to the level of a ruffian civilization," Wendell Phillips lamented.

At a meeting in Boston's Faneuil Hall, filled to capacity with thousands overflowing to the street, Governor Gardner insisted the attack had been carried out "with a grossness and brutality which history, until now, has never had written upon her pages." Many Northern conservatives were now convinced that the South would stop at nothing, Colonel A. D. Brewster warning the meeting, "The duty of the North is to arm to the teeth, and submit no more to such indignities as have been heaped upon her."

Northern resentment was intensified by the fact that the South almost universally supported the attack. "The vulgar abolitionists . . . have grown saucy, and dared to be impudent to gentlemen!" proclaimed the *Richmond Enquirer*. ". . . They must be lashed into submission." And it added: "In the main, the press of the South applauds the conduct of Mr. Brooks without condition or limitation."

Congressman Savage of Tennessee announced that Sumner not only "deserved what he received but every honest hand on earth

Proud grandparents: John Murray Forbes (left), anti-slavery financier, and Ralph Waldo Emerson, who led Brahmin intellectuals against slavery, with their grandson, Ralph Emerson Forbes *(From personal collection, Edward W. Forbes)*

Colonel Robert Gould Shaw, commander of 54th Massachusetts Regiment, first regiment of free Negroes in the Union Army, as depicted in a monument by Augustus Saint-Gaudens on Boston Common. Shaw was killed on the ramparts at Fort Wagner, Charleston, S. C., and virtually deified by New England as the embodiment of anti-slavery chivalry.

ought to have a whip to scourge the villain around the world."

During House debate on the attack, Anson Burlingame of Massachusetts cried, "What! strike a man when he is pinioned,— when he cannot respond to a blow! Call you that chivalry?" Brooks immediately assumed his reputation had been impugned and challenged his critic to a duel. Much to Brooks's surprise, Burlingame accepted, selecting a Canadian location. But Brooks backed down under the excuse he would have to go through Northern territory—neglecting to mention he could have reached Canada by ship!

The Southern bloc was so resentful of any slur on Brooks that when Wilson branded it "a brutal, murderous and cowardly assault," Senator Butler retorted, "You are a liar!" and rushed toward the Massachusetts Senator.

Brooks was sent a testimonial cane by students at the University of Virginia, its gold head inscribed with a laudatory message. Soon canes, silver goblets, and other testimonials poured on him from all over the South.

The House opened its official investigation while Sumner, who at first recovered rapidly, suffered a serious relapse. Brooks admitted he had planned the attack carefully with Keitt and Representative Edmundson of Virginia, that he had waited for Sumner twice in front of the Capitol until Edmundson persuaded him an assault on the steps placed him at a disadvantage. Former Senator Thomas H. Benton of Missouri, an opponent of the Kansas Bill, told a correspondent acidly, "This is not an assault, sir, it is a conspiracy. . . ."

Yet when the House voted to expel Brooks, only one Southern representative supported the resolution. The vote lacked the necessary two-thirds for expulsion and Brooks, censored by a 121 to 95 majority, resigned his seat, went back to his district, and was triumphantly reelected with only six votes against him. In his trial before a sympathetic Circuit Court in Washington, he was fined three hundred dollars and not even jailed for a day.

Less than seven months later, ironically, Brooks died from a pulmonary infection.

Meanwhile, Sumner began his agonizing struggle for recovery.

His brain and spinal column had been affected by the blows. "He walks . . . like a man who has not altogether recovered from paralysis . . . ," Seward reported in July. "My brain and whole nervous system are jangled and subject to relapse," Sumner wrote in October. At the Republican convention, the New York delegation proposed him vigorously as Frémont's running mate, but his friends knew his health could not stand the strain and withdrew his name. In November, Sumner had recovered enough to return to Boston where he was greeted tumultuously in the flag-draped streets. Although the Legislature knew he could not take his seat for some time, it reelected him to the Senate by an overwhelming margin—a unanimous vote in the State Senate, 333 to 12 in the House. "Where is there a Senator who holds by such a tenure?" Dana exultantly wrote him.

Sumner now sought to speed his recuperation with a trip to France. But at the end of 1857, he wrote Parker, ". . . I feel like a man of ninety." He returned to the Senate momentarily in April, 1858, but after another relapse, went back to France for painful medical treatment of his spine. Not until December, 1859, was he well enough to sit in the Senate permanently. Sumner had fought virtually alone against slavery in 1856; now he was one of twenty-four Republican Senators.

WHEN NEWS of the assault on Sumner reached Boston, Josiah Quincy, tough and irascible at eighty-two, angrily condemned "the outrages of the slaveholders at Washington; outrages which, if not met in the spirit of your fathers of the Revolution (and I see no sign they will be), our liberties are but a name, and our Union proves a curse."

Even in Kansas, compromise had already infiltrated the Free State leadership. While Marshal Donaldson's "posse" converged on Lawrence, a defense meeting was held at the Free State Hotel at midnight on May 20, 1856. Pomeroy and other leaders agreed not to resist Federal authority—although the marshal's authority rested on the guns of Border Ruffians. "I insisted," Pomeroy explained four years later, "though our town was threatened with destruction—and the invading army was then within 12 *miles* of Town! and numbered over 1200 men—well armed—that we should give the Government a fair opportunity to protect us. . . ."

On May 24, three nights after the sack of Lawrence, John Brown decided to strike back in an act of violence that would become a turning point in Kansas and forever plunge his name in controversy. When Brown and his six-man band that night massacred five pro-slavery settlers on Pottawatomie Creek, a man and a myth would become inseparable. Brown, the guerrilla fighter, would become inextricably merged with Brown, the avenging fury of Puritanism. At Pottawatomie he created an implacable and bloody symbol against compromise. Only a few months later Gerrit Smith would write, "There was a time when slavery could have been ended by political action. But that time has gone by—and, as I apprehend, for ever." For good or evil, the North had been waiting for Brown. It needed a symbol, a mystique of total commitment.

Brown has been called "the last of the Puritans" by Franklin Sanborn, "a Puritan of Puritans" by Julia Ward Howe. His roots were in the Puritan past, but such characterizations hardly explain the violent march toward Harpers Ferry. Born in 1800 in Torrington, Connecticut, Brown believed his family could trace its ancestry to the *Mayflower*. Both his grandfathers fought in the Revolution. The marks of his boyhood were poverty and discipline. When the family moved to Ohio, there was still so little money, Brown admits in a fragment of autobiography, that his prized toy, a yellow marble, was given him not by his parents but by "a poor *Indian boy*." When he lost his treasure, it was not replaced. Brown concluded, "*It took years to heal the wound. . . .*"

His father instilled in him both abolitionism and a reverence for the Bible. None of the Puritan attributes, however, helped Brown earn more than a marginal living. He tried his hand at a score of ventures, including farming and sheep raising, and failed miserably, leaving a tangle of debts and lawsuits behind him. Not until 1848, when he settled on the tract Gerrit Smith had reserved for free Negroes at North Elba, New York, did he bring even slight stability to his peregrinating family.

The enigma of Brown is that he seems to be born out of time and place, possessed by a violence that separates him from all other abolitionists. His God was an angry God, and Brown exists as an instrument of vengeance. He read the Bible constantly, sitting up late before battle to mark passages from the Gospels and Psalms. His favorite text was, "Without the shedding of blood, there is no remission of sins." He was unshakably certain that his mission had to be accomplished in blood and that God had chosen him for this purpose. It consumed him to the point where he eliminated all other reason for existence. From the moment in 1851 when he formed the League of Gileadites to oppose the Fugitive Slave Law (incorporating Biblical grandeur even in this name), he was swept inescapably forward to the appointed judgment at Harper's Ferry.

From his Connecticut Puritanism, Brown certainly inherited the Calvinist sense of sin and inflexible morality that underlie the abolition tradition. At the same time, he belongs to many worlds. His voice clangs from the mountaintop like a Hebrew prophet. He combines the frenzy of the Salem witch-burner with that rare fusion of soldier and mystic that became the backbone of Cromwell's army.

He knew how to keep a flash of Biblical lightning around his head. His brief statements before or after battle have an Old Testament eloquence, and he exploited this image through the press, his letters to New England supporters, his speech before the Massachusetts Legislature, and his final words from Harpers Ferry. Ascetic and self-denying, he patterned his company after Cromwell's. No drinking or swearing was tolerated. The men chose their own officers, and discipline was self-imposed.

If his frenzy seems close to megalomania, it was a frenzy of purpose, not plan or execution. Although recent biography has made much of a strain of insanity in Brown's family, he pursued his objectives with eminent rationality. Dr. Howe considered him "an enthusiast, yet cool, keen and cautious." At the battles of

Black Jack and Osawatomie, his strategy was flawless. Nothing could have been more logical than the plan of a slave escape in the Virginia mountains. Months of harassment and delay, however, warped his judgment in selecting Harpers Ferry and clinging to his position instead of following his original hit-and-run tactics.

Brown's massacre at Pottawatomie must be judged against the desperate condition of the Free State party in May, 1856. Many years afterward, his son, Salmon, insisted, "Cato was responsible for killing these five men—Cato and nobody else." And while Salmon was obviously intent on clearing his own and his father's name, Judge Cato and the Lecompton grand jury had clearly embarked on a campaign to break Free State resistance. Robinson had already been arrested, other leaders forced to flee. Brown and his family were the next targets. Following the sack of Lawrence, the Border Ruffians were ready to sweep Kansas.

"We must have help on the Pottawatomie," a messenger told Brown. "We have been ordered to leave in three days or die." Admittedly, the source of this message has never been identified. But two reasonably reputable witnesses, Edward F. Bridgeman and Luke F. Parons, testified that Brown replied, "Has it come to this? One party or the other must leave their homes in three days. Well, I accept the challenge." H. A. Williams, a lieutenant in the Pottawatomie company, then handed Brown a list of names "necessary to pick off to prevent the utter destruction of the whole community." Brown's supporters later claimed that his plan was approved not only by a council of companies and bands in the area but inferentially by the Free State leadership. Although such evidence is still as obscure as almost all facts surrounding Pottawatomie, the crisis at that moment still gave Brown reasonable cause for the massacre which Governor Robinson, later a critic of Brown's, called "a justifiable act which saved the homes from threatened raids of the pro-slavery party."

The first reactions of even Free State men were "considerably divided," according to Judge James Hanway. Jason Brown himself condemned the killings. But once the shock wore off, and the terror of Brown's name became a significant asset against

raids from the Border Ruffians, Hanway admitted that community
approval swung sharply toward Brown. Higginson never reconciled himself to the killings, but on his Kansas trip a few
months later concluded that everyone he spoke to approved
them. In his 1860 letter, Pomeroy insisted, ". . . we all then *en-
dorsed them*—and from *that hour*, the invaders fled." Later he
stated, "That one act struck terror into the hearts of our enemy,
and gave us the dawning of success."

Even as conservative and hard-headed an analyst as Amos A.
Lawrence did not let Pottawatomie shake his faith in Brown.
" 'Old Brown of Osawatomie,' as he is called, has done and suffered more to keep slavery out of Kansas," he wrote later, "than
any other man except perhaps Robinson."

No matter how much ethical guilt clings to Brown from Pottawatomie, the fact remains that violent causes have often demanded violent solutions. If it was as essential to save Kansas
from slavery as for the Jewish settlers of Palestine to create their
own free state, Brown's decision in 1856 was no more harsh than
the bombings of the Irgun underground in 1948. Both were crucial in the anguished days before freedom. In Kansas, almost two
hundred lives had already been lost, about two million dollars'
worth of property destroyed. Governor Shannon and Judge Cato
had conclusively demonstrated that the Federal Government had
abandoned Free State communities to pillage. Brown's drastic
blow not only served notice that the Free State men were willing to take an eye for an eye. It aroused the President to the
necessity of bringing order out of chaos and appointing an im-
partial and iron-willed Governor.

Moreover, Brown's guerrilla tactics proved increasingly successful as the fighting approached its climax. At Black Jack
Springs, his small band, no more than twenty-eight and probably
smaller, captured at least twenty of a far superior Ruffian force.
At the end of August, Brown learned that Buford was advancing
on Osawatomie with four hundred men from Kansas City. With
less than forty in his company, Brown surprised and outgeneraled
him, and killed, wounded, or captured about seventy of the
Ruffians suffering only small losses himself.

This shift in Free State fortunes helped inspire a final surge of Massachusetts fund-raising. An emergency Faneuil Hall Committee collected ten thousand dollars quickly in June. The Massachusetts Kansas Aid Committee with George L. Stearns, the Medford manufacturer as chairman, raised another forty-eight thousand dollars (a rough estimate since its finances interlocked with the Faneuil Committee), and almost thirty thousand dollars in clothing. Franklin Sanborn, only a year out of Harvard, secured seventeen thousand dollars in Middlesex County alone.

Pierce was finally forced to replace Shannon as Governor with John W. Geary of Pennsylvania who set out boldly to suppress both warring factions. In September, Atchison marched on Lawrence with the greatest army of Ruffians yet assembled, at least two thousand five hundred men and a battery of 6-pounders. Geary ordered four hundred Federal troops to Lawrence. On September 15 he faced the Missourians in their camp and ordered them to disband. Atchison, realizing that the showdown had come, retreated compliantly. It was the last invasion of Kansas from Missouri, and although sporadic fighting continued, even the Ruffian leaders slowly awakened to the fact that Kansas was lost to slavery.

A year later the Free State settlers would vote down the pro-slavery Lecompton Constitution, and Robinson wrote Amos A. Lawrence, "Thank God, the battle is over in Kansas and victory is won." In July, 1858, Kansas would adopt a new constitution prohibiting slavery. In January, 1861, it joined the Union as a free state.

John Brown, however, had left Kansas to prepare his final blow. He arrived in Boston early in January, 1857, dressed in an ancient brown coat, a waistcoat buttoned nearly to his throat, and wide brown trousers that Sanborn thought gave him "the air of a respectable deacon in a rural parish." The rest of his life would be closely linked to six prominent abolitionists, five of them from Boston. It is surely a sign of these desperate days that this secret committee comprised two men of exceptional wealth, two noted divines, a brilliant educator and philanthropist, and a school principal, four being Harvard graduates. They would spend the next two years financing the plot that led to the gallows at Harpers Ferry and come perilously close to prosecution for treason themselves.

CHAPTER XVII

John Brown and the Boston Plotters: 1857–1859

IN THE first week of January, 1857, John Brown appeared unexpectedly in the Boston offices of the Kansas State Committee, presenting to Franklin Sanborn a letter of introduction from Sanborn's brother-in-law and Governor Chase of Ohio. The formality was hardly necessary. Sanborn instantly recognized the "tall, slender, and commanding" guerrilla captain. His respect for Brown, whom he credited with "virtually rescuing the Territory from the slaveholders," already approached idolatry.

Brown was welcomed enthusiastically by other members of the committee. When Sanborn brought him to Concord for a public meeting, Brown showed the enraptured audience the chains worn by his son John while being dragged four miles by Federal cavalry under the broiling Kansas sun. On a later visit to Concord, he dined with Thoreau; Emerson dropped in after dinner; Brown's deep metallic voice held them fascinated with his harsh description of Kansas warfare.

As an official hero, Brown was invited to address the Massachusetts Legislature in support of a petition giving ten thousand dollars to the Kansas settlers. The petition failed. But more important for Brown's own plans, he won the financial backing of the key members of the committee. Henceforth, Howe, Higginson, Parker, Sanborn, and Stearns, as well as Gerrit Smith of New York, would be inextricably linked to the guerrilla captain in the tangled plot that led to Harpers Ferry.

Brown was given five hundred dollars on two different occasions and a seven-thousand-dollar letter of credit for the subsistence of his company from Stearns personally, which was never used. Stearns, in addition, donated thirteen hundred dollars for the purchase of two hundred revolvers. Amos A. Lawrence, who lauded Brown as "as true representative of the Puritanic warrior," made a small personal gift and joined Stearns in contributing over half of a thousand-dollar fund to buy Brown's family a home at North Elba. "The family of 'Captain John Brown of Osawatomie' shall not be turned out to starve in this country," Lawrence wrote Brown on March 20, "until Liberty herself is driven out."

Above all, Brown needed the two hundred Sharps rifles which had been purchased by the Massachusetts Committee, turned over to the National Kansas Committee, and were now stored at Tabor, Iowa. This necessitated a complex transaction. The Massachusetts men first had to convince the National meeting in New York on January 24 that they should regain possession of the rifles. Then Stearns as chairman transferred the rifles, four thousand ball cartridges, and thirty-one thousand caps to Brown in a letter of April 15. The rifles, eventually captured at Harpers Ferry, would become a constant storm center for the Boston plotters.

Brown fretted at these long months of preparation, once snapping at a group of abolitionists, "These men are all talk; what is needed is action, action!" He hurried to Collinsville, Connecticut, and signed an order with a local foundryman for a thousand pikes, eight-inch blades attached to the end of six-foot poles. These weapons were far better suited to untrained slaves than the crack marksmen of Brown's own company. After Brown reached Tabor and took possession of the rifles, he wrote Stearns on August 10, "I am in *immediate want* of from five hundred to one thousand dollars for Secret Service and no questions asked." The Boston group might well have suspected that "Secret Service" meant a raid into the border states and a slave uprising at which Brown had hinted. But as late as November 7, Stearns expected the blow in Kansas, warning Brown in a letter, "Don't attack *them*, but if they attack you, 'Give them Jessie' and Frémont besides."

Sanborn would always insist Brown had kept his plans well hidden. "All through 1857 and the early part of 1858, however," he wrote later, "none of Brown's Massachusetts friends knew that he had any designs against Virginia."

The accidental eruption of the plot that fall finally convinced the Boston group they were involved in a far more dangerous conspiracy than they may have intended. In New York, Brown had met Hugh Forbes, an English adventurer who had fought with Garibaldi in Italy and bestowed on himself the title of "Colonel." Brown had been impressed with his knowledge of guerrilla warfare and contracted with him to train his company at one hundred dollars a month. Now Brown was hard pressed for money, and Forbes, who had a wife and family in Paris, nagged him insistently. Forbes seems to have grown cynical of Brown's ability to direct the promised blow. Vain and pompous, he may have coveted leadership of the venture himself.

In December, Forbes began to deluge Sanborn and Howe with a series of letters, describing in intimate detail Brown's scheme for a daring raid into Virginia. If they had not been previously convinced that Brown's target was no longer Kansas, the Boston group certainly knew it now—at least four or five months before the date Sanborn later admitted. Worried by the "abusive" nature of Forbes's letters, they tried to parry the threats. When Forbes got no satisfaction from them, he wrote directly to Senator Sumner and warned Sanborn he would expose the whole plot. The Boston group instantly summoned an emergency meeting, and asked Brown to hurry East.

AT FIRST glance, it seems inexplicable that men of such national prominence in business and intellectual circles would risk a flirtation with treason. Parker was at the height of his fame, Higginson already his acknowledged heir to the leadership of the liberal ministry. Smith had not only helped found the Liberty party and been elected Congressman, but his vast landholdings extended his influence throughout the East. Sanborn, although still young, had proved his executive ability on the Kansas Committee and would soon become a prominent public official.

Stearns, a shrewd, self-made industrialist, conservative enough to criticize "the women in bloomer costumes and other peculiar-looking persons who attach themselves to this branch of the movement," was an early prototype of the Horatio Alger legend. His father, a descendant of Puritan stock and a Harvard graduate, died when his son was eleven, leaving the family slim resources. He secured a job in Boston as a store boy and later as book-keeper, walking five miles to Medford each Saturday evening to see his mother and five miles back Sunday evening. Such disci-pline was evident in his dress even at the peak of his success, for he always fastened his shoes only with leather thongs and wore no ornament but a simple watchchain.

His one flamboyant touch was a still-unfashionable, flowing, ruddy-brown beard, which his doctor had ordered to protect his throat and chest against frequent bronchial infections.

After ten years of drudgery, Stearns borrowed $20,000 to go into the linseed oil business, and in six years had made a tidy fortune. He expanded into ship chandlery, and then securing a new patent for the manufacture of lead pipe, became its largest producer in New England. When he married a niece of Lydia Maria Child in 1843, a friend enthused to her, "How excellent he is, how full of all Christian graces and virtues. . . ."

Stearns applied the same diligence, self-effacement, and courage that had brought him a fortune to the abolition movement. In 1840 he was the only citizen of Medford to vote the Liberty ticket. When the Fugitive Slave Bill was passed, he purchased a revolver and announced quietly that no fugitive would ever be taken from his house. Although he hid many, one for almost a week while deputy marshals prowled in the neighborhood, none was ever taken!

Stearns had joined the Conscience Whigs in 1848, but the as-sault on Sumner drove him full time into the movement. "He crowded forty-eight hours into twenty-four," Wendell Phillips said. He worked behind the scenes, never seeking praise or lime-light. After the Kansas Committee had exhausted its usual fund-raising sources, Stearns with his wide contacts among shopkeepers and plumbers all over the state developed the idea of tapping thousands of modest earners for small contributions. Disgusted by rich friends who complained of empty pockets, he continually searched for "someone who would go without dinner for Kansas."

Dr. Howe was a more complex personality, descended from the same impeccable Puritan stock but with an overlay of sophistication, "a cavalier grace" and "easy, frank, high-spirited and courteous manners," as Sanborn described them, that made him unique among abolitionists. Howe had an almost Byronic quality, and Whittier considered him the representative American hero of his time. Along with Garibaldi, Dr. Bowditch ranked him "the *manliest* man it has been my good fortune to meet in this world."

Like Byron, Howe joined the Greek struggle for liberation against the Turkish Empire, a grueling enlistment of almost five years that established his reputation even before his formal career began. Only recently out of Harvard Medical School, he worked relentless hours, "dressing the wounded until exhausted, then throwing himself upon the ground & resting a few moments, he would again resume his labour," another volunteer wrote. Howe claimed he had dressed more wounds in Greece than he could have done in a lifetime in Boston. He came under occasional gunfire and was critically ill with malaria. He organized hospitals, distributed American relief supplies, and even directed the construction of harbor facilities.

Howe returned home, honored as a Chevalier of the Order of St. Savior by the King of Greece after independence, and bringing Byron's cavalry helmet which he always kept on the hat tree at his door. The aura of romantic adventure always clung to him, and his friends subtly recognized it by calling him "Chev." The aura was brightened considerably in 1832 when he was arrested mysteriously in Berlin and held incommunicado in a tiny dungeon, possibly because of his assistance to the Poles against the Prussian government which Lafayette praised in a public statement.

Howe had just been appointed director of the Perkins Institution and Massachusetts School for the Blind. Adapting advanced European methods to his own radical techniques, he not only made Perkins the nation's outstanding center for the blind, but advanced its frontiers to include the deaf blind. After his first report on Laura Bridgman in 1838, Howe and his remarkable pupil would become world famous. Laura was considered a modern miracle, her name virtually a household word. By 1843,

Howe had developed similar schools in many states. He would go on to support Dorothea Dix in her reforms of prisons and institutions for the insane. And next to Horace Mann, he would become the foremost advocate of public education in Massachusetts.

A strikingly handsome man almost six feet tall, with a mass of brown hair worn in the loose, flowing style of the period, Howe's ebullient charm extended his popularity far beyond abolition circles. In 1843 he married Julia Ward, eighteen years younger than himself, the brilliant daughter of a socially prominent New York banker, known with her sisters as "the three graces of Bond Street." His closest friends were the "Five of Clubs," an informal association including not only the radical Sumner and Longfellow but two stanch Hunker Whigs, Cornelius Felton and George Hillard. An early convert to Free Soil, he ran for Congress, later helped elect Sumner to the Senate, and worked diligently in the Vigilance and Kansas Committees. But "while his political associates were ostracized in Boston by the rich and Toryish families," Sanborn shrewdly noted, Howe's popularity was so wide that he "could never be sent to Coventry. . . ."

While abolition had become respectable by 1857, and even Brown's Kansas guerrillas could be supported by pillars of society like A. A. Lawrence, the Virginia plot was another matter. All six members of the secret committee assumed grave risks. And it is extremely doubtful that they would have threatened their business and professional standings merely because Brown represented "the fulfillment of their imaginary drama," as a recent critic has claimed.

Drama there was. And Howe, Higginson, and Sanborn always had a taste for it. But such cautious businessmen as Stearns and Smith would hardly play at treason for thrills. Nor was this simply a neurotic attempt to live dangerously through another man. Higginson and Howe particularly had already tested their courage. Almost all had faced years of abuse without flinching.

The reason for what seems like an improbable gamble lies more in their judgment of the slavery crisis. The desperate extremes of the Missouri Ruffians proved that the slavery bloc would never settle for the *status quo*, the confinement of slavery to its present boundaries, which was the aim of most Republicans.

In March, 1857, moreover, while Brown visited the secret committee, the crisis was intensified by the Dred Scott decision. The case, seemingly on the simple point of whether a slave who had been taken by his master into Illinois and Minnesota, where the Northwest Ordinance and Missouri Compromise made him free, could claim his freedom on returning to Missouri, resulted in a Supreme Court opinion far beyond the issue of Scott's status. It decreed that, "Congress has no power to abolish or prevent slavery in any of the territories." Thus it opened a new holocaust far greater than Kansas. For even Douglas's doctrine of popular sovereignty would be destroyed. The settlers of a new territory could hardly establish a free soil constitution if Congress had no power to enforce it.

The Boston plotters certainly recognized that the Virginia raid was a calculated gamble. It would not only infuriate the South; it could bring the nation close to war. The pressure of the Dred Scott decision seemingly justified the gamble. If slavery not only could not be abolished, but no longer confined, the only alternative was to weaken it violently by slave raids. And rightly or wrongly, the secret committee had unlimited faith in Brown to execute them.

On his way East, Brown stopped off first to visit Frederick Douglass at Rochester. Years later, Douglass would recall Brown's infatuation with the natural advantages of guerrilla warfare in the Alleghenies in a conversation as far back as 1847. Brown had insisted then, "They are full of natural forts where one man for defense will be equal to a hundred for attack. . . . [I] could take a body of men into them and keep them there despite of all the efforts of Virginia to dislodge them."

Forbes's threats had now forced Brown to travel incognito, all letters from the plotters addressed to him as N. Hawkins. Brown wanted the Boston group to meet with him and Gerrit

Smith at Peterboro, but only Sanborn could make the trip. Brown arrived on February 18, Sanborn on the 22nd. And there in Smith's sprawling ancestral mansion, sitting up past midnight, Brown at last told his accomplices, including Edwin Morton, a classmate of Sanborn's at Harvard who served as Smith's secretary, his daring plan for a slave raid in the Alleghenies.

Sanborn later claimed they listened with "astonishment and almost dismay." The council put forward a series of cogent obstacles, all of which Brown swept aside. A year of delay had only quickened his aggressive temper. His iron will had become rigid inflexibility. Sanborn wrote later that, "No objective moved him from his purpose. . . ." Walking together at sunset over the snow-covered hills, Smith told Sanborn, "We cannot give him up to die alone; we must stand by him." Sanborn returned to Boston to tell Howe, Parker, and Higginson of the plan. None objected enough to its dangers to withdraw support. Brown arrived in Boston early in March to inform Stearns directly in a secret meeting at the American House.

While Brown hurried to Chatham, Canada, to present twelve white and thirty-four Negro supporters with an elaborate constitution he expected to enforce in his guerrilla domain in the Alleghenies, the plotters were feverishly concerned with Forbes. After the embittered Englishman had threatened full disclosure, Sanborn wrote Higginson on May 5, "It looks as if the project must, for the present, be deferred. . . ." Smith agreed. "I never was convinced of the wisdom of his [Brown's] scheme," he wrote Sanborn on May 7. "But as things now stand, it seems to me it would be madness to attempt to execute it." Higginson stood fast, writing Parker on May 9, "I regard any postponement as simply abandoning the project."

The danger, however, was now accelerated by the fact that Forbes had informed Senators Wilson, Seward, and Hale of the plot, even forcing his way into Wilson's presence on the Senate floor. Fortunately, only Wilson, who had some inkling of the involvement of the Boston conspirators, took Forbes seriously. Wilson was particularly concerned that if Brown used the Sharps rifles in a blow at Virginia, the whole Kansas Committee would be incriminated. The Kansas Committee, whose membership was virtually identical with that of the secret committee, therefore invented a flimsy subterfuge to protect its name. Since Stearns had made many personal advances to the Committee, it voted to turn over the rifles to him as "security" for his loans. The transfer was formalized in a letter, and although Howe destroyed the original after Harpers Ferry, a copy with Brown's endorsement was found among his papers at North Elba after his death.

As personal owner of the rifles, Stearns wrote Brown on May 14 that they were to be used only for the defense of Kansas and that Brown should "hold them subject to my order as Chairman of Said Committee." Howe then informed Senator Wilson of this transaction, and the Boston plotters seemed to have convinced themselves that the problem had been neatly erased. Later Sanborn tried to prove that "the transaction by which the arms were pledged to Mr. Stearns really took place long before any of us knew of the Virginia plans." This stretched the truth considerably, for the plotters certainly knew the general vicinity where the blow was to be struck, although Brown had only mentioned Harper's Ferry to sound out their opinion.

The secret committee now held a hurried meeting at the Revere House in Boston on May 24. They agreed Brown's attack should be postponed until the spring of 1859 and that Brown should return to Kansas to dispel Forbes's suspicions. Brown arrived four days later. He heard the decision sorrowfully but gave his consent. His sorrow was tempered by another donation of five hundred dollars and the pledge of a few thousand more next spring.

The plotters were already indulging in verbal gyrations to hide their complicity. Smith assured Sanborn by letter on July 26, "Whenever he shall embark in another of these contests I shall again stand ready to help him; and I will begin with giving him a hundred dollars. I do not wish to know Captain Brown's plans. I hope he will keep them to himself." Despite Smith's later denials, he had already met Brown twice at Peterboro and once in Boston and contributed handsomely to the raid. Sanborn too would insist, "the alleged property of the Kansas Committee [its rifles] was to be so transferred as to relieve the Committee of all responsibility, and the secret committee were, in future, to know nothing in detail of Brown's plans."

The plotters, however, were too deeply involved to make such thinly veiled attempts to remain half in and half out of the raid. Sanborn later defended the rifle transfer as "mainly a blind to satisfy Senator Wilson and other Republican politicians." This may well have been true. But the insistence that Brown should keep his future plans to himself, the assumption that the secret committee could supply him with arms and money and refuse responsibility for their use, was their first show of weakness.

Brown returned to Kansas in June and began preparing his slave raid into Missouri. He struck on December 20, 1858, releasing eleven or twelve slaves whom he transported to freedom in Canada. It was a minor maneuver, in effect, a practice run for Harpers Ferry. For the number of slaves rescued was not Brown's main concern. His theory was that such raids would keep the planters under unbearable pressure. "His object," Douglass pointed out, "was to make slavery unprofitable by making it insecure."

In early April, 1859, Brown visited his wife at North Elba for the last time and reached Gerrit Smith's home on April 11. Smith always expressed his devotion to the guerrilla captain profusely. The previous August he had written, "To no man living is so much praise due for beating back the tide of border ruffianism and slavery as to my old and dear friend, John Brown of Osawatomie." At this meeting, he proclaimed, "If I were asked to point out—I will say it in his presence—to point out the man in all this world I think most Christian, I would point to John Brown."

Later that summer, only a few months before Harpers Ferry, he would indirectly reaffirm his support of the Virginia plan, telling a colored meeting in Syracuse, "For insurrections then we may look any year, any month, any day. A terrible remedy for a terrible wrong! But come it must. . . ."

Brown went on to Boston, registering in his own name at the United States House, strolling calmly down Court Street, peeling an apple with a jackknife despite curious stares from pedestrians at the lanky rustic figure with the flowing white beard. The Governor of Missouri had put a three-thousand-dollar price on his head after the recent raid, the President had added two hundred and fifty dollars. But although he was always armed and accompanied by a bodyguard, Brown attempted no concealment on this trip.

In fact, he addressed a public meeting at Concord's Town Hall on his last birthday, attended a Bird Club dinner at the Parker House, and spoke to another assemblage at Boston's Tremont Temple. John Andrew, soon to be Governor of the Commonwealth, met Brown and gave him twenty-five dollars, noting that he seemed "entirely self-possessed, sufficient to himself."

Brown stayed over one night at the home of John Murray Forbes in Milton. By an almost freak coincidence, the Governor of Missouri arrived the next day to discuss railroad construction with the financier and slept in the same room that Brown had just occupied.

At Brown's final conference with the secret committee, the promised two thousand dollars was given him, over half donated by Stearns alone. Brown now stopped at Collinsville, Connecticut, to pay for the pikes which were shipped to Chambersburg, Pennsylvania. The last the secret committee heard from him was in August when his money ran out and he asked for another three hundred dollars. It was sent to Chambersburg in small drafts to avoid suspicion. Brown himself, meanwhile, had rented the Kennedy farm as his headquarters on the Maryland side of the Potomac River, five miles from Harpers Ferry. There his men joined him.

Sanborn later claimed he thought the raid would be made from Ohio rather than Washington or Maryland. Yet the Boston plotters obviously knew Brown's Chambersburg address and may even have divulged it to a few Boston confidants. Lewis Hayden, in fact, met Francis Jackson Merriam on the street shortly afterward and asked for a contribution. "If you tell me John Brown is there," Merriam replied, "you can have my money and me along with it."

Merriam, grandson of that early Garrisonian, Francis Jackson, was a young man of twenty-two who had traveled widely in Europe and the West Indies. He had inherited a small estate, and when he arrived in Chambersburg on October 9, he brought six hundred dollars in gold, immediately used to replenish the dwindling supplies. Untrained in guerrilla tactics, and unstable in temperament, he was left to guard the arms in a schoolhouse on the Maryland side of the river during the raid. After Brown's capture, he escaped in a harrowing march across the mountains, finally reaching Canada in safety.

Douglass, already privy to the general plan, was implicated further at the last minute when Brown summoned him to Chambersburg. At their meeting place, an old stone quarry outside town, Brown arrived, disguised as a fisherman, and proceeded to describe the Harpers Ferry attack in detail. "I at once opposed the massacre with all the arguments at my command . . . ," Douglass stated later. "He was not to be shaken by anything I could say. . . . " Brown implored him to join his company, but Douglass was adamant.

As a result of the Chatham conference, the Forbes disclosures, and possible gossip by Brown's own company, the plot was now known to a dangerously large circle. It is little wonder that a warning letter reached Secretary of War John B. Floyd on August 20, stating that a "secret organization" for "the liberation of the slaves of the South" would soon "enter Virginia at Harpers Ferry." The informant might have been Forbes himself, but more likely an Iowa friend of Brown's who hoped to avoid what he considered certain disaster by stopping the attack beforehand. Misled by the erroneous mention of a nonexistent Maryland armory, Floyd, a man not easily ruffled, considered the letter the work of a crank and filed it away.

Brown was troubled by increasing information leaks. In addition, the restlessness of his company in the confines of the farmhouse and Merriam's arrival, solving the money shortage, may have made him move up his schedule. A chill mist was rising from the Potomac on the night of Sunday, October 16, when he gave the order, "Men, get your arms; we will proceed to the Ferry."

By midnight, Brown's company had taken the town, cut the telegraph wires, and barricaded itself in the armory and other strong points. Brown sent out a scout party to capture prominent citizens from the neighborhood as hostages. Their slaves, immediately freed, would form the nucleus of the uprising. Already church bells were sounding the alarm, and messengers had reached nearby Charles Town. The next morning the Jefferson Guards boarded a train for the Ferry. Troops were coming from Fredericksburg and Fort Monroe. Colonel Robert E. Lee commanded a company of Marines from Washington.

Still Brown delayed although John Kagi begged him to retreat to the mountains as planned. Instead, he withdrew the remnants of his company to the enginehouse. He insisted the wounded could not be left behind. One son was dead, another dying. Almost no support had come from the neighboring slaves. Brown had misjudged the area; the slaves were few and widely scattered. His final error was to make a fortress of the enginehouse, cutting off any last chance of escape. On the morning of October 18, the Marines battered through its door. Of the original band of twenty-two, six were seized with Brown, ten were dead or dying, only five had escaped.

DOUGLASS was filling a speaking engagement in Philadelphia when blaring headlines announced the Harpers Ferry raid. His letters had been found in a carpetbag at the Kennedy farm, which Brown had foolishly left, giving no orders to his guards to destroy them in case of a catastrophe. Now they were turned over to Governor Wise of Virginia. Hurrying to New York, Douglass telegraphed his son at Rochester to hide all crucial correspondence. By the time he reached home, his friends were convinced that New York might allow Virginia to requisition his presence at Brown's trial. As an escaped slave, he would be in serious jeopardy. Douglass, therefore, fled to Canada and then sailed for England. "I have been informed that several United States Marshals were in Rochester in search of me within six hours after my departure," he wrote later.

The names of Gerrit Smith and other plotters were found among Brown's papers at almost the same time. On October 21, the *New York Herald* accused them of being "accessories before the fact" in treason. Smith immediately destroyed all pertinent letters and sent his son-in-law to Boston and to the Ohio home of John Brown, Jr., to eradicate as much evidence as possible. He grew panicky, hardly sleeping or eating. His servants went around the house armed. Friends guarded the doors. A *Herald* reporter who visited him found him highly overwrought, his eyes "bloodshot and restless as [those] of a startled horse." Only the year before, he had been a candidate for Governor, and he still had political ambitions. But it was not fear alone that affected his mind. A deeply religious man, he held himself responsible for the Harpers Ferry disaster. On November 7, five days after Brown had been sentenced to death, he broke down completely. His doctor confined him to New York State Asylum for the Insane at Utica.

Smith was able to return home before the end of the year, and in January, 1860, the Senate Committee of Investigation under Senator James Mason of Virginia summoned him to testify. His doctor pleaded illness, and Smith never appeared. All this is understandable. But after recovering his health, Smith launched a startling campaign to disassociate himself from Brown and the Boston plotters. In May, 1860, a committee of prominent citizens in New York released a report describing the activities of Smith and the secret committee in fairly accurate detail. Smith dispatched a long letter to the *Herald*, admitting only that he had given Brown money and denying all complicity with the raid. He demanded a retraction from the committee. When it was not made, he brought suit. The committee, in turn, threatened to prove its contentions in court but finally backed down.

Even two years after the war, Smith was still protesting his innocence in lawsuits and libel actions, one against John Brown, Jr., who testified in 1867 that Smith "aided by advice and money and counsel. . . . No attempt at concealment in any degree was had in the interviews with Mr. Smith." Sanborn, too, stated that Smith "knew as much as anybody did, sympathized as much and aided as much. A check for $100 . . . found in Brown's possession at his capture and sent by Smith to Chambersburg . . . establishes the fact that his presence there was known to Smith. . . ."

When Sanborn asked Smith's cooperation as late as 1872 in preparing an accurate report on the raid, Smith concluded his unfortunate retreat by refusing even to discuss the affair. "In every fresh turn I fear a recurrence of my insanity," he pleaded.

Dr. Howe and Stearns, with an unnecessarily hasty discretion, since it was unlikely Governor Banks would have allowed Virginia to requisition their presence at the trial, also fled to Canada. Both returned, however, to face the Senate Investigating Committee and boldly parried all Senator Mason's attempts to find "where this money was supplied." Stearns made a particularly vigorous defense of Brown, proclaiming, "I believe John Brown to be the representative man of this century, as Washington was of the last—the Harpers Ferry affair, and the capacity shown by the Italians for self-government, the great events of the age."

While still in Canada, Howe issued a "card" to the newspapers on November 19, protesting that, "The outbreak at Harpers Ferry was unforeseen and unexpected by me. . . ." It was hardly as extreme as Smith's disclaimers, but at the same time an unexpected compromise. In a letter of January 22, 1860, to Parker, who had gone to Italy long before the raid in a futile attempt to save his crumbling health, Smith repeated the old evasions, insisting his last words to Brown had been, "Captain Brown, don't tell me what you are about or where you are going, and let me advise you not to tell anyone else."

To Sumner, Howe insisted he had issued his "card" so that by disassociating Brown from the secret committee, the Virginia courts might be more inclined to spare his life. To Parker, Howe explained sorrowfully, "that my 'card' seems to have conveyed an impression stronger than I meant it to do—that of a total disclaimer." Higginson, however, unmoved by such excuses, criticized "the extreme baseness in us to deny complicity with

Captain Brown's general scheme" and snapped at Howe, "Is there no such thing as *honor* among confederates?"

As always, Higginson stood firm. Refusing either to flee to Canada or testify before the Senate Committee, he busied himself collecting funds for Brown's defense counsel. Somehow he escaped unscathed, but Thaddeus Hyatt, president of the National Kansas Committee was not as lucky. Refusing to answer a Senate subpoena, he was arrested and jailed for three months. James Redpath, the newspaper correspondent and close friend of Brown's, avoided a subpoena by going into hiding. John Brown, Jr., promptly fortified his home and announced that they would have to drag him to Washington to testify at gunpoint.

Sanborn, who had taken a brief, six-day refuge in Canada, was the only Boston plotter who resorted to violence in resisting a Senate subpoena. Two United States marshals came to Concord one afternoon, and hiding in an old barn near the school, kept him under surveillance. After Sanborn went home to dinner, they were joined by two more marshals, bringing a carriage to his door. They presented the subpoena and started to drag him to the carriage. But Sanborn, a powerful man, resisted furiously. Hearing his cries, his sister Sarah slashed at the horses with a whip, so that it was almost impossible for the officers to force their prisoner into the careening carriage. The neighbors, meanwhile, rushed down the street, pounding on doors. Soon the clanging church bell alerted the town.

Judge Rockwood Hoar, a prominent Republican, issued a writ of *habeas corpus* on the spot, and the Sheriff deputized everyone in sight, including Emerson, to assist him in wresting Sanborn from the marshal's clutches. After the rescue, a special town meeting honored Miss Sarah for her bravery. When the government's case against Sanborn came to trial in Boston, it was quashed on a technicality.

Although Andrew and Sewall worked determinedly on the legal brief which formed the basis of George Hoyt's defense before the Virginia court, Higginson was convinced that only a rescue could save Brown. The immediate problem was making contact with the prisoner. John W. LeBarnes of Boston, an associate of

Higginson's, expected Hoyt to function more as a spy than a defense counsel. Hoyt was only twenty-one. Instead of disarming suspicion, however, his youthfulness helped alert the Virginia authorities. No one was allowed to enter Brown's cell without a guard present. Stearns wanted to finance a plot that would bring Mary Partridge, a friend of Brown's, from Kansas to Charles Town. Throwing her arms around the prisoner's neck, she would force a wad of paper with the rescue plan into his mouth. Although Lydia Maria Child probably had no connection with Higginson's maneuvers, she begged Governor Wise to let her nurse Brown but was bluntly rejected. Rebecca Buffum Spring was finally allowed into his cell and complained of "the rabble, ever hanging about the Court House and prison, fearful that we were plotting treason inside. . . ."

Higginson even made a special trip to North Elba to convince Mrs. Brown to visit her husband, thinking she might be useful as a contact. But it was not until December 1 that she was permitted in Charles Town. And then a reporter noted, "her clothing was searched for concealed weapons, or other means which the morbid suspicion of the Virginia army of occupation suggested Mrs. Brown might surreptitiously convey to her husband."

Even a contact was meaningless after Brown insisted to Hoyt and Judge Thomas Russell of Boston that he opposed all rescue plots. He not only felt a deep obligation to the kindness of his jailer, Captain John Avis, but seemed intent on martyrdom. "I am not sure that it would not be better for me to die at this time," he told a *New York Tribune* reporter. When Samuel Pomeroy visited him, he repeated, "I am worth infinitely more now to die than to live."

Without Brown's cooperation, the only chance of rescue was direct assault by a large force. Higginson, Howe, and Sanborn hurriedly began to collect men and money, but they soon found the cost far beyond their reach. Besides, Governor Wise was taking infinite precautions. Almost every day, as scare warnings inundated his office, he shuttled fresh companies of infantry and artillery back and forth from Richmond and Petersburg. Almost a thousand troops were constantly kept in Charles Town. Nervously, he begged Buchanan to send three hundred Federal artillerymen and kept the town virtually under martial law. In case of a rescue attempt, the guards had orders to shoot Brown immediately. Five fires had already been set in the neighborhood, and the Richmond papers constantly carried new reports. The authorities considered them the work of antislavery agents. More likely they had been set by slaves.

The surrounding planters, fearing a slave uprising, slept in town at night, and sentry lines were extended farther and farther from the jail. The soldiers had grown so jittery that when a grazing cow one night approached the lines, a sentry demanded the countersign, and receiving no reply, shot the bovine intruder.

As a last resort, Higginson and LeBarnes accepted the plan proposed by Lysander Spooner, the veteran Boston abolitionist, to kidnap Wise and hold him as hostage against Brown's life. They would take a fast steamboat up the James River with a highly trained guerrilla band, recruited from Kansas or New York, which would capture the Governor at his home at night and spirit him down the river before Virginia troops could give chase. By November 20, Spooner had even hired a boat and pilot. On November 27, LeBarnes wrote Higginson from New York that he had secured the rescue party. But the cost, particularly the necessity of providing for the men's families in case of death, would reach at least fifteen thousand dollars. Higginson could raise nowhere near that amount, and time was running out. Besides, they recognized the odds against them, for even if the kidnaping succeeded, there was no surety that Virginia would guarantee Brown's life for the Governor's. At the last minute, the plot was abandoned.

Higginson's tough, agile mind, however, refused to admit defeat. Even after Brown and four of his band went to the gallows, he concocted one more plot that came remarkably close to saving the last survivors, Aaron D. Stevens and Albert H. Hazlett.

This time he collected almost two thousand dollars. Charles P. Tidd, who was hiding in Ohio after his escape from Harpers Ferry, was summoned to Boston for consultation. To lead the rescue, Higginson recruited Captain James Montgomery, who had known Brown in Kansas and built an enviable record himself as a guerrilla fighter.

Montgomery brought five men from Kansas and Iowa, but his key assistants were Amasa Soule and two compatriots who had engineered the daring rescue of Dr. John Doy from the St. Joseph, Missouri, jail not long before. Doy had been caught while helping a slave escape and sentenced to five years at hard labor. Soule had gained admission to the jail on the excuse of bringing a message from Doy's wife, and by distracting the guard for a moment, informed Doy of the prison break that night. Shortly before midnight, when crowds were pouring out of the theater across the street, Soule's band dragged an accomplice into jail whom they accused of being a horse thief. As the jailer opened the iron grate, they held him prisoner at gunpoint, snatched Doy from his cell, and disappeared into the throng of revelers outside.

After Montgomery met Higginson on February 16, 1860, at Harrisburg, Pennsylvania, they agreed to follow the same technique in the Charles Town rescue. Higginson listed the major obstacles in a memorandum: a week's journey through mountainous country, traveling only at night; penetration of the sentry lines; scaling a fourteen-foot-high wall; retreat with the prisoners and possible wounded by daylight.

Montgomery and Soule first decided to reconnoiter the jail and its surroundings. Soule's accent aroused no suspicions since he had been born in Kentucky. He impersonated a drunken Irishman so successfully that he was immediately arrested and locked in the same jail with the Harper's Ferry prisoners. Charming the jailer with his Irish songs, he had no trouble reaching Stevens and Hazlett.

The two men, however, insisted that the heavy prison guard imposed an extreme risk on the rescue party. Montgomery, too, found the surrounding country efficiently patrolled. Even then, they might have gone ahead except for one insurmountable obstacle. A heavy snowstorm came up, covering the ground with such deep drifts that escape through the mountains would have been hazardous at best and impossible if any of the party had been wounded. In a melancholy conference at Harrisburg, Higginson and Montgomery agreed to give up the attempt. Higginson concluded in his diary, "The effort to rescue Stevens and Hazlett—undertaken on my sole responsibility—restored my self-respect. It did not fail like the Brown rescue through the timidity of others—but simply through the impossibility of the thing."

Almost twenty years later, Higginson visited the Charles Town jail, and his wife and biographer, Mary Thacher Higginson, wrote, "When he looked at the high and apparently impregnable wall, he felt fully convinced that Montgomery's judgment was sound."

ALOOF FROM the rescue plots, John Brown waited for death, evoking from the violence of his last years a dignity and almost joy that reached the nation in letters that flowed constantly from his pen. "I am awaiting the hour of my public murder with great composure and cheerfulness," he wrote in his last letter to his family, "feeling the strongest assurance that in no other possible way could I be used to so much advance the cause of God and of humanity. . . . I have now no doubt that our seeming disaster will ultimately result in the most glorious success."

On December 2, he was awake early, reading his Bible. Outside the jail, his black coffin was placed on a wagon surrounded by three companies of infantry. Brown seated himself on the coffin for the final ride. In the field where fifteen hundred Virginia militia were massed, among them a private named J. Wilkes Booth, Brown mounted the scaffold. For twelve minutes he stood quietly with the noose around his neck while the militia formed in a great hollow square. The trap was sprung. His body jerked and dangled from the rope for twenty minutes.

As he had left his cell that morning, he had handed an attendant his last message: "I, John Brown, am now quite certain that the crimes of this *guilty land: will* never be purged *away;* but with Blood."

In Boston a hushed and overflow audience waited at Tremont Temple. A photograph of John Brown against a huge black cross dominated the hall. At the scheduled moment of his execution, people wept openly; Emerson told them, Brown has "made the gallows glorious like a cross." In the evening at the same hall, Garrison proclaimed, "Today Virginia has murdered John Brown; tonight, we here witness his resurrection. . . ."

Boston had received its ultimate martyr. Already Judge Russell's wife had brought back a blood-soaked pin from Brown's cell as the first "relic" and letters and pieces of Brown's clothing were being hawked at mounting prices. Soon, the 12th Massachusetts Regiment would march through the city, singing the John Brown Song, improvised by four of its members, "His soul goes marching on."

"It is the John Brown in every man's conscience that the South is afraid of," Phillips shrewdly predicted.

"Whether the enterprise of John Brown and his associates in Virginia was wise or foolish, right or wrong," John Andrew concluded, "I only know that whether the enterprise was the one or the other, John Brown himself is right."

CHAPTER XVIII

Jubilee Year and the Puritan Radicals: 1860–1863

EVEN CONSERVATIVE Republican leaders like Samuel Bowles of Springfield were appalled by Andrew's "John Brown sympathies and speeches." The chubby-faced, red-cheeked, immoderately boyish-looking lawyer was "a genuine, 'regular built' antislavery man . . . 'clear down to his boots,' " said Warrington, the political columnist. He had defended Higginson and other abolitionists after their indictment in the Burns case in 1854. He had directed John Brown's legal defense, represented Sanborn in his trial for evading arrest by the United States Marshal, and proudly told the Senate investigating committee he had contributed money to Captain Brown. When Andrew was picked to run for Governor in 1860, Republican politicians begged him to renounce the guerrilla captain. Andrew insisted, "I sympathize with the man; I sympathize with the idea; because I sympathize and believe in the Eternal Right."

Two conventions had failed to hold the Democratic party together, and its Southern wing was running Vice President John C. Breckinridge of Kentucky; its Northern wing, Senator Douglas of Illinois. In addition, remnants of the old Whigs, now called the Constitutional-Unionists, supported Senator John Bell of Tennessee. Andrew's opponents, determined to destroy him with the John Brown label, sent swarms of boys through the streets, chanting "Tell John Andrew, Tell John Andrew, Tell John Andrew, John Brown's dead." But even the wily Caleb Cushing, still gambling on his planter friends in the Breckinridge movement, had underestimated the grip of radical Republicanism on the Commonwealth. Lincoln and Andrew swept the state.

The Republicans' 107,000 votes, in fact, gave them a decisive plurality over all other parties; Douglas polling thirty-four thousand; Bell, twenty-two thousand; and Breckinridge about six thousand. It was now established that the coalition of farmers and mechanics, which had steadily deserted Jacksonian democracy in the last decade, had joined the Republicans en masse.

No sooner had clanging church bells rung out the news when South Carolina announced its intention of leaving the Union. In Boston, crowds of well-dressed merchant-clerks, Bell and Breckinridge men, strikingly similar to the mob which had once chased Garrison, poured into State Street. A new panic, a secession panic, seized the city, making abolition its scapegoat. For four months it was almost as if the clock had been turned back to 1835.

On DECEMBER 3, a year and a day after John Brown went to the gallows, the rioters invaded a commemorative meeting at Tremont Temple. They drowned out the first speaker, Franklin Sanborn, with what one reporter described as "beastly bellowings" and "serpent-like hisses." They interrupted every sentence with cheers for Bell, for Tennessee, for Georgia, for one of their own local candidates, Richard S. Fay who stood in the gallery, hurling seat cushions at the platform. There was a comic opera quality to these interruptions. "Where's John Brown?" demanded one voice. "He's safe," shouted a second voice, "the devil has him!" Then Fay challenged the platform to elect a permanent chairman. More shouts of approval. Fifty policemen had arrived, but made no attempt to bring order. A vote was called, and since the rioters outnumbered the guests, they elected Fay permanent chairman. Fay climbed to the platform, promptly announced that the meeting was adjourned, and called on the police to clear the hall.

Frederick Douglass, insisting that he have the chance to be heard, managed to shout one sentence: "This is one of the most impudent (shouts: Order! Order!), barefaced (Knock him down!), outrageous acts on free speech (Stop him!) that I have ever witnessed in Boston or elsewhere." At this point one reporter noted that "the uproar which had been perfectly deafening for some minutes increased so much that the speaker was inaudible." Cushions rained on the platform, chairs were smashed in heaps. The police finally seized on a unique solution: they hustled Douglass from the hall. Meanwhile, the mayor had arrived and decided that instead of protecting the meeting, he would close Tremont Temple.

That night the meeting convened at the Joy Street Church with Wendell Phillips as the main speaker. The police succeeded in keeping the mob outside, but when Phillips left the building, almost two thousand rioters surrounded him. Fortunately, forty young abolitionists had designated themselves as a bodyguard. With police assistance, they got him home safely, the mob cursing at their heels and showering them with stones. "D_____n him!" shouted one rioter, according to the Worcester *Spy*. "He has depreciated stocks three million dollars by his slang!"

That part of the business community which had supported Bell and Breckinridge now vented its fury on the abolitionists for the Republican victory and the increasing failure of Southern trade. Northern merchants had at least 200 million dollars in debts among the slave states. With Western trade still crippled by the 1857 panic, Boston and other Eastern ports were heavily dependent on the South. The stock exchanges fluctuated wildly. Many New England manufacturers closed their factories or cut their employment rolls. As Southern states canceled orders, shoemakers in Lynn, Haverhill, and Marblehead, Massachusetts, went on strike against wage cuts. "Boston streets today are full of discharged workmen," the *Daily Courier* wrote on December 3. The Reverend J. J. Bowen of Pittsfield, Massachusetts, announced two weeks later, "I firmly believe that in ninety days the doors of every mill will be closed. . . ." John Murray Forbes warned Sumner, "Our money people have been badly frightened and many decent-looking men . . . would try to have a kind of compromise made. . . ."

To bolster their dwindling profits, some Northern shippers revived the illegal slave trade, making at least half a million dollars from a single voyage. "No wonder Boston, New York and

Philadelphia have so much interest in the business," wrote the American consul at Key West.*

Die-hard Cotton Whigs like Nathan Appleton were still convinced the crisis could be blinked away. "I say to the North, the Free States," he wrote former Senator William C. Rives of Virginia, "why agitate and discuss at all the question of slavery? . . . To the South I would say . . . why trouble yourself about slavery in the territories to which it is not suited?"

On Sunday, December 16, when Phillips was invited to address Theodore Parker's congregation, a mob surrounded the Music Hall. This time the police had taken the precaution of stationing units not only outside but around the platform. Phillips's bodyguard and a wedge of hundreds of policemen broke through the mob and managed to escort him home. Phillips and his friends now carried pistols. A permanent guard was maintained at his Essex Street house. Without the police that Sunday, one official told reporters, "he never would have got home alive."

On January 24, 1861, the mob invaded Tremont Temple where the Massachusetts Antislavery Society was holding its annual meeting. The new mayor had sent only a token police force, and the rioters quickly took over the galleries. "Such yelling, screeching, stamping and bellowing I never heard," wrote Lydia Maria Child. "Mr. Phillips stood on the platform for a full hour trying to be heard. Whenever the storm lulled a little, they cried, 'Throw him out!' 'Throw a brickbat at him!' "

Finally the rioters poured down to the main floor and made a rush for Phillips. His bodyguard beat them back, and Phillips shouted above the din, "We will have free speech yet. Massachusetts is not conquered; the Capitol is not owned by State Street and whoever is Mayor of Boston, John A. Andrew is Governor of the Commonwealth."

Phillips immediately went to the governor's office and insisted he should protect the rights of the Society to transact its business and present its speakers. Much as he supported the meeting, Andrew asked what he could do. Call out the State militia to

* House Executive Documents No. 7, 36th Congress, 2nd Session, p. 450, quoted in Philip Foner, *Business and Slavery*, p. 167.

put down the rioters, Phillips answered. Andrew brought out a copy of the Revised Statutes of Massachusetts. What statute gave him this power? Phillips insisted that free speech was a common law right, but the governor shook his head. Phillips stomped angrily out of the office.

By midafternoon the rioters had taken complete possession of the Society's meeting. The mayor finally arrived with police reinforcements. But instead of imposing order, he insisted the session be terminated, promising, however, to protect the evening speeches with a heavy guard. An hour later, he secretly countermanded the order and had the police chief close Tremont Temple. The rioters decided to celebrate by marching a thousand strong on Phillips's house, shouting, "Hoe him out! Carve him out!" His bodyguard held them off until the police arrived and battled for hours to clear the streets. For weeks thereafter mobs roamed the neighborhood. Phillips's home was a fortress under siege.

THE BOSTON mobs were only the surface manifestation of a deeper panic that swept the North as South Carolina prepared to leave the Union. Fear penetrated the highest levels of Republicanism, and the party often seemed ready to break apart. "My best energies have been devoted to keep our men *firm*, FIRM, FIRM," Sumner told Dr. Howe. Lincoln not only lacked a majority of the popular vote; the Republicans had failed to gain control of either the Senate or House. As Southern states poured out their grievances, pointing particularly at the Personal Liberty Acts which nullified the Fugitive Slave Law, at least five Northern governors hastened to promise that the acts would be repealed. Although the Massachusetts act had been the model for the nation, even Banks, the outgoing governor, joined the parade of timidity.

As soon as Andrew took office, he came out against repeal. But the conservatives put heavy pressure on him. Andrew began to waver, fearing he might lose control of a third of his party at the start of his term. In March he agreed to modify the law.

Maine and Vermont followed the same pattern; Rhode Island under a Democratic governor repealed its law outright.

Such compromises, however, were ignored by the South. The extremists, who had made it clear in October that Lincoln's election meant secession, listened to nothing. Still, Senator John J. Crittenden of Kentucky, aspiring to Clay's mantle of peacemaker, proposed his drastic amendments on December 18, 1860. One would extend the Missouri line of 36° 30′ to California, opening everything south of it to slavery. Another would forbid any future change by Congress of the status of slavery.

The Crittenden amendments were hardly a compromise; they were almost a complete surrender, giving up "the advanced position for freedom which had been gained after long years of conflict," as Forbes lamented, giving the South guarantees it had never dared claim before. South Carolina, however, was determined to reject even the most sweeping supplications. On the day Crittenden addressed the Senate, it seceded from the Union.

The same Boston merchants, the Bell and Breckinridge men who had urged the rioters on Phillips, drew up a petition with almost twenty-three thousand signatures in favor of the Crittenden Compromise. Senator Douglas and many of his supporters also backed it. But Lincoln stood firmly on the moderate Republican platform, opposing any further extension of slavery into the territories, writing one Congressman, "The instant you do [compromise], they have us under again: all our labor is lost and soon or late must be done over again."

Sumner wrote on January 26, 1861, "Mr. Lincoln is perfectly firm. He says that the Republican party shall not with his assent become 'a mere sucked egg, all shell and no meat,—the principle all sucked out.' "

Lincoln was well aware that acceptance of the Compromise would destroy the foundation on which the Republican administration had been elected. It would hardly postpone the crisis, and in many ways would intensify it. For given free rein below the Missouri line, the slave system would inevitably engage in an increasingly desperate race to counter the North with incursions into Mexico and Central America.

Yet despite Lincoln's opposition, and even without the votes of seceding Senators, the Senate turned down the Compromise only 20 to 19. The House defeated it by the more decisive margin of 113 to 80.

Behind the endless threats and debates stood only one real issue: the South would have to accept the Republican platform of containment and agree that slavery was a temporal institution. It could have maintained slavery in fifteen states for many decades under Lincoln's moderate program of emancipation. For even later in the war emergency, the President clung to his offer of federal reimbursement and inch-by-inch emancipation that would have stretched past 1900.

What brought the crisis to a head was the refusal of Southern extremists to accept any alternative but uncontrolled expansion of the slave system. In their view, they had reached a point of no return. No longer controlling the Administration through a subservient President, losing their base of power in the Senate, and with the Republicans pledged to containment of slavery, they had no further use for the Union. Secession was hardly popular in large segments of the South, particularly in small-farm communities. Tennessee, Arkansas, and North Carolina all turned down calls for secession conventions. In Alabama, Georgia, and particularly Louisiana, the Unionists rolled up significantly high minority votes against secession. But the extremists dominated the state governments, swept forward by visions of an ever-expanding Confederacy with "sources of wealth, property and power," as Senator Iverson of Georgia described it, "unsurpassed by any nation on earth."

Even after Mississippi, Florida, and Alabama followed South Carolina out of the Union, many key Republicans continued their frantic overtures to the South. On January 12, Seward, the dominant figure in the party until Lincoln's nomination, and now the Secretary-of-State-designate, made his plea for compromise.

His proposal, among other things, would guarantee slavery forever in the existing slave states. Reading the speech beforehand, Sumner protested violently, writing Dr. Howe, "I supplicated him to say no such thing."

When the amendment, guaranteeing slavery forever in fifteen states, reached the floor of Congress, the Springfield *Republican*, voice of the Massachusetts conservatives, rushed to give its blessing. Even after seven states had seceded, the amendment was passed by the House on February 28, by the Senate a few days later. Buchanan signed it; Ohio, Maryland, and Illinois ratified it. After the firing on Fort Sumter, however, it was buried in the government archives, an ironic memorial to a panicky Congress which actually passed two Thirteenth Amendments, one perpetuating slavery in 1861, the other, the ratified Amendment, abolishing slavery in 1865.

Even after Lincoln's inauguration, the Massachusetts party was sharply divided over Virginia's invitation to a Peace Conference. Adams insisted on grasping the last straw and converted most of the Congressional delegation to his position. Sumner, Andrew, and the radicals at first opposed it. Andrew, "a noble horse harnessed in with the mules," Dr. Howe described him, finally gave way to Adams. The Conference, meeting the same day as the Confederacy was being established at Montgomery, Alabama, soon bogged down in futile oratory over the old Crittenden proposals.

After the firing on Sumter on April 13, the abolitionists became superpatriots in their demands for prosecution of the war. "And when I said I would not sustain the Constitution because it was 'a covenant with death and an agreement with hell,'" Garrison wittily explained his shift, "*I had no idea that I should live to see death and hell secede.*"

Garrison and Phillips immediately realized that war offered the one decisive means of hastening emancipation and wiping out the "Southern slave oligarchy." Garrison particularly defended Lincoln and the Republicans from "minute criticism" and glorified them as "instruments in the hands of God to carry forward and help achieve the great object of emancipation." The abolitionists would continue to snap at Administrative delays, but they were essentially constructive critics. And despite Garrison's long record of pacifism, he never "laid a straw in [his] way" when his eldest son, George, sought and secured a commission in a Massachusetts regiment. The sons and relatives of many abolitionists, in fact, soon entered the Army, the list including the Tappans, Dr. Bowditch, Birney, Gerrit Smith, Frederick Douglass, William Jay, and Samuel May, Jr.

Garrison insisted he had not altered his nonresistant principles by supporting the war. In May, 1858, when Higginson and Parker both concluded that the slavery issue would be settled only by bloodshed, Garrison told his followers, "Perhaps blood will flow —God knows, I do not; but it shall not flow through any counsel of mine."

At the crowded Tremont Temple meeting on December 2, 1859, he supported John Brown and any future slave revolts, proclaiming, "Success to every slave insurrection at the South, and in every slave country. And I do not see how I compromise or stain my peace profession in making that declaration."

Even deeper contradictions had affected his personality in the past thirty years. At his first public speech in Boston, the Reverend May had counseled him, "Oh my friend, do try to moderate your indignation to keep more cool; why you are all on fire." Garrison had replied, "Brother May, I have need to be all on fire, for I have mountains of ice about me to melt."

But if his inflexible wrath, his air of moral infallibility, and the violent attacks he unleashed against all opposition even in the movement was the image known to the public, his grandson, Oswald Garrison Villard, still insisted, "His heart was the heart of a child even when he denounced a whole class in language of complete immoderation." At home with his wife and four sons and a daughter, he was an exuberantly affectionate father. He loved swimming, skating, and in later years, a game of croquet or whist with his family. Above all, he enjoyed filling his house with music "unless, indeed," Phillips observed, "a baby and playing with it proved metal even more attractive."

He was unquenchably generous although pressed for money all his life. Once when he was called from the dinner table by a man begging for clothes, he decided that since he had just bought a new pair of trousers, he would donate the pair he was wearing. When he told his wife, she protested, "If you gave him the pair you had on, you gave him your *new* trousers." Garrison only laughed at his error, insisting that the beggar "has a good pair anyhow."

He battled constantly against the restrictions and tyrannies of the church, and Elizabeth Cady Stanton later testified, "To Garrison, we owe, more than to any other man of our day, all that we have of religious freedom." None of his children was baptized. His daughter, coming home from school one day after being branded by classmates "the daughter of an infidel," asked her father if it were true that she lacked this qualification. "No, my darling," Garrison replied, "you have had a good bath every morning, and that is a great deal better."

MONTHS BEFORE Sumter, Governor Andrew hastily began buying arms and equipment for the Massachusetts militia. The Bell and Breckinridge men screamed "provocation." But after patiently suffering the compromise frenzies of his own party, Andrew had returned to an unshakable radical policy. He worked exhausting hours, his friends forced to drag him from the office to dinner at midnight. When Lincoln issued his call for troops, Andrew had 3120 men ready for action, more than the Commonwealth's quota. Attacked by mobs as it marched through Baltimore, the 6th Massachusetts suffered the first Union casualties and was the first regiment to reach Washington before the city was temporarily cut off from the North.

Phillips appointed himself the great gadfly of the Administration. When Lincoln placated the border states by returning fugitive slaves, Phillips branded him "a slave hound." The abolitionists insisted the war could not be prosecuted successfully unless based on a grand design of freedom for the colored race. As always, they were ahead of public opinion. Lincoln, on the other hand, consumed with only one purpose, that of holding the Union together, told his friends when Sumner broached emancipation, "It would do no good to go ahead any faster than the country could follow." Phillips retorted, "His theory of Democracy is that he is the servant of the people, not the leader."

Lincoln not only waited for the right political winds; he was still handicapped by old prejudices in favor of colonization as an over-all solution to slavery. When he pressed his same colonization and Federal compensation plans in his December message, even Garrison, who had restrained himself consistently, snapped, "He has evidently not a drop of antislavery blood in his veins."

The abolitionists kept up the din: not merely emancipation but "annihilating that oligarchy which rules the South." If the President was waiting for public opinion, they would organize it and make Lincoln recognize it. "I must educate, arouse and mature a public opinion which shall compel the Administration to adopt and support it in pursuing the policy I can aid," Phillips proclaimed. He hurried from city to city, speaking almost incessantly. The Boston *Post* called him, "a nuisance, a pest." But in a few months at the close of 1861, he probably addressed fifty thousand people and reached another 5 million through his printed speeches. He was soon the popular symbol of an emancipation crusade that extended far beyond the abolitionists. Only a little more than a year after he had been mobbed in Boston, he entered Washington triumphantly, was received at the White House and entertained at a gala dinner by Speaker of the House, Galusha Grow.

The abolitionists were not just critics and goads. Garrison had strong ties in Great Britain whose aristocratic and commercial classes, heavily dependent on Southern cotton, were leaning dangerously toward recognition of the Confederacy. He secured the help of George Thompson, principal target of the Boston riot in 1835, now an influential Member of Parliament. Supported by John Stuart Mill, Richard Cobden, and many British liberals, Thompson formed an Emancipation Committee which became a major factor in holding British support behind the Union.

Sumner and Andrew hardly lagged behind Phillips in maintaining pressure on the President. Sumner, as chairman of the Senate Committee on Foreign Relations, had ready access to the White House. Andrew's record in rallying every resource of the Commonwealth and New England behind the war put him high in

Lincoln's esteem. When General Frémont in Missouri emancipated the slaves of residents who had taken up arms against the government, and General David Hunter freed the slaves in coastal areas of Florida, South Carolina, and Georgia held by Union troops, Sumner and Andrew supported them vigorously.

Lincoln revoked both orders, fearful of antagonizing the border states. But radical pressure soon brought results. In March, 1862, the President forbade his officers to return slaves to the Confederate lines. In April, he abolished slavery in the District of Columbia, in June in the territories. A month later, the Confiscation Act finally carried out Frémont's order by emancipating slaves of any citizen in the Union convicted of treason or rebellion. Seward admitted to Phillips, "You make opinion and we use it."

Sumner pleaded with Lincoln to issue an Emancipation Proclamation on July 4. Instead, the President again urged gradual, compensated emancipation on Congress. Phillips remarked bitterly, ". . . I think the present purpose of the government, so far as it has now a purpose, is to end the war and save slavery."

The abolitionists were particularly exasperated by Lincoln's reply to Horace Greeley's demand for emancipation. "If I could save the Union without freeing any slaves, I would do it—if I could save it by freeing all the slaves, I would do it—and if I could do it by freeing some and leaving others alone, I would also do that," the President wrote on August 22.

Andrew sent a special emissary to the White House to impress the President with the extent of emancipation sympathy in New England. Lincoln listened gravely, making no comment. "A slow moving machine," Phillips called him.

The President, however, had almost made up his mind to hazard a preliminary step when Andrew helped initiate a conference of governors at Altoona, Pennsylvania, to explore means of hastening emancipation and expediting the war. Lincoln waited only the decisive moment which came at Antietam. A few days after McClellan had beaten off the Confederates, Lincoln issued his preliminary Emancipation Proclamation on September 24. It was actually a warning, putting the Confederate States on notice that unless they returned to the Union by January 1, 1863, their slaves would be freed. It was a limited warning at that, exempting not only the border states but parts of Louisiana, Virginia, and the Carolinas already occupied by Union forces. ·

Informed of the Proclamation en route to Altoona, Andrew called it "a poor *document* but a mighty *act:* slow, somewhat halting, wrong in its delay till January, but grand and sublime after all." Still, the Governor celebrated the news after his return to Boston by marching around his office with a friend, singing the "John Brown Song."

But when the Congressional elections in November went against the Administration, many radicals feared Lincoln would never issue the final proclamation. He ignored it in his annual message in December aand harked back to his colonization plans. The radicals in Congress countered by pressuring the President openly, even threatening to block appropriations for the Army. Sumner practically haunted the White House. Christmas passed, and Boston waited gloomily while abolitionists bombarded Sumner with queries on Lincoln's state of mind. On December 28, he assured Dr. Howe, "The President is firm."

THE New Year swept in along the whole Atlantic seaboard with a storm of snow and rain. In Boston, a distinguished audience— Longfellow, Josiah Quincy, Jr., Whittier, many of New England's most glittering names—crowded the Music Hall, ostensibly to hear a concert, primarily to await the President's Proclamation. The news was expected around noon. People listened patiently to Beethoven's Fifth Symphony and Handel's Hallelujah Chorus. Emerson recited his "Boston Hymn," Dr. Oliver Wendell Holmes, his "Army Hymn." Darkness was coming on, and the expectancy grew painful. A rumor began to circulate that the President had decided against the Proclamation after all.

At Tremont Temple, the Union Progressive Association had called a similar meeting. The audience, which had listened to

Frederick Douglass and a long list of speakers since early that morning, stirred restlessly.

No word had come from Washington that the President had written the Proclamation that morning and sent it to the State Department to be engrossed. All afternoon Lincoln had shaken thousands of hands in his New Year's Day reception. After the last caller had gone, Seward brought in the Proclamation. Lincoln's hand was limp and exhausted when he signed it. The signature appeared a trifle shaky, but he studiously used both names, not just the usual "A. Lincoln," telling Sumner who stood at his shoulder, "I know very well that the name connected with this document will never be forgotten."

An attendant came out of the wings of the Music Hall, halted the music and announced that the Proclamation was coming over the wire. On Boston Common, as in Pittsburgh, Chicago, and many cities, hundred-gun salutes began to boom over the rooftops. The Music Hall was suddenly a mass of shouting, dancing figures. "A storm of enthusiasm followed such as was never before seen from such an audience in that place," the *Liberator*'s reporter described it. "Shouts arose, hats and handkerchiefs were waved, men and women sprang to their feet to give more energetic utterance to their joy." Three tumultuous cheers were given for the President. Then someone called for Harriet Beecher Stowe, who was sitting in the gallery. Looking into a sea of beaming faces, she could only bow and dab at her eyes with a handkerchief. The audience shouted for Garrison. He stood quietly while the cheers echoed around him, his final triumphant moment after thirty-two years.

The audience at Tremont Temple was close to hysteria. Douglass stood up and began to sing, "Blow Ye Trumpets, Blow!" Everyone joined him. They called for Garrison, but he had left for Medford to unveil a bust of John Brown at the home of George Stearns. The celebration went on till midnight when the hall closed. Then it adjourned to the "Fugitive Slave Church" nearby where the singing and dancing continued through the night.

"A great historic event, sublime in its magnitude . . . ," Garrison hailed the Proclamation the next day. From London, Henry Adams wrote, "The Emancipation Proclamation has done more for us here than all our former victories and all our diplomacy."

WHAT A handful of abolitionists had begun in 1831 had now been completed. Lincoln never stinted in judging their contribution, telling Daniel H. Chamberlain in April, 1865, "I have only been an instrument. The logic and moral power of Garrison, and the antislavery people of the country and the army, have done all." Garrison, of course, was cited as the symbol of a whole movement. Still, Lincoln's tribute is worth noting today when most abolition leaders have been consigned to oblivion.

Even when remembered by historians, they have either been damned as fanatics who incited a needless conflict, or dismissed as a windy rabble whose effusions had little impact on the crisis. Neither extreme comes near the truth. By virtue of the fact that they exposed the most sensitive nerve in our history, we are still wary of the abolitionists. They disturb us too much. They are easier to neglect than understand. Any movement that makes us face the crucial flaw in our own soul is a jarring reminder not only of past failures but of unfinished responsibilities.

Insistently and furiously, the abolitionists moved the nation toward its greatest moral decision. They were the vanguard of a cause that involved every individual more deeply and agonizingly than we have ever been involved since the Revolution. They took the issue of slavery out of dark corners and jabbed and provoked an essentially indifferent people into solving its responsibility.

Although long vilified as troublemakers, they did not make the trouble. It had been built into the Constitution. They simply made the nation come to grips with a decision that had been postponed since 1787. In a larger sense, they forced us to decide what kind of government we really wanted.

For the very existence of slavery threatened the meaning of the Republic. It had created two diametrically opposed societies, one with a ruling class of three hundred forty-seven thousand slaveholders out of 8 million whites in 1850; and at the top of the pyramid, a planter aristocracy of only eight thousand families, each owning over fifty slaves. The slave system itself had largely walled itself off from the spirit of the age.

The abolitionists were not only the heirs of the Revolution but the creators of a second revolution. They became, in fact, our first great radical sect. For they struck equally at human property in the South worth hundreds of millions of dollars and at merchants and manufacturers in the North whose prosperity was inextricably linked to the slave system.

They have been accused of sacrificing little themselves. And it is true that except for Southerners like Birney and a few Northerners like Dr. Palfrey, who gave up inherited slaves, they would lose no human property by emancipation. On the other hand, they stood to lose their businesses and professions through boycotts and ostracism at home. They were mobbed and beaten. Risking imprisonment and heavy fines by aiding fugitive escapes in defiance of the law, they put their lives in the balance, and many paid dearly.

If radicalism and the Puritan tradition seem contradictory on the surface, the abolitionists had preserved only the vital center of Puritanism after the dead husk of Calvinism had been stripped away. What they had left was furious moral energy, relentless devotion to principle, and refusal to compromise where their consciences forbade it.

The radical Puritan, in fact, gradually became a unique New England hero type in the decades before 1860. Lovejoy, John Quincy Adams, Parker, and Higginson, to name a few, took surprising hold of the public imagination. And John Brown was turned into folk legend within a year of his death.

We might call them heroes in spite of themselves, for they had few qualities that warm the human audience. They were generally grim, insufferably self-righteous, and unshakably rigid. They were violent extremists, recognizing no shadings of black or white, attacking clergymen, relatives, or bosom friends for any deviation from antislavery principles. They turned their hatred of the planter aristocracy into a cult, disturbing even devoted associates with the fury of their words.

What they lacked most was laughter. The dreary procession of hymn-singings, which was the chief recreation at Garrison's fireside, or their aversion to theater, so pronounced in the Tappan brothers that they fired any employee caught buying a ticket, reflected their endless concentration on the evils of slavery. It is little wonder that the frustration limit of many abolition wives was severely taxed and that the first Mrs. Higginson, Mrs Wendell Phillips, and Angelina Grimké Weld, to cite a few, were confined to their chambers for an excessive amount of time with "sick headaches" and "nerves."

While the abolitionists have been criticized, and often rightly, for failing to practice racial equality at home, the Bostonians generally worked against such prejudices. They dined frequently with Negro leaders like Lewis Hayden and Frederick Douglass. Sewall took a young Negro lawyer into his office. And they effectively broke down Massachusetts color bars in public education and transportation and legal restrictions against intermarriage.

Their most serious failure, however, was in another area, a blind and often purposefully hostile neglect of the problems of the working class and union organization in the North. It is an ironic reflection on Puritan radicals that they had no formulated system of economic progress. In their consuming hatred of slavery, they were blind to the grievances of their own exploited class. Dedicated to the destruction of a feudal system in the South, they had nothing to offer at home except the fulfillment of the principles of their grandfathers, which seemed to tell them nothing about a twelve- or fourteen-hour day in New England mill towns.

There were, of course, individual exceptions. Parker preached increasingly on industrial democracy in the years before his death. Higginson dabbled in Socialist theory after Harvard. Phillips would become a militant spokesman for labor—after the war! But the abolitionists as a class were so deeply concerned in every reform from jails, poorhouses, and mental institutions to the blind, deaf, and alcoholic, that they had little excuse for shunning the working class except from deep psychological hostility.

The roots of hostility were both political and religious. Their fathers had been mostly Federalist; they themselves, if they voted, voted Whig until 1840 and even after. Thus they inherited a natural antipathy to Jacksonian democracy which was intensified when the planters shifted into the party and made it the slave party of the South. When the Irish emigrants in Boston and the big New England towns entered the Democratic party almost to the last man, the antipathy was sealed.

The Irish emigrant in politics, and the leaders who used their votes like Caleb Cushing in Boston and James Gordon Bennett in New York, quickly raised the specter of Negro competition in the labor market. After 1856 they harangued against the danger of emancipation and the flood of slaves that would invade the North. Many Roman Catholic clergymen supported this thesis so consistently that it was largely accepted as dogma.

If the Know-Nothings in New England took out their frustrations against slavery on the emigrants, the bitter circle was completed when the Irish turned on the Negroes. Its climax came at the start of the army draft in 1863 when workers in New York and to a lesser extent Boston and New England cities, tortured and killed hundreds of Negroes in days of rioting.

If the abolitionists had concentrated on the factory towns as vigorously as they did the rural areas, where they swung a large segment of New England's farmers and mechanics from the Democratic to the Republican party, they might have effected a rapprochement before the war. As it was, the failure was shrewdly exploited by the South, Alabama planters during the factory layoffs of 1855, for example, raising relief funds among their own slaves for the "white slaves" of the North.

What Lincoln called "the logic and moral power" of Garrison was the ultimate contribution of the abolitionists despite all other deficiencies. Through their refusal to compromise they prepared the nation for the crisis ahead. They were inexhaustible gadflies. They hung on, they stuck, they hurt. In effect, they created the moral framework. They molded "the emotions, habits, attitudes, and ideas which define the character of the stimulus and select the path of response" in what Professor Lewis S. Feuer has called the "psychoeconomic" causation of history.*

Undoubtedly, the antislavery friction between the sections was intensified by economic and political factors after 1840. The protective tariff for Northern industry, the Northern monopoly on coastal shipping which raised freight charges in the South, the hard-money policy which made the South a debtor economy— all these, to name a few, were valid Southern grievances which contributed to the split. They were valid, but *not crucial*. And they might have been adjusted, as Nullification was adjusted in 1833 by the Compromise Tariff, if they had been an isolated phenomenon. It was the genius of the abolitionists that they saw from the start that every significant economic and political grievance sprang from the slave system itself and that nothing could be *really* solved apart from the central, inescapable issue.

What Congress attempted to compromise could never be compromised as long as the inherent nature of the slave system demanded ceaseless expansion. Before 1820, the nation had gambled that slavery would fade away. The Compromise of 1820 destroyed the illusion. Once the South had won admission of slavery into new territories below the Missouri line and gained control of the Senate through the principle of balancing new free states with slave states, the nation was effectively divided into two parts.

The only hope of avoiding eventual conflict was gradual revolution within the South itself and acceptance of a long-range plan of emancipation. But the dominant planter faction made certain in the decade or so after 1820 that the South would be sealed off from any interference, inside or out, with its system. Scores of Southern antislavery societies were broken up. Abolitionists like Birney were forced into exile. Drastic laws against abolition literature, or even discussion of the issue, destroyed

* *Marx and Engels, Basic Writings on Politics and Philosophy,* Anchor Books, New York, 1959, p. XVI.

forever the development of an informed public opinion. In Congress, the petition Gag Rule of 1836 was the final assertion that the South intended to isolate its system from debate even in the nation's forum.

When John Quincy Adams presented his resolution for gradual emancipation to the House in 1839, he was rudely ignored. The conflict had passed the point of internal reform.

While abolition, except for a few survivors like Cassius Clay, had been purged from the South, it took hold firmly in New England after 1831, spreading westward through the "burned-over" district of New York to the Ohio Reserve. The Puritan conscience was particularly susceptible to its humanitarian attack on slavery. And it was on humanitarian grounds alone that Massachusetts became the first state to protect fugitives seized on its soil with its Personal Liberty Law of 1843. It was, in effect, a selfish protest. It was an attempt to keep the stain of slavery from its borders, not a challenge to the expansion of slavery.

Only when slavery became as much of a threat to the Puritan pocketbook as the Puritan conscience would New England take an aggressive stand. It was the admission of Texas that poised the threat, created the Liberty party and forced New England to vote as well as think against slavery. It was Texas that made the alliance between moral and political antislavery, split the Conscience Whigs from the Cotton Whigs and led to the Free Soil party in 1848.

What was proved in these crucial years between 1839 and 1848 was that abolition "defined the character of the stimulus" while economic necessity molded it into a political reality. Neither could exist by itself. The Liberty party, limited to its abolition plank, would inevitably have to be broadened into the Free Soil movement before the fears of the small businessman in the face of the Southwest's expanding power and the demands of the farmer for cheap homesteads in the West could be given a common basis of economic unity against the slave system.

This basis became the Republican party in which all "psycho-economic" factors eventually coalesced. It was a remarkably short process, hastened to a great extent by the abolitionists, who marked the path with dazzling clarity and spoke out relentlessly like a knife in the American conscience. Between 1840 and 1854, between the Liberty and Republican parties, their moral power was transformed into the political power of the Republican radicals. In New England, in Massachusetts particularly, the Puritan quest had reached fulfillment. Sumner and Wilson sat in the Senate, Andrew in the State House; the radicals controlled the Legislature. They had succeeded, as closely as any movement in our history, in remaking society in their own image.

Robert Gould Shaw—
Puritan at the Ramparts: July 18, 1863

IT HAD BEEN a brilliant, cloudless morning off the South Carolina coast until the federal artillery opened up on Fort Wagner in Charleston harbor, blistering the air with gunsmoke. A week before on July 11, 1863, Major General Quincy Gillmore had made a landing on Morris Island and moved forty-one pieces of artillery within range of the fort. Supported by four ironclads, five gunboats and smaller ships of the South Atlantic Squadron, Gillmore now concentrated almost a hundred guns on Wagner, one of the heaviest bombardments of the war. Confederate Brigadier General William B. Taliaferro later claimed that nine thousand shells had been hurled against his fort.

The Union Command wanted Charleston badly, allocating ten thousand troops for the attack. The city was not only the birthplace of the rebellion but the symbolic heart of the Confederacy and its proudest aristocracy. Strategically, it was one of two major Southern ports through which Confederate armies were supplied from abroad. Federal troops controlled small strips of the Carolina and Georgia coast, but they needed Charleston to consolidate their positions.

Fort Wagner at the northern end of Morris Island lay only 2600 yards from Fort Sumter, key to the city's defenses. If Gillmore could take Wagner, he was convinced he could pound Sumter into submission and control the city.

The only approach to Wagner was a strip of sandy soil narrowing to a spit a few hundred yards wide. It was a double-bastioned fort built of palmetto-log revetments with bombproofs holding eight hundred men. Naval guns and howitzers covered the land approach; 32-pound cannon and howitzers provided flanking fire. Further, an attacking force could be swept with crossfire from Confederate batteries on Sumter, James, and Sullivan islands. Even if attackers reached the fort, they would have to clamber up its steep, 30-foot slopes to face the battle-hardened 1st South Carolina and 51st North Carolina battalions.

Although Wagner was one of the most heavily fortified points in the South, Gillmore half convinced himself the bombardment had seriously weakened its defenses. Confederate guns had answered only sporadically, and about 4 P.M. he ordered the bombardment halted. Actually, Taliaferro had carefully sandbagged his guns or buried them in the sand. None had been damaged; his men had suffered few casualties. Now he brought his guns back into position for the impending attack.

At dusk Brigadier General George C. Strong, a yellow bandanna around his neck, mounted on a gray charger, began moving the six regiments of his 1st Brigade into position. Highly respected by his men for personally leading the landings on Morris Island, he would eventually succumb to the wounds he received that night.

"At ten minutes past 6," wrote the Providence *Journal*'s correspondent, "the 54th Massachusetts is moving up the island. . . ." Engaged by superior Confederate forces on James in a bloody skirmish only two days before, it had hardly eaten or slept in fifty hours. The other regiments cheered the still-precise columns marching into position, and the *Journal* reporter noted the "modest and unassuming manner" of its slim blond colonel, Robert Gould Shaw.

At twenty-six, already a veteran of many campaigns, Shaw had just made a critical decision. Strong had offered the 54th the honor, with all its risks, of leading the assault. "The best troops can seldom be made to advance," Gillmore himself had concluded later, "under the fire of even a few well-served pieces of artillery supported by the fire of small arms." Yet Shaw had immediately accepted, his decision based on far more than bravado. He held a unique command, the first white colonel of the first free colored troops enlisted in the North. He had long wanted, and now embraced, the chance to test his men in a major battle. Despite the derision of the South and the doubts of the North, his regiment could prove that night that the Negro could equal the white man as a soldier. It would be an even larger test of the Negro's demands for equal responsibility in a nation that had just promised over four million slaves their freedom.

Shaw paced his lines, dressed in close-fitting jacket and light blue trousers, a silk sash would around his waist—"a simple suit, hardly a uniform," the *Journal* reporter described it. A New Bedford private wrote later "his lips were compressed, and now and then there was visible a slight twitching of the corners of the mouth like one bent on accomplishing or dying." It was almost 7:30, darkness coming on fast, a heavy fog drifting in from the sea. The officers of the 54th grasped each other's hands and moved their revolver holsters to the front.

LESS THAN six months before on January 30, Governor Andrew had written Francis G. Shaw, offering his son, Captain Shaw of the 2nd Massachusetts, command of the Negro regiment he was organizing. "With my deep conviction of the importance of this undertaking . . . and that its success or failure will go far to elevate or depress the estimation in which the character of the Colored Americans will be held throughout the world," Andrew wrote, "the command of such a regiment seems to me to be a high object of ambition for any officer."

The Governor had picked Shaw carefully. His grandfather had been a prominent Boston merchant; his parents among the first people of wealth to support abolition with connections by marriage to devoted antislavery men like General Charles Russell Lowell and General Francis G. Barlow. Shaw had been raised in abolition principles, and since graduation from Harvard, had made an outstanding military record in every campaign of the 2nd Massachusetts. At Winchester he had escaped serious injury when a bullet struck his watch; at Antietam his neck had been grazed by a shell.

Francis Shaw considered his son's selection so important that he carried the Governor's letter himself from New York, where he was living, to the captain's camp in Virginia. Both he and his wife wanted Shaw to take the command, although the colonel of the first Negro regiment not only faced ridicule from fellow officers, but special dangers if captured. The Confederate government had already announced that white officers of Negro troops would be denied all protection of regular prisoners under the code of war.

Whatever factors influenced his decision, Captain Shaw debated the offer for two days and then turned it down. His mother admitted it was "the bitterest disappointment I have ever experienced." She wrote the Governor, "It would have been the proudest moment of my life if I could have died satisfied that I had not lived in vain. . . . I do not understand it unless from a habit inherited from his father of self-distrust in his own capabilities."

A few days later, Shaw changed his mind and wired his father, "Please telegraph Governor Andrew that I accept." In a letter to his fiancée, Annie Haggerty of Lenox, Massachusetts, he insisted, ". . . I shan't be frightened out of it by its unpopularity; and I hope you don't care if it is made fun of."

One of Shaw's own colored recruits told his New Bedford family a few weeks later, "I doubt there could have been found a dozen men in the North holding a high position . . . who would have accepted the unenviable position of commander of the first colored regiment in the North." The philosopher, William James, two of whose brothers became officers in colored regiments, the 54th and 55th, later wrote of Shaw, "loneliness was certain, ridicule was inevitable, failure possible."

Although it favored recruitment of Negro troops, the New York *Times* on February 16 analyzed the principal causes of opposition. Most people were convinced colored soldiers would run at the first rifle shot, the first glimpse of their former masters. It was further believed that no Union regiment would fight alongside a colored unit. There were additional doubts the government could recruit enough Negro soldiers to justify the commotion. And finally, people feared the policy itself would alienate the border states and exasperate Peace Democrats in the North.

Such feelings were held even in parts of Massachusetts. When the 54th marched through Boston a few months later on its way to the front, the *Pilot*, hewing to its anti-Republican and anti-Negro line, insisted, "They are as fit to be the soldiers of this country as their abettors are to be its statesmen. One Southern regiment of white men could put twenty regiments of them to flight in half an hour."

Although thousands of Negroes had served with distinction in the Revolution and the War of 1812, the President himself opposed the first attempts to enlist them in the Union Army. When General Hunter in May, 1862, tried to bolster his depleted forces in the Department of the South by organizing former slaves into the 1st South Carolina Volunteers, the War Department made this unit disband. One company, however, was kept intact and eventually formed the basis of a new colored regiment under Colonel Thomas Wentworth Higginson, who had resigned his Worcester parish.

In Louisiana that July, General Benjamin Butler first enlisted Negroes as laborers, then reversed himself and formed his own Negro companies without official authorization. In Kansas too, James H. Lane, veteran guerrilla chieftain and United States Senator, ignored Washington's policy and took both fugitives and free Negroes into his 1st Kansas Colored Volunteers.

Even after Henry Wilson in the Senate and Thaddeus Stevens in the House pushed through a bill in July authorizing Negro recruitment, Lincoln still delayed. Governor Andrew constantly urged Negro enlistments, but only after the Emancipation Proclamation did Lincoln give his approval. The 54th was the first regiment of free Negroes authorized by the War Department, but two weeks earlier, six companies of the Kansas Volunteers were sworn into Federal Service.

The Administration's shift was as much the result of necessity as concern for Negro equality. For the Army faced a critical manpower shortage when many two-year enlistments ended in the spring. Dependence on volunteers had proved a failure. In July, Lincoln would be forced to establish the first nation-wide draft, a measure that produced riots and hundreds of deaths in New York and other major cities. "If this nation is to be saved . . . ," Edmund Quincy shrewdly predicted, "it will be by the assistance of the race which owes us no gratitude and to which the first favor we have granted is the privilege of fighting and dying in our behalf."

After weathering official obstacles and public disdain, Governor Andrew was determined to make the 54th a model for all Negro regiments. "I stand or fall, as a man and a magistrate," he insisted, "with the rise and fall in the history of the 54th Massachusetts Regiment." He and Shaw hand-picked its white officers, taking as assistant commander, Captain Norwood P. Hallowell of the 20th Massachusetts. Its company commanders, including Francis L. Higginson, Cabot J. Russel, and John W. Appleton, were drawn from the Commonwealth's most distinguished abolition families.

Shaw was equally insistent on the standard of his colored troops. "The company from New Bedford are a fine body of men, and out of forty, only two cannot read or write," he told Annie Haggerty on March 14. A few weeks later he wrote her that the mustering officer, a Virginian by birth, "tells me that he has never mustered in so fine a set of men, though about 20,000 have passed through his hands since September."

Between this patrician abolitionist and his troops there was a strong bond, based not only on their mutual cause but the respect and affection he inspired wherever he went. Shaw was a handsome man, his features "delicate and well-cut, and set off by a fine complexion and winning, merry blue eyes and golden hair," Major Henry Lee Higginson described him later. A Negro woman teacher, meeting him in July, would always remember "something in his face finer and more exquisite than one sees in a woman's face." Even men used words like "sweetness," Dr. Bowditch recalling his "sweet smile," Major Higginson calling him, "a day in June, sweet, wholesome, vigorous, breezy." R. Morris Copeland found him "wise beyond his years" but "there was no one who had such a pure, simple and spring-like nature as he."

Still, Shaw was a strict disciplinarian, drilling his troops exhausting hours, exulting to Annie by the end of March, "There is no doubt that we shall leave the state with as good a regiment as any that has marched."

The main problem was finding enough capable Negroes to fill not only the 54th but a second colored regiment that Andrew planned. Since Massachusetts lacked populous Negro communities, George L. Stearns established a special recruiting committee and hurried to Rochester to secure the help of Frederick Douglass. The Negro leader ran a series of announcements in his newspaper: "Men of Color! To Arms! . . . Who would be free must themselves strike the blow. . . . This is our golden opportunity. . . ." The first men Douglass enlisted were his own sons, Lewis and Charles.

Stearns worked ten to eighteen hours a day, establishing recruiting stations from Rochester to St. Louis, advancing ten thousand dollars of his own money to speed enlistments. In parts of Philadelphia, the resentment against Negro troops was so strong the recruiting station had to be kept secret, and men put on board the train for Boston in small parties. But by May 7, Stearns had filled the quota of the 54th and raised two hundred men toward the 55th when the Governor suddenly decided to abandon the second regiment. Stearns protested, and Andrew finally let him go ahead if he could complete the regiment in four weeks. The Medford abolitionist tirelessly met the deadline. Norwood Hallowell was transferred to command of the 55th; his brother Edward was made assistant commander of the 54th.

It was a decisive month both for Shaw and the regiment. On May 2, he was married to Annie despite preliminary objections from their families. He had strong premonitions of what lay ahead, writing his mother, "Indeed, one reason for my wishing to be married is that we are going to undertake a very dangerous piece of work, and I feel that there are more chances than ever of my not getting back. I know I should go away more happy and contented if we were married." Annie set up housekeeping at Readville near the camp, but they would have a short-lived domesticity. On May 18, the regiment was presented with its colors, nine special railway cars bringing the Governor and other dignitaries from Boston for the ceremony. On the same day, ob-

viously pressed by a shortage of troops, Stanton telegraphed
Andrew to have the 54th report to the Southern Command.

Ten days later, the 54th, armed with nine hundred fifty Enfield
rifles, boarded the train for Boston to be greeted by the most
tumultuous reception in the city's history. Sidewalks, balconies,
and windows were jammed along the route to the Common.
The superbly trained regiment marched with "an order and
morale such as I have not seen surpassed in any white regiment,"
enthused the *Republican*'s reporter. Standing at the cornor of
Park Square and Boylston, Dr. Bowditch shouted, "Three cheers
for Colonel Shaw!" and recorded in his dairy, "I got from him
that lovely, almost heavenly smile. . . ." At the Common, the
54th was reviewed by Senator Wilson and the Governor who
told them, "I know not when in all human history, to any given
thousand men in arms, has been committed a work so proud, so
precious, so full of hope and glory as the work committed to
you."

Through the same crowded streets with the band playing the
"John Brown Song," the regiment marched to its ship at Battery
Wharf. Garrison watched from the balcony of Phillips's house,
his hand resting on a bust of John Brown, tears flowing un-
ashamedly down his cheeks. Shaw, riding at the head of his men,
seemed to pause for a moment as the column passed down State
Street over the spot where Attucks had fallen in 1770 and over
which Sims and Burns had been taken back to slavery only a few
years before. "History may be searched in vain," commented
the New York *Daily Tribune*, "for a contrast or a retribution of
which the poetic or religious justice is parallel to this."

Whittier, a confirmed pacifist who avoided military parades,
found himself cheering uncontrollably as Shaw and his taut black
lines swept by. "The very flower and grace of chivalry," Whittier described the colonel, "he seemed to me beautiful and awful,
as an angel of God come down to lead the host of freedom to
victory."

If that day produced an overflow of oratory and tears, it was
an excusable climax. One way of life had ended with the Emancipation Proclamation. Now another was beginning, the Negro

entrusted with the weapons to create his own freedom, "the despised race," as Major Higginson noted, going forth "to blot out with their own blood the sin of the nation."

Even Shaw broke his usual reserve, writing his wife as the *De Molay* steamed toward South Carolina, "Just remember our own doubts and fears, and other people's sneering and pitying remarks, when we began last winter, and then look at the perfect triumph of last Thursday."

At Hilton Head, South Carolina, an island held by Union forces, the 54th began a month of wearying guard duty. Shaw had written Annie, "If the raising of colored troops prove such a benefit to the country and to the blacks as many people think it will, I shall thank God a thousand times that I was led to take my share in it." But he soon began to fret at inaction, fearful that his regiment would be relegated to labor details, little better than the loading and hauling performed by slave gangs. The only assignment given the 54th was a raiding party up the coast in which Shaw was ordered to burn and pillage the small town of Darien. Concerned that Negro troops would be tagged with the reputation of marauders, Shaw protested to General Strong, "My men are capable of better service."

At the same time, Shaw heard from Washington that Negro troops were to be paid ten dollars a month instead of the standard thirteen dollars promised by Stanton. Determined to keep his regiment on an equal footing with white troops, he wrote the Governor, "I shall refuse to have the regiment paid until I hear from you on the subject." While Andrew debated the issue with Washington, eventually winning equal payment, Stearns faithfully raised fifty thousand dollars, in part his own contribution, to make up the three-dollar difference for both Negro regiments.

Shaw kept pressing General Strong for a combat assignment, writing him, "It seems to me quite important that the colored soldiers should be associated, as much as possible, with white troops, in order that they may have other witnesses beside their own officers of what they are capable of doing." On July 8

Strong granted his request. On an hour's notice the 54th was ordered to board a small transport. For the next three days, it shuttled from island to island in the complex network rimming Charleston harbor, landing finally on James where General A. H. Terry was preparing a diversionary attack to siphon off Confederate defenders from Morris, the eventual target.

Four companies of the 54th were holding the forward line with the 10th Connecticut on the morning of July 11 when they were charged by five Confederate regiments. The 54th took the brunt of the attack, standing firm although losing at least thirty men. "One of our sergeants named [James D.] Wilson was surrounded but killed from three to six rebels before he went under," Captain Russel wrote his family. "The bullets whistled so close that I could feel the wind of them," Sergeant R. J. Simmons told his mother, whose house in New York, by grim irony, had just been plundered by draft rioters and whose ten-year-old nephew would succumb a few days later to the beating they inflicted.

"They showed no sign of fear but fought as if they were very angry and determined to have revenge," the Boston *Traveller's* correspondent described the Negro troops who had saved a white regiment from disaster. "Had the 54th given way, the retreat of the 10th would have been cut off, and they would have been absolutely annihilated or captured." Later that night, General Terry sent Shaw his official commendation.

The 54th was ordered to evacuate James in a blinding storm of lightning and rain, marching single file on the narrow path through the swamps, feeling their way over bridges only two planks wide, once "over a narrow dike so slippery as to make it almost impossible to keep one's feet," Shaw wrote his family. Their boots were heavy with clay, their uniforms soaked. It took seven hours until 5 A.M. to make four miles.

They ferried from James to Morris Island on a small boat holding only thirty men, requiring more than two dozen crossings. Shaw made each trip, often steering himself. In the morning with almost no rest, their water supply depleted, they had to march four more hours up Morris Island under a brilliant sun, "dazzling and roasting us," as Shaw wrote. "I saw them and they looked worn and weary," one correspondent informed Governor Andrew.

After the embarkation that morning, Hallowell found Shaw lying near the pilothouse of the boat. "I said, 'Bob, don't you feel well? Why are you so sad,'" he wrote later. "He turned towards me and replied, 'Oh, Ned, if I could only have a few weeks longer with my wife and be at home a little while I think I might die happy; but it cannot be; I do not believe I shall live through our next fight.'"

General Strong had already told the regimental commanders a call would be made for volunteers to take Fort Wagner. It was the opportunity Shaw had been waiting for, "a splendid chance to prove to the world that our men were worthy to be respected as soldiers," Hallowell wrote. When Hallowell saw Shaw that afternoon at their positions, "all the sadness had left him." He told his assistant commander simply, "We shall take the fort or die there. . . ."

Strong moved his brigade into position, the 54th at the head of the line, then the Connecticut and four other regiments, with two supporting brigades of less numerical strength in the rear. Gillmore had decided to wait until 7:30 P.M. to make the attackers a dimmer target. Yet the delay also gave the Confederate command ample time to reinforce the Wagner garrison from the mainland. In fact, Gillmore must have counted far too heavily on the effectiveness of the bombardment, for many normal precautions seem to have been overlooked. No engineers had been sent ahead over the narrow strip before the fort to clear obstructions. No plan of the fort had been shown the regimental officers. The scouts had also failed to report, or their reports were forgotten in the confusion, the ditch before the fort or the deep cut made by the creek and marshes in the sand strip over which they would attack.

There were only a few minutes left. Shaw ordered his men to fix bayonets. He addressed them briefly, his voice "ringing with that peculiar strength and sweetness," a reporter had noted at their Readville camp. There were no heroics in his words, only the reminder that their actions tonight would decide how the

nation judged the Negro as a soldier and his demands for equality
as a citizen. There could be no retreat, no surrenders, for the
Confederates had already sworn that any colored soldier would
be shot on the spot or sold into slavery.

The evening light was fading quickly as the Colonel drew his
sword and gave the command, "Forward!" The long blue line
moved ahead at quick time for the first hundred yards. Then
Shaw gave the order for double-quick time, and suddenly within
a few hundred yards of the fort, the Confederate guns opened up
in a sheet of flame. The line buckled, then plunged forward at
full charge as the steady fusillade of musket fire cut deep holes
in the forward companies and men reeled and dropped in their
tracks.

The regiment reached the defile where a creek cut the sandy
spit to a width of 150 yards and less. The charging lines jammed
together, companies breaking formation, piling up on the men
ahead. At the same time, the Confederate batteries on Sumter,
Sullivan, and James Island opened with a blinding crossfire,
churning the regiment to pieces and pinning down the regiments
behind them so that the 54th was virtually isolated. Still they kept
coming on, line after line, plunging into a hail of grape and can-
nister until the bodies were strewn in piles and the next lines
stumbled and leaped over crumpled forms.

Not more than fifty yards from the fort, they hit the ditch
almost 4 feet deep with water. Some never got across, but Shaw
and part of the advance company made it and started up the
pitted slope of the parapets. From behind the breastworks and
traverses, the Confederate fire poured down on them. It was 30
feet up the slope, and as the men reached and scrambled for a
foothold, howitzers raked them and grenades blasted them back
into the ditch.

Somehow Shaw and a handful of men reached the parapet and
stood momentarily silhouetted by the flash of cannon. At first
twenty, perhaps forty men, fought in a circle around him as the
Confederates met them with musket butts, handspikes, and gun
rammers. The color sergeant planted the flag on the parapet and
died before a volley of musket balls. Another sergeant managed

to grab the flag. Although wounded himself, lying on the parapet, he held the flag aloft at least fifteen minutes. Lewis Douglass, hurled from the parapet by an exploding grenade, miraculously survived. Captain Appleton crawled into an embrasure and knocked out the gun crew with his revolver. Captain William Simpkins and Captain Russel, who was killed a moment later, even reached the left bastion of the inner fort.

The men at the foot of the parapet saw Shaw for the last time, his sword flailing at the gray shapes around him, until he went down before a blast of muskets. No one knows how long the first wave held that small circle around the colonel's body, perhaps ten, at the most fifteen minutes. But they fought on the ramparts at close quarters until their bodies were strewn in mounds, and not one man was left.

At this crucial point, the supporting regiments failed. A few units of the Connecticut and New York regiments reached the southeast salient of the fort, but most of them were pinned down in front of the ditch by the crossfire from James and other batteries. Captain Luis Emilio reported later that one regiment, halting at the ditch, began firing wildly at the parapet, striking some of the 54th. Emilio held the remnants of Shaw's regiment at the foot of the parapet. They kept up a steady fire for over an hour while the Confederates rolled grenades and lighted shells down the slope.

It was too late. The momentum had been lost in those few minutes while Shaw's advance guard held the ramparts, and the regiments at the rear had failed to close the gap. There was only blood and havoc left on that small strip of sand. "The dead and wounded were piled up in a ditch together, sometimes fifty in a heap," Confederate Lieutenant Iredell Jones reported later, "and they were strewn all over the plain for a distance of three-quarters of a mile." Scattered units kept up a desultory fire until midnight, but the Union forces had been so badly crippled that another attack was impossible. Of six hundred men of the 54th, almost half were killed, wounded, or missing. The total Union losses ran over fifteen hundred. Of ten regimental commanders, seven had been killed or wounded.

That night Colonel Shaw's body was stripped of its uniform, the watch and chain stolen by a Confederate private. When General Gillmore requested the body be returned for military burial, a Confederate officer supposedly replied, "We have buried him with his niggers." Whether apocryphal or not, the scornful message was reported throughout the North, turned into a song and soon sung by thousands of Negro troops marching off to war. A captured Federal surgeon, John T. Luck, was told by Confederate General Johnson Hagood, who later denied the statement, "Had he been in command of white troops, I should have given him an honorable burial; as it is, I shall bury him in the common trench with the negroes that fell with him."

In either case, Francis Shaw opposed all attempts to recover his son's body, writing General Gillmore, "We hold that a soldier's most appropriate burial place is on the field where he has fallen."

OVERNIGHT Fort Wagner became a national symbol. "To a whole race, a holy sepulchre," the *National Antislavery Standard* described it. "It made Fort Wagner such a name to the colored race," the *New York Tribune* stated, "as Bunker Hill had been for ninety years to the white Yankees. . . ."

Few battles had so captured the imagination of the North. In defeat, Shaw had created a legend. Only the most foolhardy and bigoted critics could ever claim again that well-trained Negro troops could not hold their own against the pick of the Confederacy. ". . . Though Wagner still defies us," concluded the *Atlantic Monthly*, "public prejudice is down; and through the cannon smoke of that black night, the manhood of the colored race shines before many eyes that would not see. . . ."

In practical terms, the Administration considered its new policy more than exonerated and pushed ahead with the recruitment of Negro regiments. In the next twenty months, almost one hundred eighty thousand colored troops joined the Army and thirty-seven thousand would be killed, wounded, or missing. Almost thirty thousand enlisted in the Union Navy, which had never discriminated. This would have been a significant addition of manpower under any circumstances. But after the draft met almost frenzied resistance in some cities in the July riots, and most governors had to strain to meet their quotas, the Negro troops became a crucial factor in the North's eventual superiority.

Shaw's death was greeted with an outburst of emotion rarely equaled during the war. If Lydia Maria Child indulged in heroic oratory, proclaiming he "had gone to join the glorious army of martyrs," even grim-lipped soldiers matched such testimonials. "I have had but little opportunity to be with him, but I already loved him," General Strong stated shortly before he died of his own wounds. "No one ever went more gallantly into battle." George W. Curtis, editor of *Harper's Weekly*, wrote Thomas Wentworth Higginson, "Wherever he went, he left a lover, and I don't know whether men or women loved him most." James Russell Lowell was only one of many poets who celebrated Shaw in heroic couplets:

> But the high soul burns on to light men's feet,
> Where death for noble ends makes dying sweet.

It was not just the poetic imagination that considered Shaw's dying sweet. His father, who had wanted him to take a regiment almost certainly destined to end on some bloody rampart, would state, "He died in what was to him a moment of triumph—could we wish for him a nobler death?" It was almost as if Shaw had been offered up by the Puritan conscience as its final sacrifice against slavery. And the symbolism of a young abolitionist officer's blood, mixed forever with his dark warriors in one Southern grave, gave an inescapable grandeur to this New England version of Greek tragedy.

Shaw marked the climax of an epoch, the Puritan conscience in its finest hour. He and John Brown were contrasting products of the same Puritan quest. If Brown represented the violence of an Old Testament prophet, Shaw was "an angel of God," as Whittier saw him, stripped of all fanaticism, pure and almost childlike in his high sense of duty. He was the final embodiment of chivalry in New England's last great cause. And if troops would march off to the front singing of John Brown, Boston would enshrine Shaw at its heart, raising a great bronze bas relief of the colonel and his men directly in front of the Massachusetts State House. Even fifty years later Harvard students, passing the plaque in Memorial Hall with Shaw's name, would tip their caps respectfully.

Acknowledgments and Bibliography

It HAS BEEN my purpose to make this study as readable as possible by eliminating chapter notes and almost all footnotes. After citing manuscripts and newspapers which have been consulted, I have divided the reference works into two categories: first, those of a general nature; second, a list by chapter of those which proved particularly valuable in each period.

For simplicity, only essential reports and pamphlets have been cited—only those years from the Boston Female Antislavery Society reports, for example, which supplied a quotation or statistics used in that chapter. While it is obvious to anyone who has scanned the crowded antislavery shelves of New England's libraries that these listings are only a small part of the available materials, I have purposefully omitted hundreds of tracts and polemics which are not only generally repetitious, but would clutter any bibliography to the point of distraction.

It should be noted that I have attempted to keep a uniformity of style by spelling "antislavery" without a hyphen and "abolitionist" in lower case although the form may have differed in the original version. On the other hand, since the treatment of words like "Negro" and "African" is indicative of contemporary attitudes, I have preserved the original form in all quotations.

I want to express my lasting gratitude to Professor Edwin Rozwenc of Amherst College who read the entire manuscript and made invaluable suggestions; and to my devoted friends, Professors Lewis and Katherine Feuer of the University of California at Berkeley, in whose home the book first took shape and who have assisted unstintingly in furthering its completion.

To all those librarians, whose labors are the bulwark of any historian and biographer, I am deeply indebted; particularly to Gilbert A. Cam of the New York Public Library who made the Frederick Lewis Allen Room available to me, and the staff of the American History Room who could never do enough. I enjoyed continued courtesies from the staffs of the Widener, Houghton, and Business School Libraries at Harvard; the Women's Archives at Radcliffe; and from the Massachusetts Historical Society, the Boston Public Library, and the New York Historical Society.

In addition, I am deeply grateful to Scott Bartlett and Peter Prescott, my editors at E. P. Dutton; to Tilden Edelstein who made special materials available to me from his forthcoming dissertation on Thomas Wentworth Higginson; and to Marie K. Murphy for her typing of this manuscript.

I. Manuscripts

Adams, John Quincy. *Manuscript*. Columbia University Library (microfilm).

Andrew, John A. *Papers*. Massachusetts Historical Society.

Appleton, William, *Diaries (1826–1841)*. Harvard Business School Library.

Bostonian Society. Papers, clippings on abolition.

Bowditch, Henry I. *Latimer Journal & Papers*. Massachusetts Historical Society.

——. *Manuscripts Relating to Lieut. Nathaniel Bowditch*. Massachusetts Historical Society.

Burns, Anthony, *Papers on*. Massachusetts Historical Society and Boston Public Library.

Chapman, Maria W. *Papers*. Boston Public Library.

Child, Lydia Maria. *Papers, Correspondence*. Boston Public Library.

Dana, Richard H., Jr. *Papers*. Massachusetts Historical Society.

Forbes, John Murray. *Papers*. Harvard Business School Library and Massachusetts Historical Society.

Garrison, William L. *Papers*. Boston Public Library.

Higginson, Thomas Wentworth. *Papers*. Houghton Library, Harvard.

——. *Papers on Anthony Burns*. Boston Public Library.

Howe, Samuel Gridley. *Papers*. Houghton Library, Harvard.

Loring, Alice Gray. *Papers*. The Women's Archives, Radcliffe College.

BIBLIOGRAPHY					295

Parker, Theodore. *Letters and Notebooks.* Massachusetts Historical
	Society.
———. *Letters, Notebooks, Clippings.* Boston Public Library.
Richardson, Jeffrey. *Account Books.* Harvard Business School Library.
Sumner, Charles. *Papers.* Houghton Library, Harvard.

II. Newspapers

Boston: *Atlas, Bee, Columbian Centinel, Commonwealth, Daily Adver-
	tiser, Evening Times, Journal, Liberator, Morning Post, Times*
Springfield, Mass.: *Republican*
New York: *American, Daily Times, Daily Tribune*

III. General Reference Works

Aaron, Daniel. *Men of Good Hope.* New York, Oxford University
	Press, 1951.
Adams, Alice D. *The Neglected Period of Antislavery in America,
	1808–1831.* Boston, Ginn & Co., 1908.
Adams, Charles F. *Richard Henry Dana.* 2 vols. Boston, Houghton
	Mifflin Co., 1895.
Adams, James Truslow. *New England in the Republic, 1776–1850.* Bos-
	ton, Little, Brown & Co., 1926.
Adams, John, and Adams, John Quincy. *Selected Writings,* ed. by
	Adrienne Koch and William Peden. New York, Alfred A. Knopf,
	1946.
Adams, John Quincy, *Memoirs of, Comprising Portions of His Diary
	from 1795 to 1848,* ed. by Charles Francis Adams. 12 vols. Phila-
	delphia, J. B. Lippincott Co., 1874–1877.
———. *Writings,* ed. by W. C. Ford. 7 vols. New York, The Mac-
	millan Company, 1913–1917.
American Antislavery Society. *Annual Reports.* New York, 1834–1861.
Andrews, Ethan A. *Slavery and the Domestic Slave Trade.* Boston,
	Light & Stearns, 1836.
Aptheker, Herbert. *American Negro Slave Revolts.* New York, Co-
	lumbia University Press, 1943.
———. *Negro in the Abolitionist Movement.* New York, International
	Publishers, 1941.
———. "Quakers and Negro Slavery," *Journal of Negro History,* Vol.
	XXV, 1940.

Barnes, Gilbert H. *The Antislavery Impulse*. New York, D. Appleton–Century Co., 1933.

Bassett, J. S. *Antislavery Leaders of North Carolina*. Baltimore, Johns Hopkins Press, 1898.

Beard, Charles A. and Mary R. *Rise of American Civilization*. 2 vols. New York, The Macmillan Company, 1927.

Bearse, Austin. *Reminiscences of Fugitive Slave Days in Boston*. Boston, W. Richardson, 1880.

Birney, James G. *Letters*, ed. by Dwight L. Dumond. 2 vols. New York, D. Appleton–Century Co., 1938.

Birney, William. *James G. Birney and His Times*. New York, D. Appleton–Century Co., 1890.

Bowditch, Vincent Y. *Life and Correspondence of Henry I. Bowditch*. 2 vols. Boston, Houghton Mifflin Co., 1902.

Bowditch, William I. *The Antislavery Reform*. Boston, Robert F. Wallcut, 1850.

———. *Slavery and the Constitution*. Boston, Robert F. Wallcut, 1849.

Brown, William Wells. *Narrative of William Wells Brown*. London, Charles Gilpin, 1849.

Buckmaster, Henrietta. *Let My People Go*. New York, Harper & Brothers, 1941.

Cash, W. J. *The Mind of the South*. New York, Alfred A. Knopf, 1941.

Chadwick, John W. *William Ellery Channing*. Boston, Houghton Mifflin Co., 1903.

Chamberlain, Allen. "Old Passages of Boston's Underground Railroad," *Magazine of History*, Vol. XXXI, No. 4, extra No. 124. Tarrytown, New York, 1926.

Channing, William Ellery. *Emancipation*. Boston, Peabody, 1840.

———. *Slavery*. Boston, Munroe & Co., 1836.

Chapman, John J. *Memoirs and Milestones*. New York, Moffat, Yard & Co., 1915.

———. *William L. Garrison*. New York, Moffat, Yard & Co., 1913.

Child, Lydia M. *Letters*, collected by Harriet W. Sewall. Boston, Houghton Mifflin Co., 1883.

Clarke, James F. *Antislavery Days*. New York, Lovell & Co., 1883.

———. *Autobiography, Diary and Correspondence*, ed. by Edward E. Hale. Boston, Houghton Mifflin Co., 1892.

Commager, Henry S. *Theodore Parker*. Boston, Little, Brown & Co., 1936.

Craven, Avery. *The Coming of the Civil War*. New York, Charles Scribner's Sons, 1942.

———. *The Repressible Conflict*. Baton Rouge, Louisiana State University Press, 1939.

Crawford, Mary C. *Old Boston Days and Ways*. Boston, Little, Brown & Co., 1909.

Curtis, George T. *Daniel Webster*. New York, D. Appleton & Co., 1870.

Darling, Arthur B. "The Workingmen's Party in Massachusetts, 1833–34," *American Historical Review*, Vol. XXIX, 1924.

Deane, Charles. "Letters and Documents Relating to Slavery in Massachusetts," *Collections*, Ser. 5, Vol. III, Massachusetts Historical Society.

DeVoto, Bernard. *The Year of Decision: 1846*. Boston, Little, Brown & Co., 1943.

Dodd, William E. *The Cotton Kingdom*. New Haven, Yale University Press, 1921.

Donald, David. *Lincoln Reconsidered*. New York, Alfred A. Knopf, 1956.

Douglass, Frederick, *Life and Times*. Hartford, Park Publishing Co., 1882.

Drake, Samuel A. *Old Landmarks and Historic Personages of Boston*. Boston, Roberts Bros., 1876.

Du Bois, W. E. B. *Suppression of the African Slave Trade*. New York, Longmans, Green & Co., 1896.

Dumond, Dwight L. *Antislavery Origins of the Civil War in the United States*. Ann Arbor, University of Michigan Press, 1939.

Edgell, David P. *William Ellery Channing*. Boston, Beacon Press, 1955.

Elkins, Stanley M. *Slavery, A Problem in American Institutional and Intellectual Life*. Chicago, University of Chicago Press, 1959.

Emerson, Ralph W. *Journals*, ed. by Edward W. Emerson and Waldo E. Forbes. 10 vols. Boston, Houghton Mifflin Co., 1912.

Foner, Philip S. *Business and Slavery*. Chapel Hill, University of North Carolina Press, 1941.

Franklin, John H. *From Slavery to Freedom*. New York, Alfred A. Knopf, 1947.

Fuess, Claude M. *Caleb Cushing*. New York, Harcourt, Brace and Company, 1923.

———. *Daniel Webster*. 2 vols. Boston, Little, Brown & Co., 1930.

———. "Daniel Webster and the Abolitionists," *Proceedings of Massachussetts Historical Society*, Vol. LXIV, 1932.

Gabriel, Ralph H. *The Course of American Democratic Thought*. New York, The Ronald Press Co., 1940.

Garrison, Wendell P. and Francis J. *William L. Garrison*. 4 vols. New York, The Century Co., 1885–1889.

Garrison, William L. *Principles and Mode of Action of the American Antislavery Society*. London (undated).

Garrison, William L., Jr. "Boston Antislavery Days," *Bostonian Society Publications*, Vol. II, 1905.

Handlin, Oscar. *Race and Nationality in American Life*. Boston, Little, Brown & Co., 1957.

Hart, Albert B. *Slavery and Abolition*. New York, Harper & Brothers, 1906.

Hart, Albert B., ed. *American History Told by Contemporaries*. 5 vols. New York, The Macmillian Company, 1901–1902.

———. *Commonwealth History of Massachusetts*. 5 vols. New York, States History Co., 1927–1930.

Herbert, Hilary A. *The Abolition Crusade and Its Consequences*. New York, Charles Scribner's Sons, 1912.

Higginson, Mary T. *Thomas Wentworth Higginson*. Boston, Houghton Mifflin Co., 1914.

Higginson, Thomas Wentworth. *Cheerful Yesterdays*. Boston, Houghton Mifflin Co., 1898.

———. *Contemporaries*. Boston, Houghton Mifflin Co., 1899.

———. *Letters and Journals*, ed. by Mary T. Higginson. Boston, Houghton Mifflin Co., 1921.

———. *Margaret Fuller Ossoli*. Boston, Houghton Mifflin Co., 1893.

———. *Wendell Phillips*. Boston, Lee & Shepard, 1884.

Hoar, George F. *Autobiography of Seventy Years*. 2 vols. New York, Charles Scribner's Sons, 1903.

von Holst, Hermann E. *The Constitutional and Political History of the United States*, trans. from the German. 8 vols. Chicago, Callaghan & Co., 1876–1892.

Howe, Julia W. *Reminiscences*, Boston, Houghton Mifflin Co., 1899.

Howe, M. A. De Wolfe. "Edmund Quincy," *Proceedings of Massachusetts Historical Society*, Vol. LXVIII. Boston, 1952.

Hughes, Sarah F. *Reminiscences of John Murray Forbes*. Boston, George H. Ellis Co., 1902.

Hughes, Sarah F., ed. *Letters and Recollections of John Murray Forbes*. 2 vols. Boston, Houghton Mifflin Co., 1899.

Hume, John F. *The Abolitionists*. New York, G. P. Putnam's Sons, 1905.

Jackson, Francis. *Account Book of the Vigilance Committee of Boston*. Boston, reproduced by The Bostonian Society.

Jay, William. *Miscellaneous Writings on Slavery*. Boston, J. P. Jewett, 1853.

Jefferson, Thomas. *Writings*, ed. by Paul L. Ford. 10 vols. New York, G. P. Putnam's Sons, 1892–1899.

Kaplan, Sidney. "The *Moby Dick* in the Service of the Underground Railroad," *Phylon*, Vol. XII, No. 2, 1951.

Kelly, Ralph. *Boston in the 1830's—and the 'William Penn,'* New York, Newcomen Society, 1947.

Korngold, Ralph. *Two Friends of Man.* Boston, Little, Brown & Co., 1950.

Lloyd, Arthur Y. *The Slavery Controversy, 1831–1860.* Chapel Hill, University of North Carolina Press, 1939.

✓Lowell, James Russell. *Antislavery Papers.* Boston, Houghton Mifflin Co., 1902.

Macy, Jesse. *The Antislavery Crusade.* New Haven, Yale University Press, 1919.

Madison, James. *Writings,* ed. by G. Hunt. 9 vols. New York, G. P. Putnam's Sons, 1900–1910.

Mandel, Bernard. *Labor: Free and Slave.* New York, Associated Authors, 1955.

Martin, Asa E. *Antislavery in Kentucky Prior to 1850.* Louisville, Standard Printing Co., 1918.

———. "Pioneer Antislavery Press," *Mississippi Valley Historical Review,* II, No. 4, March, 1916.

Martyn, Carlos. *Wendell Phillips.* New York, Funk & Wagnalls, 1890.

May, Samuel J. *Discourse on the Life and Character of Rev. Charles Follen.* Boston, Henry L. Devereux, 1840.

———. *The Fugitive Slave Law and Its Victims,* New Series, No. 15. New York, American Antislavery Society, 1861.

———. *Some Recollections of Our Antislavery Conflict.* Boston, Fields, Osgood Co., 1869.

McDougall, Marion G. *Fugitive Slaves (1619–1865).* Boston, Ginn & Co., 1891.

Memorial History of Boston, ed. by Justin Winsor. 4 vols. Boston, James R. Osgood & Co., 1881.

Moore, George H. *Notes on the History of Slavery in Massachusetts.* New York, D. Appleton & Co., 1866.

Mumford, Thomas J. *Memoir of Samuel J. May.* Boston, Roberts Bros., 1873.

Nevins, Allan. *The Emergence of Lincoln.* 2 vols. New York, Charles Scribner's Sons, 1950.

———. *Ordeal of the Union.* 2 vols. New York, Charles Scribner's Sons, 1947.

———. *War for the Union,* Vol. I. New York, Charles Scribner's Sons, 1959.

Nye, Russel B. *Fettered Freedom.* East Lansing, Michigan State College Press, 1949.

———. *William L. Garrison.* Boston, Little, Brown & Co., 1955.

Old Antislavery Days. Danvers (Mass.) Historical Society, 1893.

Olmstead, Frederick L. *The Cotton Kingdom.* 2 vols. New York, Mason Bros., 1861.
——. *A Journey in the Seaboard Slave States.* 2 vols. New York, G. P. Putnam's Sons, 1907.
Parrington, Vernon L. *Main Currents in American Thought.* 3 vols. New York, Harcourt, Brace and Company, 1930.
Pearson, Henry G. *John Murray Forbes.* Boston, Houghton Mifflin Co., 1911.
Phillips, Wendell. *Can Abolitionists Vote or Take Office Under the Constitution?* New York, American Antislavery Society, 1845.
——. *The Constitution, A Pro-Slavery Compact.* New York, American Antislavery Society, 1856.
Pierce, Edward L. *Memoirs and Letters of Charles Sumner.* 3 vols. Boston Roberts Bros., 1893.
Pike, James S. *First Blows of the Civil War.* New York, American News Co., 1879.
Preston, E. Deloros, Jr. "Genesis of the Underground Railroad," *Journal of Negro History,* Vol. XIII, 1928.
Quincy, Edmond. *Life of Josiah Quincy.* Boston, Ticknor & Fields, 1868.
Quincy, Josiah P. "Memoir of Edmond Quincy," *Proceedings of Massachusetts Historical Society,* 2nd Series, Vol. XVIII, 1903–1904.
Rhodes, James F. *History of the United States from the Compromise of 1850.* 7 vols. New York, The Macmillan Company, 1902–1907.
Richards, Laura E. *Samuel Gridley Howe.* New York, Appleton-Century Co., 1935.
——. *Stepping Westward.* New York, D. Appleton & Co., 1931.
Richards, Laura E., ed. *Letters and Journals of Samuel Gridley Howe.* 2 vols. Boston, Dana Estes & Co., 1909.
Robinson, William W. ("Warrington"). *Pen Portraits, 1848–1876.* Boston, H. J. Robinson Co., 1877.
Sanborn, Franklin B. *Dr. Samuel G. Howe.* New York, Funk & Wagnalls, 1891.
Sanborn, Franklin G. *Recollections of Seventy Years.* 2 vols. Boston, Richard G. Badger, 1909.
Sandburg, Carl. *Abraham Lincoln: The War Years.* 4 vols. New York, Harcourt, Brace and Company, 1939.
Savage, W. Sherman. *Controversy Over Distribution of Abolition Literature.* Washington, D.C., Association for the Study of Negro Life and History, 1938.
Schlesinger, Arthur M., Jr. *The Age of Jackson.* Boston, Little, Brown & Co., 1945.
Schouler, William. *A History of Massachusetts in the Civil War.* 2 vols. Boston, 1868–1871.

Schwartz, Harold. "Fugitive Slave Days in Boston," *New England Quarterly*, June, 1954.
———. *Samuel G. Howe*. Cambridge, Harvard University Press, 1956.
Shaw, Warren C. *The Fugitive Slave Issue in Massachusetts Politics, 1786–1837*. Doctoral Thesis, Urbana, University of Illinois Press, 1938.
Sherwin, Oscar. *Prophet of Liberty, The Life and Times of Wendell Phillips*. New York, Bookman Associates, 1958.
Siebert, Wilbur H. "Underground Railroad in Massachusetts," *Proceedings of American Antiquarian Society*, New Series Part I, Vol. XLV, April 17, 1935.
———. *Underground Railroad from Slavery to Freedom*. New York, The Macmillan Co., 1899.
———. *Vermont's Antislavery and Underground Railroad Record*. Columbus, Ohio, Spahr & Glenn Co., 1937.
———. *Vigilance Committee of Boston*. Boston, The Bostonian Society, 1953.
Stampp, Kenneth. "The Fate of the Southern Antislavery Sentiment," *Journal of Negro History*, Vol. XXVIII, No. 1, January, 1943.
Stanton, Elizabeth C., Anthony, Susan B., and Gage, Mathilda J., eds. *History of Woman Suffrage*. 3 vols. Rochester, Charles Mann, 1881
Still, William. *The Underground Railroad*. Philadelphia, Porter & Coates, 1872.
Storey, Moorfield. *Charles Sumner*. Boston, Houghton Mifflin Co., 1900.
Tappan, Lewis. *Life of Arthur Tappan*. New York, Hurd & Houghton, 1877.
Tharp, Louise H. *Until Victory: Horace Mann and Mary Peabody*. Boston, Little, Brown & Co., 1953.
Thomas, Benjamin P. *Theodore Weld*. New Brunswick, N.J., Rutgers University Press, 1950.
Tiffany, Nina M. *Samuel E. Sewall*. Boston, Houghton Mifflin Co., 1898.
———. "Stories of the Fugitive Slaves," *New England Magazine*, New Series, Vol. II, March, May, and June, 1890.
Tyler, Alice F. *Freedom's Ferment*. Minneapolis, University of Minnesota Press, 1944.
Villard, Oswald G. "Wendell Phillips After Fifty Years," *American Mercury*, Vol. XXXIV, No. 133, January, 1935.
Ware, Ethel K. "Lydia Maria Child and Antislavery," *Boston Public Library Quarterly*, October, 1951.
Weeks, S. B. *Southern Quakers and Slavery*. Baltimore, Johns Hopkins Press, 1896.

Weld, Theodore D. *American Slavery As It Is*. New York, American
   Antislavery Society, 1839.
Whittier, John G. "The Antislavery Convention of 1833," *Atlantic
   Monthly*, February, 1874.
——. "Introduction to Oliver Johnson," *William L. Garrison and
   His Times*. Boston, B. B. Russell & Co., 1880.
——. *Writings*. 7 vols. Cambridge, Riverside Press, 1888.
Wilson, Henry. *History of the Rise and Fall of the Slave Power in
   America*. 3 vols. Boston, James R. Osgood & Co., 1874–1877.
Wiltse, Charles M. *John C. Calhoun*. 3 vols. Indianapolis, Bobbs-
   Merrill Co., 1944–1951.
Wolf, Hazel C. *The Martyr Complex in the Abolition Movement*.
   Madison, University of Wisconsin Press, 1952.
Woodson, Carter G. *The Negro in Our History*. Washington, D.C.,
   Associated Publishers, Inc., 1922.

IV. Special Reference Works

Chapter I: Garrison's Bloody Year
Ames, Ellis. "Garrison Mob," *Proceedings of the Massachusetts His-
   torical Society*, Vol. XVIII, February, 1881.
The Boston Mob, Proceedings of the Antislavery Meeting, Stacy Hall,
   Boston, Twentieth Anniversary of the Mob. Boston, R. F. Wallcutt,
   1855.
Chapman, Maria Weston. *Right and Wrong in Boston*. 1836.
Lyman, Theodore, 3rd, ed. *Papers Relating to the Garrison Mob*. Cam-
   bridge, Welch, Bigelow & Co., 1870.
Morison, Samuel Eliot. *Life and Letters of Harrison Gray Otis*. 2 vols.
   Boston, Houghton Mifflin Co., 1913.
Second Annual Report, Boston Female Antislavery Society. Boston,
   1836.

Chapter II: Seeds of Violence
Bancroft, George. *History of the Formation of the Constitution of
   the United States*. 2 vols. New York, D. Appleton & Co., 1882.
Beard, Charles. *An Economic Interpretation of the Constitution*. New
   York, The Macmillan Company, 1913.
Curtis, George T. *History of the Constitution of the United States*.
   2 vols. New York, Harper & Brothers, 1859.
Elliott, Jonathan, ed. *The Debates in the Several State Conventions on
   the Adoption of the Federal Constitution*, rev. 5 vols. Published
   under Sanction of Congress, Washington, D.C., 1836–1845.

Farrand, Max. *The Framing of the Constitution of the United States.* New Haven, Yale University Press, 1913.

Farrand, Max, ed. *The Records of the Federal Convention of 1787.* New Haven, Yale University Press, 1911.

Ford, Paul Leicester, ed. *Essays on the Constitution of the United States.* Brooklyn, Historical Printing Club, 1892.

———. *Pamphlets on the Constitution of the United States.* Brooklyn, Historical Printing Club, 1888.

Lyon, Hastings. *The Constitution and the Men Who Made It.* Boston, Houghton Mifflin Co., 1936.

Rowland, Kate Mason. *The Life of George Mason.* 2 vols. New York, G. P. Putnam's Sons, 1892.

Swisher, Carl Brent. *American Constitutional Development.* Boston, Houghton Mifflin Co., 1943.

Van Doren, Carl. *The Great Rehearsal.* New York, Viking Press, 1948.

Warren, Charles. *The Making of the Constitution.* Boston, Little, Brown & Co., 1928.

Chapter III: Conspiracy of Silence

Drew, Thomas R. *Review of Debates in the Virginia Legislature of 1831 and 1832.* Charleston, S.C., 1852.

Eaton, Clement. "A Dangerous Pamphlet in the Old South," *Journal of Southern History,* Vol. II, No. 3, August, 1936.

Josephson, Hannah. *The Golden Threads.* New York, Duell, Sloan & Pearce, 1949.

Lawrence, George A. "Benjamin Lundy, Pioneer of Freedom," *Journal of the Illinois State Historical Society,* Vol. VI, No. 2, July, 1913.

Lundy, Benjamin. *Life, Travels and Opinions of Benjamin Lundy.* Philadelphia, Parish & Co., 1847.

Martineau, Harriet. *Society in America.* New York, Percy Reed, Printer, 1837.

Phillips, Ulrich B. *Life and Labor in the Old South.* Boston, Little, Brown & Co., 1929.

Proceedings of the Antislavery Convention at Philadelphia in 1833. New York, Dorr & Butterfield, 1833.

Snodgrass, Joseph E. "Benjamin Lundy," *Northern Weekly,* Vol. II, No. 5. New York, March, 1868.

Sydnor, Charles S. *Development of Southern Sectionalism (1819–1848).* Baton Rouge, Louisiana State University Press, 1948.

Turner, Frederick J. *The Frontier in American History.* New York, Henry Holt & Co., 1920.

———. *Rise of the New West, 1819–1829.* New York, Harper & Brothers, 1920.

Wadlin, Horace G. "The Growth of Manufacturers," *Twentieth An-*

nual Report of the Massachusetts Bureau of Statistics of Labor. Boston, Wright & Potter Printing Co., 1890.

Webster, Daniel. *Memorial to the Congress of the United States, December 3, 1819.* Boston, Sewall, Phelps Co., 1819.

Weston, George M. *Progress of Slavery in the United States.* Washington, D.C., 1857.

Chapter IV: Mobs and Mad Women and *Chapter V: The Grimké Sisters*

Abdy, Edward S. *Journal of a Residence and Tour in the United States of North America,* Vol. 1. London, John Murray, 1835.

Anthony, Katherine. *Susan B. Anthony.* New York, Doubleday & Company, Inc., 1954.

Birney, Catherine H. *Sarah and Angelina Grimké.* Boston, Lee & Shepard, 1835.

Blatch, Harriet S. and Stanton, Theodore S. *Elizabeth C. Stanton.* New York, Harper & Brothers, 1922.

Chace, Elizabeth B. *Antislavery Reminiscences.* Central Falls, R.I., E. L. Freeman & Sons, 1891.

Child, Alfred T., Jr. "Prudence Crandall and the Canterbury Experiment," *Bulletin of Friends' Historical Association,* Vol. XXII, No. 1, Spring, 1933.

Child, Lydia M. *An Appeal in Favor of That Class of Americans Called Africans.* Boston, Allen & Ticknor, 1833.

———. *Antislavery Catechism.* Newburyport, Mass., C. Whipple, 1836.

———. *Letters.* Boston, Houghton Mifflin Co., 1882.

Fall River Antislavery Society. *Report of Delegates to Antislavery Convention of American Women in Philadelphia, May, 1838.* Boston, I. Knapp, 1838.

Grimké, Angelina. *Appeal to the Christian Women of the South.* New York, American Antislavery Society, 1836.

———. *Appeal to the Women of the Nominally Free States.* New York, American Antislavery Society, 1839.

———. *Letters to Catherine E. Beecher.* Boston, I. Knapp, 1838.

Hallowell, Anna D. *James and Lucretia Mott.* Boston, Houghton Mifflin Co., 1896.

Harper, Ida H. *Susan B. Anthony.* 3 vols. Indianapolis, Bowen-Merrill Co., 1899–1908.

Jones, F. Dudley. "The Grimké Sisters," *Proceedings of the South Carolina Historical Association,* 1933.

Kimball, John C. *Connecticut's Canterbury Tale.* Hartford, Plimpton Press, 1888.

Larned, Ella D. *History of Windham County.* 2 vols. Worcester, Mass., C. Hamilton Co., 1874–1880.

Martineau, Harriet. *The Martyr Age of the United States*. Boston, Weeks, Jordan & Co., 1839.

McCarron, Anna T. "The Trial of Prudence Crandall," *The Connecticut Magazine*, Vol. XII, No. 2, 1908.

Sillen, Samuel. *Women Against Slavery*. New York, Masses & Mainstream Inc., 1955.

Small, Edwin W. and Miriam R. "Prudence Crandall," *New England Quarterly*, Vol. XVII, No. 4, December, 1944.

Steiner, Bernard. *Slavery In Connecticut*. Baltimore, Johns Hopkins University Press, 1893.

Tracts on Slavery, "Report of the Trial of Prudence Crandall." Brooklyn, 1833.

Ware, Ethel K. "Lydia Maria Child and Antislavery," *Boston Public Library Quarterly*, October, 1951.

Weld, Theodore D., Angelina Grimké Weld, and Sarah Grimké, Letters of, ed. by Gilbert H. Barnes and Dwight L. Dumond. New York, D. Appleton–Century Co., 1934.

Wormley, G. Smith. "Prudence Crandall," *Journal of Negro History*, Vol. VIII, January, 1923.

Chapter VI: Boston Rebels and the Martyrdom of Lovejoy

Beecher, Edward. *Narrative of the Riots at Alton*. Alton, Ill., G. Holton, 1838.

Dugan, Frank H. "An Illinois Martyrdom," *Papers in Illinois History*. Illinois State Historical Society, Springfield, Ill., 1939.

Krum, John M. "Death of Elijah P. Lovejoy," *Journal of the Illinois State Historical Society*, Vol. IV, No. 4, January, 1912.

Lovejoy, Joseph C. and Owen. *Memoir of Reverend Elijah P. Lovejoy*, New York, Taylor, 1838.

Parker, Theodore. *An Humble Tribute to William Ellery Channing*. Boston, C. C. Little and J. Brown, 1842.

Seventh Annual Report. Boston Female Antislavery Society. Boston, 1840.

Tanner, Henry. *The Martyrdom of Lovejoy*. Chicago, Fergus Printing Co., 1881.

Chapter VII: John Quincy Adams

Adams, Charles F. "John Quincy Adams: His Connection with Emancipation Under Martial Law (1819–1842)," *Proceedings of Massachusetts Historical Society*, January, 1902.

Bemis, Samuel F. *John Quincy Adams and the Foundations of American Foreign Policy*. New York, Alfred A. Knopf, 1949.

——. *John Quincy Adams and the Union*. New York, Alfred A. Knopf, 1956.

Carroll, E. Malcolm. *Origins of the Whig Party*. Durham, N.C., Duke University Press, 1925.

Clark, Bennett C., *John Quincy Adams*. Boston, Little, Brown & Co., 1932.

Cole, Arthur C. *The Whig Party in the South*. Washington, D.C., American Historical Society, 1913.

Lipsky, George A., *John Quincy Adams*. New York, Crowell, 1950.

Morse, John T., *John Quincy Adams*. Boston, Houghton Mifflin Co., 1892.

Quincy, Josiah. *Memoir of the Life of John Quincy Adams*. Boston, Phillips, Sampson Co., 1885.

Seward, William H., *Life and Public Service of John Quincy Adams*. Auburn, N.Y., Derby, Miller & Co., 1849.

Third Annual Report. Boston Female Antislavery Society, 1837.

Chapter VIII: Torrey and the Proper Price of Liberty

Bigelow, John P. *Report on the Condition of Certain Branches of Industry in Massachusetts*. Boston, 1838.

Bird, Francis W. *A Memoir by His Children*. Boston, Privately Printed, 1897.

Correspondence Between Nathan Appleton and John G. Palfrey. Boston, Eastburn's Press, 1846.

Cross, Whitney. *The Burned-over District*. Ithaca, N.Y., Cornell University Press, 1950.

Hazel, John T., Jr. *Trade, Riots and Abolition*. Unpublished Honors thesis, Harvard College, 1951.

Lovejoy, Joseph C. *Memoir of Reverend Charles T. Torrey*. Boston, John P. Jewett Co., 1847.

Our First Men: A Calendar of Wealth, Fashion and Gentility. Boston, 1846.

Parker, Theodore. *Additional Speeches*. 2 vols. Boston, Little, Brown & Co., 1855.

Trial and Imprisoment of Jonathan Walker. Boston, New England Antislavery Society, 1845.

Chapter IX: Slave Hunt in Boston—the Come-Outers

Austin, Elbridge G. *Statement of Facts Connected with the Arrest and Emancipation of George Latimer*. Boston, J. H. Eastburn, 1842.

Birney, James G. *The American Churches: The Bulwarks of American Slavery*. Newburyport, Mass., C. Whipple, 1842.

Bowditch, Henry I. *The Latimer Case and Anti-Manhunting League*. Manuscript in Massachusetts Historical Society, 1842.

Chapman, Maria W. *Right and Wrong In Massachusetts*. Boston, Dow & Jackson, 1839.

Filler, Louis. "Parker Pillsbury," *New England Quarterly*, Vol. XIX, No. 3, September, 1946.

Foster, Stephen S. *The Brotherhood of Thieves; or A True Picture of the American Church and Clergy*. New London, Conn., W. Bolles, 1843.

Goodell, William. *Come-Outerism—The Duty of Secession From A Corrupt Church*. Boston, 25 Cornhill, 1845.

———. *Slavery and Antislavery*. New York, pub. by the author, 1853.

———. *Views of American Constitutional Law Bearing Upon Slavery*. Utica, N.Y., Jackson & Chaplin, 1844.

Pillsbury, Parker. *Acts of the Antislavery Apostles*. Boston, Cupples, Upham & Co., 1884.

Tracy, Cyrus, *et al. History of the County of Essex*. Essex, Mass., 1872.

Chapter X: The Political Plunge

Darling, Arthur B. *Political Changes in Massachusetts (1842–48)*. New Haven, Yale University Press, 1925.

Drayton, Daniel. *Personal Memoir*. Boston, Bela Marsh, 1855.

Frothingham, Octavius B. *Gerrit Smith*. New York, G. P. Putnam's Sons, 1878.

Harlow, Ralph V. *Gerrit Smith*. New York, Henry Holt & Co., 1939.

Hesseltine, William B. *Rise and Fall of Third Parties*. Washington, D.C., Public Affairs Press, 1848.

Morrow, R. L. "The Liberty Party in Vermont," *New England Quarterly*, Vol. II, No. 2, April, 1929.

Nash, Howard P., Jr. *Third Parties in American Politics*. Washington, D.C., Public Affairs Press, 1959.

Palfrey, John G. *Papers on the Slave Power*. Boston, Merrill, Cobb & Co., 1846.

Smith, Theodore C. *The Liberty and Free Soil Parties*. New York, Longmans, Green & Co., 1897.

———. *Parties and Slavery*. New York, Harper & Brothers, 1906.

Chapter XI: Parker's "Law" and the Crisis of 1850

Chadwick, John W. *Theodore Parker, Preacher and Reformer*. Boston, Houghton Mifflin Co., 1900.

Commager, Henry S. "The Dilemma of Theodore Parker," *New England Quarterly*, Vol. VI, No. 2, June, 1933.

———. "Tempest in a Boston Tea Cup," *New England Quarterly*, Vol. VI, No. 4, December, 1933.

Frothingham, Octavius B. *Theodore Parker*. Boston, James R. Osgood & Co., 1874.

The Fugitive Slave Bill, Its History and Unconstitutionality. New York, William Harred Co., 1850.

Holmes, John Haynes. *The Social Message of Theodore Parker*. New York, Unitarian Fellowship for Social Justice, 1913.

Ladu, Arthur I. "The Political Ideas of Theodore Parker," *Studies in Philology*. University of North Carolina Press, XXXVIII, No. 1, January, 1941.

Mead, Edwin D. *Emerson and Theodore Parker*. Boston, American Unitarian Association, 1910.

Russel, Robert R. "What Was the Compromise of 1850?" *Journal of Southern History*, XXII, No. 3, August, 1956.

Weiss, John. *Life and Correspondence of Theodore Parker*. 2 vols. New York, D. Appleton & Co., 1864.

Chapter XII: The Vigilance Committee and Shadrach Rescue

Greenough, Charles P. "Rendition of Thomas Sims," *Proceedings of Massachusetts Historical Society*, Vol. LV, June, 1922.

Parker, Theodore. *The Boston Kidnapping*. Boston, Crosby, Nichols & Co., 1852.

Shlakman, Vera. *Economic History of a Factory Town*. Northampton, Mass., Smith College Studies in History, XX, Nos. 1–4, 1935.

U.S. Circuit Court, *1st Circuit, Massachusetts: Report of the Proceedings At the Examination of Charles G. Davis, Esq*. Boston, White & Potter, 1851.

Winthrop, Robert C. *Memoir of Hon. Nathan Appleton*. Boston, John Wilson & Son, 1861.

Chapter XIII: Uncle Tom and the Capture of Thomas Sims

Baldwin, James. "Everybody's Protest Novel," *Partisan Review*, June, 1949.

Bentzon, Theodore. *A Typical American: Thomas Wentworth Higginson*. London and New York, Howard W. Bell Co., 1902.

Bowen, Edwin W. "Thomas Wentworth Higginson," *Sewanee Review*, XXXIII, 1915.

Edelstein, Tilden. *Strange Enthusiam: Thomas Wentworth Higginson*. (Book in progress).

———. "Thomas Wentworth Higginson: His Ante-Bellum Years," *Proceedings of Cambridge Historical Society*, XXXVI, 1959.

Foster, Charles H. *The Rungless Ladder: Harriet Beecher Stowe and New England Puritanism*. Durham, N.C., Duke University Press, 1954.

Gilbertson, Catherine. *Harriet Beecher Stowe*. New York, D. Appleton–Century Co., 1937.

Higginson, Thomas Wentworth. "Antislavery Days," *Outlook*, LX, September 3, 1898.

———. *The New Revolution*. Boston, R. F. Wallcutt, 1857.

———. *Travellers and Outlaws*. Boston, Lee & Shepard Co., 1889.

Hintz, Howard W. *Thomas Wentworth Higginson*. New York, New York University Press, 1939.

Rourke, Catherine M. *Trumpet of Jubilee*. New York, Harcourt, Brace & Co., 1927.

Stowe, Harriet Beecher. *The Key to Uncle Tom's Cabin*. Boston, J. P. Jewett & Co., 1853.

———. *Life and Letters*, ed. by Annie Fields. Boston, Houghton Mifflin Co., 1897.

———. *Uncle Tom's Cabin*. 2 vols. Boston, J. P. Jewett & Co., 1852.

Stowe, Lyman Beecher. *Saints, Sinners and Beechers*. Indianapolis, Bobbs-Merrill Co., 1934.

Turner, Lorenzo D. *Antislavery Sentiment in American Literature*. Washington, D.C., Association for the Study of Negro Life and History, 1929.

Ward, Theodora V. W. "Emily Dickinson and Thomas Wentworth Higginson," *Boston Public Library Quarterly*, January, 1953.

Chapter XIV: Sumner and Kansas—New England Battleground

Bradford, Gamaliel, "Charles Sumner," *Yale Review*, V, April–July, 1916.

Isely, W. H. "The Sharps Rifle Episode in Kansas History," *American Historical Review*, XII, No. 3, April, 1907.

Johnson, Samuel A. *Battle Cry of Freedom—New England Emigrant Aid Company in the Kansas Crusade*. Lawrence, Kan., University of Kansas Press, 1954.

Lawrence, William L. *Life of Amos A. Lawrence*. Boston, Houghton Mifflin Co., 1899.

Schurz, Carl. *Charles Sumner*, ed. by Arthur R. Hogue. Urbana, Ill., University of Illinois Press, 1951.

Sumner, Charles. *His Complete Works*. 20 vols. Boston, Lee & Shepard Co., 1910, Vols. V and VI.

Thayer, Eli. *A History of the Kansas Crusade*. New York, Harper & Brothers, 1889.

———. *New England Emigrant Aid Company*, Worcester, Mass., Franklin P. Rice, 1887.

Chapter XV: The Reverend Storms the Court House

Boston Slave Riot and Trial of Anthony Burns. Boston, Fetridge & Co., 1854.

Bowditch, William I. *The Rendition of Anthony Burns*. Boston, R. F. Wallcutt, 1854.

Higginson, Thomas Wentworth. *Massachusetts In Mourning*. Boston, J. Munroe & Co., 1854.

Parker, Theodore. *The New Crime Against Humanity*. Boston, B. B. Mossey & Co., 1854.
Sherwin, Oscar. "Sons of Otis and Hancock," *New England Quarterly*, June, 1946.
Stevens, Charles E. *Anthony Burns*. Boston, J. P. Jewett & Co., 1856.
Swift, John L. *Speech on the Removal of Edward G. Loring*. Boston, W. White, 1855.

Chapter XVI: Senate Blood and Ruffian Blood
Bean, William G. *Party Transformation in Massachusetts, 1848–60*. Unpublished Doctoral thesis, Harvard University, 1922.
Billington, Ray A. *The Protestant Crusade*. New York, The Macmillan Company, 1938.
Brown, Salmon. "John Brown and Sons in Kansas Territory," *Indiana Magazine of History*, XXXI, No. 2, June, 1935.
Haynes, G. H. "A Know-Nothing Legislature," *American Historical Association Reports*, 1896.
Malin, James C. *John Brown and the Legend of Fifty-Six*. Philadelphia, *Memoirs of the American Philosophical Society*, XVII, 1942.
Parson, Luke F. and Bridgman, Edward P. *With John Brown in Kansas*. Madison, Wisc., J. N. Davidson, 1915.
Redpath, James. *The Public Life of Captain John Brown*. Boston, Thayer & Eldridge, 1860.
Rice, Madeleine H. *American Catholic Opinion in the Slavery Controversy*. New York, Columbia University Press, 1944.
The Sumner Outrage: Speeches at the Meeting of Citizens in Cambridge, June 2, 1856. Cambridge, John Ford, 1856.
Thoreau, Henry D. *A Yankee In Canada, With Antislavery and Reform Papers*. Boston, Houghton Mifflin Co., 1881.
Villard, Oswald G. *John Brown*. Boston, Houghton Mifflin Co., 1911.
Ware, Edith E. "Political Opinion in Massachusetts During the Civil War and Reconstruction," *Studies In History, Economics and Public Law*, LXXIV, No. 2, Whole No. 175. New York, Columbia University, 1916.

Chapter XVII: John Brown and the Boston Plotters
Harlow, Ralph V. "Gerrit Smith and the John Brown Raid," *American Historical Review*, XXXVIII, No. 1, October, 1932.
Hinton, Richard. *John Brown and His Men*. New York, Funk & Wagnalls, 1894.
Keeler, Ralph. "Owen Brown's Escape From Harpers Ferry," *Atlantic Monthly*, March, 1874.
Sanborn, Franklin B. "John Brown In Massachusetts," *Atlantic Monthly*, April–July, 1872 (unsigned).

————. *John Brown, Life and Letters.* Boston, Roberts Bros., 1891.
————. "The Virginia Campaign of John Brown," *Atlantic Monthly,* January–May and December, 1875.
Seay, Virginia C. "Pioneers of Freedom," *Kansas Magazine,* 1943.
Stearns, Frank P. *Cambridge Sketches.* Philadelphia, J. B. Lippincott, 1905.
————. *Life and Public Service of George L. Stearns.* Philadelphia, J. B. Lippincott, 1907.
Thoreau, Henry D. "A Plea for Captain John Brown," *Works.* Boston, New Riverside Edition, 1893.
Warren, Robert Penn. *John Brown, The Making of a Martyr.* New York, Payson and Clarke Co., 1929.

Chapter XVIII: Jubilee Year and the Puritan Radicals
Adams, Henry. "The Great Secession Winter of 1860–61," *Proceedings of Massachusetts Historical Society,* Vol. XLIII, 1910.
Appleton, Nathan. *Letters to the Hon. William C. Rives of Virgina on Slavery and the Union.* Boston, J. H. Eastburn Co., 1860.
Browne, Albert G. Jr. *Sketch of The Official Life of John A. Andrew.* New York, Hurd & Houghton, 1868.
Chandler, Peleg W. *Memoir of Governor Andrew.* Boston, Roberts Bros., 1880.
Craven, Avery. "Coming of the War Between the States, An Interpretation," *Journal of Southern History,* II, No. 3, August, 1936.
Dumond, Dwight L. *The Secession Movement.* New York, The Macmillan Company, 1931.
Geyl, Pieter. "The American Civil War and the Problem of Inevitability," *New England Quarterly,* XXIV, No. 2, June, 1951.
Helper, Hinton R. *The Impending Crisis.* New York, Burdick & Co., 1860.
Lord, Daniel. *The Effect of Secession Upon The Commercial Relations Between The North and South.* New York, *New York Times,* 1861.
Marx, Karl and Engels, Frederick. *The Civil War in the United States.* New York, International Publishers, 1937.
Pearson, Henry G. *Life of John A. Andrew.* 2 vols. Boston, Houghton Mifflin Co., 1904.
Rhodes, James F. *Lectures on the American Civil War.* New York, The Macmillan Company, 1913.
Stampp, Kenneth M. *And the War Came.* Baton Rouge, Louisiana State University Press, 1950.
Tchertkoff, V. and Holah, F. *A Short Biography of William Lloyd Garrison.* London, Free Age Press, 1904.
Villard, Fanny Garrison. *William Lloyd Garrison On Non-Resistance.* New York, The Nation Press, 1924.

Wilbur, Henry W. *President Lincoln's Attitude Towards Slavery and Emancipation*. Philadelphia, W. R. Jenkins Co., 1914.

End of an Epoch

Aptheker, Herbert. *The Negro in the Civil War*. New York, International Publishers, 1938.

Bowditch, Henry I. "Memorials Of Our Martyr Soldiers." Manuscript in Massachusetts Historical Society.

Brown, William W. *The Negro In The American Rebellion*. Boston, Lee & Shepard, 1867.

Cornish, Douglas T. *The Sable Arm*. New York, Longmans, Green & Co., 1956.

Emilio, Luis F. *The Assault on Fort Wagner*. Boston, Rand Avery Co., 1887.

———. *A Brave Black Regiment—History of the 54th Massachusetts Regiment*. Boston, Boston Book Co., 1891.

———. *Manuscript Records of the 54th Massachusetts Regiment*. Massachusetts Historical Society.

Headley, J. T. *The Great Riots of New York, 1712-1873*. New York, E. B. Treat & Co., 1873.

Higginson, Henry L. *Four Addresses*. Boston, D. B. Updike, 1902.

Higginson, Thomas Wentworth. *Army Life in a Black Regiment*. Boston, Fields, Osgood & Co., 1870.

———. Harvard Memorial Biographies. 2 vols. Cambridge, Sever & Francis, 1866.

James, Garth W. *The Assault on Fort Wagner*. Milwaukee, 1891.

The Monument to Robert Gould Shaw; Its Inception, Completion and Unveiling. Boston, Houghton Mifflin Co., 1897.

Robert Gould Shaw Memorial. Cambridge, Mass., University Press, 1864.

Shaw, Robert Gould. *Letters*. Cambridge, Mass., University Press, 1864.

———. "Letters from Camp," *Magazine of History*, XVIII & XIX, 1914.

Sutherland, George E. *The Negro In The Late War*. Milwaukee, Burdick, Armitage & Allen, 1888.

Williams, George W. *History of the Negro Troops In The War of The Rebellion*. New York, Harper & Brothers, 1888.

Wilson, Joseph T. *The Black Phalanx*. Hartford, American Publishing Co., 1882.

Index